3/00

ALEXANDER POPE
World and Word

Alexander Pope, the portrait engraved in his *Works*, 1717, based on the painting by Charles Jervas, *c*. 1714.

PROCEEDINGS OF THE BRITISH ACADEMY · 91

ALEXANDER POPE
World and Word

Edited by
HOWARD ERSKINE-HILL

Published for THE BRITISH ACADEMY
by OXFORD UNIVERSITY PRESS

Oxford University Press, Great Clarendon Street, Oxford OX2 6DP

Oxford New York
Athens Auckland Bangkok Bogota Bombay
Buenos Aires Calcutta Cape Town Dar es Salaam
Delhi Florence Hong Kong Istanbul Karachi
Kuala Lumpur Madras Madrid Melbourne
Mexico City Nairobi Paris Singapore
Taipei Tokyo Toronto Warsaw

and associated companies in
Berlin Ibadan

British Library Cataloguing in Publication Data
Data available

ISBN 0–19–726170–1
ISSN 0068–1202

Typeset by Intype London Ltd
Printed in Great Britain
on acid free paper by
Bookcraft (Bath) Ltd
Midsomer Norton, North Somerset

Contents

List of Plates   vi

Notes on Contributors   vii

Preface   ix

Introduction   1
HOWARD ERSKINE-HILL

Pope and Slavery   27
HOWARD ERSKINE-HILL

Pope's Homer: The Shadow of Friendship   55
HESTER JONES

Heroic Notes: Pope's Epic Idiom Revisited   69
CLAUDE RAWSON

From Text to Work: The Presentation and Re-presentation of
Epistles to Several Persons   111
JULIAN FERRARO

The Ambitious Pursuit: Pope, Gay and the Life of Writing   135
DAVID NOKES

Reception, and *The Rape of the Lock*, and Richardson   147
THOMAS KEYMER

Index   177

List of Plates

Frontispiece. Alexander Pope, the portrait engraved in his *Works*, 1717, based on the painting by Charles Jervas, *c.* 1714.

Between page 54 and page 55

1. Pallas Athene and Odysseus on the coast of Ithica, plate from John Ogilby's translation of the *Odyssey* (1665), probably known to Pope as a child.

2. The frontispiece from *Pope Alexander's Supremacy and Infallibility Examin'd* (1729), an attack responding to Pope's *Dunciad Variorum*, published in that year. By permission of the British Library.

3. The autograph leaf of the opening of Pope's Epistle *To Burlington.* By permission of the Pierpont Morgan Library, New York, MA 36.

4. The titlepage of *Pamela: Or, The Fair Imposter. A Poem, in Five Cantos* (1744). By permission of the British Library.

Notes on Contributors

Howard Erskine-Hill is Professor of Literary History in the English Faculty at Cambridge University. His chief books are *The Social Milieu of Alexander Pope: Lives, Example and the Poetic Response* (New Haven and London, 1975), *The Augustan Idea in English Literature* (London, 1983), *Poetry and the Realm of Politics* (Oxford, 1996) and *Poetry of Opposition and Revolution* (Oxford, 1996). He has edited with Richard A. McCabe, *Presenting Poetry: Composition, Publication, Reception, Essays in Honour of Ian Jack* (Cambridge, 1995) and is the author of numerous articles on the writings and life of Pope.

Dr. Julian Ferraro is a British Academy Postdoctoral Fellow in English at Liverpool University. His principal area of research is the poetry of Pope, and he is at present working on a new edition of Pope's *Epistles to Several Persons*. Among his publications are: 'Political Discourse in Alexander Pope's *Episode of Sarpedon*: Variations on the Theme of kingship', *Modern Language Review*, 1993; 'The Satirist, the Text and "The World Beside": *The First Satire of the Second Book of Horace Imitated*', *Translation and Literature*, 1993; and 'Taste and Use: Pope's *Epistle to Burlington*', *British Journal for Eighteenth-Century Studies*, 1996. He is working also on early Modernism, in particular Conrad and Wyndham Lewis.

Dr. Hester Jones is Lecturer in English at the University of Liverpool, having previously held a Junior Research Fellowship at Trinity College, Cambridge. She is working on a book about friendship in seventeenth- and eighteenth-century literature. She works also on Emily Dickinson, Rose Macaulay, Elizabeth Bowen and Adrienne Rich.

Dr. Thomas Keymer is Elmore Fellow in English at St. Anne's College, Oxford, and a Lecturer of the University. His publications include *Richardson's Clarissa and the Eighteenth-Century Reader* (Cambridge, 1992), editions of Sterne's *A Sentimental Journey* (London 1994) and Fielding's *The Journal of a Voyage to Lisbon* (London, 1996), and recent essays on poets of the period including Macpherson and Smart. He is currently writing a book about intertextuality and politics in eighteenth-century fiction.

David Nokes is Reader in English Literature at King's College, London. His principal publications include *Jonathan Swift, a Hypocrite Reversed* (Oxford, 1985) and *John Gay, A Profession of Friendship* (Oxford, 1995). He is currently writing a new biography of Jane Austen. He has also written screenplays for BBC television dramatisations of Samuel Richardson's *Clarissa* and Anne Brontë's *The Tenant of Wild-fell Hall*.

Claude Rawson is the Maynard Mack Professor of English at Yale University, Chairman of the Yale Boswell Editions, and an Honorary Professor at the University of Warwick. He is a former president of the British Society of Eighteenth-Century Studies. His publications include *Henry Fielding and the Augustan Ideal under Stress, Gulliver and the Gentle Reader* and *Order from Confusion Sprung: Studies in Eighteenth-Century Literature from Swift to Cowper*. His most recent book is *Satire and Sentiment, 1660–1830* (Cambridge, 1994) and he is, with H. B. Nisbet, editor of the forthcoming eighteenth-century volume of the Cambridge History of Literary Criticism, a series of which he is a general editor.

Preface

THE ESSAYS WHICH COMPOSE this volume were, with the exception of the Introduction, papers originally given at the Symposium on Alexander Pope: World and Word, held at the British Academy in May 1994, to mark the two hundred and fiftieth anniversary of Pope's death. Each paper has since been supplemented and revised.

While one reason for the Introduction is, naturally, to introduce the essays which follow, it seemed useful also to survey the work on Pope which had been published during the last twenty-five years, since G. S. Rousseau produced a similar survey as the Introduction to *Alexander Pope,* which Peter Dixon edited for the Writers and Their Background Series in 1972. Like G. S. Rousseau's review, mine does not pretend to mention every book and article on Pope which has appeared during a quarter of a century. It claims only to sketch the salient features of a fertile and various terrain.

Acknowledgements are due, in the United Kingdom, to the British Academy for helping to make the 1994 Pope Symposium such a successful and enjoyable occasion. I am grateful also to Dr. Iain G. Brown, Professor H. T. Dickinson, Dr. David Husain, Dr. D. K. Money and Dr. Kevin van Anglen for their kind information and advice. I acknowledge the assistance of the British Library; the Bodleian Library, Oxford; Cambridge University Library; the National Library of Scotland; the Library of the Society of Antiquaries; the Trustees of the Chatsworth Settlement; Chetham's Library, Manchester; Durham University Library; the Hertford County Record Office; the Lambeth Palace Library; the Leeds University Library (Brotherton Collection); the Wren Library, Trinity College, Cambridge; and the Library of Worcester College, Oxford, in helping me locate and often in sending me copies of poems on the Treaty of Utrecht. Acknowledgement is gratefully made for similar assistance from the following libraries in the United States of America: the Beinecke Library, Yale University; the Folger Library; the Harry Ranson Humanities Research Center at the University of Texas at Austin; the Lilly Library, Indiana University; the Houghton Library, Harvard University; the Huntington Library, San Marino, California; and the Newberry Library, Chicago.

I am grateful to Chadwyck-Healey Ltd. for assisting me in making various searches in its English Poetry Data Base, and to Mr. Ian Baker for compiling the Index.

18 May 1996   H. H. E.-H.

Proceedings of the British Academy, **91**, 1–26

Introduction

HOWARD ERSKINE-HILL

1

POPE UNDOUBTEDLY HAD a vision of the world. It was initially a vision of place, where virtually every name — whether of land, sea, river, region or city — carried its legend of antiquity or its tale of the present.[1] His imagination, holding past and present in mind, that city, for example where

> Tyber, now no longer Roman, rolls,

produced, thus, a vision of time, ideas of the processes of the world, notions of the patterns of history, of the cycles of civilisations, within which hopes of progress, fears of decline and fall, could be urged, averted, at least understood. Through the ways of the world in history works were disseminated, sometimes relegated. As a consequence some modern minds enjoyed contact with the past, though some were impoverished for the lack of it. In so far as this was a living contact, so far was it possible for modern minds to assess their world in the light of the past. These were the conditions of Pope's view of his world, ancient and modern.

Pope may be regarded as a moralist alone, that is to say, as an author read solely, or primarily, for the content of his writings, his human wisdom. Indeed, it is the opinion of the present writer that discussion of Pope in recent decades has been chiefly concerned with his thought, his views and his judgement, and only perfunctorily or occasionally with the salient fact that his most famous works were written in verse, and usually in a particular kind of verse. If this is so, it is only part of a wider trend in Western literary culture, which is

[1] I am grateful to Mr. Jonathan Pritchard, of Trinity College, Cambridge, for his discussions of the importance of place and place names in Pope.

concerned with the writings of poets, dramatists, even novelists, as if they were all essayists or didactic prose-writers. Modern critical discussion has not only been losing control of an older technical idiom which made discussions of the craft of poetry possible, but, unfortunately, has also often lost compelling ways in which to explain that an inspiring or a drastic judgement —

And wretches hang that jury-men may dine—

owes something to form as well as something to ethics, owes everything, in fact, to a moral and aesthetic mastery of poetic language which it can never finally be intelligent to separate into content and form. Peter France, however, reminds us that perhaps the most influential translation of Pope's *Works* into French was in prose and, further, that this was not at all unusual practice in eighteenth-century France when it came to translating poetic masters in verse from other languages.[2] It is thus worth reviewing what seems to have been the wisdom of Pope, the thought of Pope the moralist, as perceived in the later twentieth century, irrespective of the literary forms, whether in verse or prose, in which he chose to cast his thoughts. Thus it would be possible to say that, in a conciliatory and familiar mode, Pope synthesised the literary theory of Aristotle, Horace and Longinus, in *An Essay on Criticism* (1711). In *Windsor-Forest* (1713) he explored the themes of warfare, conquest, slavery in a range of senses, peace and freedom, as they seemed to arise from a survey of British history past and present. Unlike the author of any other poem on the Treaty of Utrecht, Pope confronted the practice of slavery in its literal sense and repudiated it as inconsistent with his vision of peace.[3] In a further conciliatory and discursive exploration, *An Essay on Man*, Pope sought to review and combine those arguments which relate the earthly to the heavenly, the physical with the metaphysical, the personal impulse with the social impulse, the passions with reason, and man's contingent state with his

[2]See Peter France, 'The French Pope' in Colin Nicholson, ed. *Alexander Pope: Essays for the tercentenary* (Aberdeen, 1988), pp. 117–19.
[3]See the first essay in the present volume, 'Pope and Slavery', pp. 27–53. It is remarkable that Pope should stand in the poetic record as an exception. If we ask why this should be, it may at least be suggested that Pope may have known Jean Bodin's *Six Livres de la République*, with its chapter opposing slavery (I. v), for Bodin is praised (albeit in a different connection) in one of Pope's favourite books, Charles Cotton's translation of Montaigne's *Essays* (Ch. 69). Montaigne himself may have swayed Pope's view of slavery in the New World: see Pope's annotations in his copy of Cotton's Montaigne as recorded in Maynard Mack, *Collected in Himself: Essays Critical, Biographical, and Bibliographical on Pope and Some of His Contemporaries* (London, 1982), p. 430.

hopes of happiness. While affirming the divine more fully than regular eighteenth-century deism, Pope's poem circled around but never mentioned the specific Christian Revelation, though the poet originally planned to open his first epistle with an address to Christ.[4] In *The Dunciad* and many of his satires and epistles (whether imitations of Horace or not) Pope drew on and powerfully contributed to the widespread opposition culture which in the 1720s and 1730s was being directed against the long régime of Sir Robert Walpole, and against the Hanoverian court under the first two Georges. This opposition culture was underpinned ideologically by several authors, ancient and modern; Virgil and Horace, but also Tacitus and, from the Renaissance, Machiavelli, whom Pope's friend and mentor, Henry St. John, Viscount Bolingbroke, specifically drew on to analyse the ills and fears of Britain in the 1720s and 1730s as he saw them. Above all in the potent image and concept of corruption, both moral failure and a process of historical decay, Pope's later poetry derived from Machiavelli a dominant idea which made coherent some of the most radical poetry of opposition English literature has known. More important, perhaps, than all these areas of thought and teaching in Pope, are those predominantly later poems, indebted to Horace if not formal imitations of him, in which Pope, with irony and humour, mixes personal life with public life, playing a variety of parts, as Maynard Mack has shown in one of the best essays on Pope this century.[5] The poet who admired Erasmus, the poet who was an early student of Montaigne, found in Horace the liberating example which encouraged him not to speak a public or an intellectual language only, but, in well-contrived autobiographical mode, a personal language too. Strange as it may seem, Pope is the most autobiographical poet in English literature up to his own time. Donne and Marvell, masters of dramatic *personae*, more so than Pope, are, so far as we can tell, less close to autobiography. By comparison with these two earlier poets, Pope more commonly mingles different *personae* within the same text, with the result that the reader begins to develop the idea of a character behind or above the various parts he plays.

It is in the context of these relations between personal, social and public that Pope's presentation of women should be seen. His poetry moves decisively away from that dichotomy according to which the

---

[4] J. M. Osborn, ed. *Observations, Anecdotes, and Characters of Books and Men*, 2 vols. (Oxford, 1966), I. 135 (item 305).
[5] Maynard Mack, 'The Muse of Satire', *Yale Review*, XLI (1951–2), pp. 80–92.

woman is either mistress or saint. His prose letters to Lady Mary
Wortley Montagu, on an uneasy frontier between extravagant performance and ill-controlled irony, are perhaps the nearest thing we find in
Pope to seventeenth-century poetry of courtship. That is supplanted
by a poetry of friendship, between man and woman, also between man
and man. Within the range of feeling here involved are to be found
affection, amusement, ironic awareness, candour and admiration. They
exist within a more equal and open relationship than that between, for
example, Marvell's male lover and his Coy Mistress, or between Dryden
and Anne Killigrew, easy though it is to oversimplify and undervalue
those seventeenth-century poems. Some feminist criticism, more concerned to fight late twentieth-century battles than achieve an
understanding of Pope, has charged him with misogyny and a merely
patronising politeness towards women. On similar grounds one could
charge him with a similar treatment of men. On each side this is a part,
but far from the whole, truth. This is a subject prone to programmatic
distortion. By contrast, Hester Jones's essay in the present collection,
'Pope's Homer: The Shadow of Friendship' discusses male and female
relations in Pope with exceptional sensitivity, and brilliantly links
Pope's presentation of Ulysses and Athena in *Odyssey*, Book XIII,
with his address to Martha Blount at the end of his Epistle *To a Lady*.

It will be noticed that Pope's most famous early poem, *The Rape
of the Lock* (1714, 1717) has not featured in this survey of Pope's
'thought'. This is because the poem is, at first sight, deceptively easy
to reduce to a summary of attitudes and a moral. It seems to sum itself
up, after all, in Clarissa's speech at the opening of Canto V. In fact
this heroi-comical poem is harder to reduce to 'thought' than any other
of Pope's major works save *The Dunciad*. Of course Pope displays the
human muddle when manners cease to be morals and become mere
fashions. Of course, in Clarissa's speech the reader is confronted with
a sombre vision of life as a series of irresistible deprivations. This
has led generations of readers to suppose that the poem advocates
submission. With the sudden advent of a new feminist criticism, some
twenty years ago, this was speedily transformed into the conclusion
that the poem advocated the subordination of women. There was in
fact a further ground for such a conclusion, for had not almost every
text of *The Rape of the Lock* since Warburton's 1751 Edition of Pope's
Works appended to Clarissa's speech the footnote: '*Clarissa* / A new
Character introduced in the subsequent Editions, to open more clearly
the MORAL of the Poem, in a parody of the speech of Sarpedon to

Glaucus in Homer.'[6] It is one of the most widespread misconceptions about Pope, and by no means easy to rectify from the relevant volumes of the Twickenham Edition, to think that Pope wrote the main part of this well-known footnote. He did not. All that he wrote in his lifetime was that the speech was a parody of that of Sarpedon to Glaucus. Clarissa was not a new character (see III. 127–8). In the circumstances it is highly conjectural that Warburton had Pope's authority for the 1751 footnote in which this 'moral' first appeared. It is rather part of the posthumous reception of the poem. Clarissa's speech is thus not the moral of the poem but a moral *in* the poem, to be interpreted in the light of the total poetic work. This in turn means that it is extremely difficult to generalise the 'thought' of the poem. *The Rape of the Lock* is now revealed as a finely balanced aesthetic structure in which notions of active resistance and passive obedience are kept in play, responsive to each episode of the action and each action of the poetry. The reader is kept in suspense until the poem's final, comic, move: the apotheosis of the Lock. What the reader makes of this depends on the transformations of poetic tone in the whole of the foregoing text. If it ratifies Belinda's resistance to the Baron, which I am inclined to suppose, it does so in a vulnerably comic manner. We should probably conclude that *The Rape of the Lock* is a poem which resists any but the most complex moral summary. We should conclude also that there is no way in which Pope's poem advocates the subordination of women to men, however surprising that might seem in view of the regular patterns of eighteenth-century social history.

The Rape of the Lock is an example which demonstrates the relative inadequacy of attempting to reduce complex aesthetic structures to statements of presumed intention, or to morals too simple to be believed. There is a case for studying poets such as Spenser, Milton, Pope or Wordsworth as moralists, as writers notable for their thought alone, but, by contrast with writers whose practice is closer than that of these poets to the ratiocinative and didactic, such as Berkeley, or Shaftesbury, such an approach is one-eyed to a circumspect, Ulyssean, poetic text. Thus it is that recent Pope criticism, concentrating as it has predominantly done, on attitude and opinion, has often failed to do justice to the subtle and circumspect knowledge of the poem.

---

[6]*The Twickenham Edition of the Poems of Alexander Pope*, ed. John Butt *et al.* 11 vols. (London, 1939–69), II. 199, n. 7.

2

These two interdependent aspects of Pope, his thought and his art, are represented by the two terms in the title of the present collection: world and word. Pope's knowledge and judgement of his world — to some extent still also our world — and his art in the choice of word in relation to available vocabulary, to situations described, to paragraph, to metre, to rhyme, to the aesthetic structure of the whole poem, afford us a critical pattern with which to review the varieties of work on Pope and his world which has been produced during the last twenty-five years. The purpose of this Introduction is to provide such a review, and to place the different contributions to the present volume in relation to foregoing work on Pope.

In his Introduction to Peter Dixon's collection of essays, *Alexander Pope* (1972), George Rousseau surveyed the then state of learning about Pope, and his significance for twentieth-century culture. The most important thing, probably, which Rousseau emphasised was the survival of Pope's poetic and other, manuscripts. The chief feature of this part of his discussion is the lost Chauncy MS of *The Dunciad*: the first edition containing Pope's own 'corrections, comments and additions in his handwriting' which seems to have been available to Elwin and Courthope, Pope's Victorian editors, but which has subsequently disappeared.[7] This volume has not, so far as I know, been rediscovered, but something of similar significance has since been published in facsimile by Maynard Mack: the record made at Pope's request by Jonathan Richardson the younger of passages drafted for or deleted from the 1729 *Dunciad*. This and other poetic MSS of Pope have now been published by Professor Mack, in his major collection *The Last and Greatest Art: Some Unpublished Poetical Manuscripts of Alexander Pope* (1984), which comprises the copious *Essay on Man* MSS previously published by Mack for the Roxburgh Club, and all other poetic MSS of Pope known to have survived at the time of publication save those previously published by others: *An Essay on Criticism*, ed. R. M. Schmitz (1962), *Windsor-Forest*, ed. R. M. Schmitz (1952) and the Epistle *To Bathurst*, ed. E. R. Wasserman (1962), and with the further exception of the important and significant Homer MSS in the British Library. With *The Last and Greatest Art*, then, the MSS of *The Pastorals* (the Preface, 'Spring', 'Summer', 'Autumn',

---

[7] G. S. Rousseau, 'On Reading Pope' in Peter Dixon, ed. *Alexander Pope, Writers and their Background* (London, 1972), pp. 1–59.

and 'Winter', but not the 'Messiah') were published; *Sapho to Phaon*; the Epistle *To Jervas*; *The Dunciad* (Richardson's collations of the first and second 'Broglio MSS'; the Epistle *To Burlington* (including the Chatsworth version and the Mapledurham Fragments); *The First Satire of the Second Book of Horace, Imitated* (To Fortescue); *An Essay on Man* (the Pierpont Morgan Library and Houghton Library MSS); and the Epistle *To Arbuthnot*. All these were in 1984 made available in facsimile and with transcripts on the facing page, Introductions and Commentaries. Subsequently David L. Vander Meulen published *Pope's Dunciad of 1728. A History and Facsimile* (1991), which contributes graphically to our understanding of how *The Dunciad* developed, since it includes a record of Pope's early drafts in annotations by Jonathan Richardson the younger. It is fair to say that critical discussion of Pope's art has barely begun to assimilate this mass of intricate but highly revealing material.[8] It is also true to say that the Homer MSS in the British Library demand the same attention that Maynard Mack has given the poetic manuscripts listed above. Meanwhile Dr. Julian Ferraro, whose essay 'From Text to Work: The Presentation and Representation of *Epistles to Several Persons*' is included in the present collection, is among those younger scholars who have begun to think afresh about the study of poetic manuscripts, and their particular significance in the case of Pope. The suggestion that MS versions may not represent different stages towards an ultimately desired aesthetic form, but rather different poems in themselves each responding to subtly different circumstances, is one which deserves much discussion as the study of Pope's manuscripts proceeds.

A similar concept, perhaps, dominates the second great development in Pope studies since G. S. Rousseau's essay. In 1975–6 David Foxon delivered the Lyell Lectures at the University of Oxford on the subject of Pope and the Early Eighteenth-Century Book Trade. For a decade and a half these important lectures were consulted as circulated by the generosity of the author, or as deposited in certain major research libraries, chiefly the British Library. Then in 1991 they were published, revised and edited by James McLaverty, by the Clarendon Press, Oxford.[9] Several salient suggestions emerge from Foxon's research, and I shall focus here on a few only. First, the copy-text

---

[8] Maynard Mack, *The Last and Greatest Art: Some Unpublished Poetical Manuscripts of Alexander Pope* (London, 1984).
[9] David Foxon, *Pope and the Early Eighteenth-Century Book Trade*, The Lyell Lectures, Oxford 1975–6, Rev. and ed. James McLaverty (Oxford, 1991).

philosophy promulgated by W. W. Gregg and generally followed by Fredson Bowers, produced to cope with the problems of the printed versions of Elizabethan and early Jacobean drama, is inappropriate to the printed works of Pope, who had unusual control over the printed form of his works, early and late, and seems to have changed his views on the typographical and broader visual presentation of his works as the years went by, and as particular publishing opportunities presented themselves. Foxon then tends to support that editorial method which honours the author's last considered intentions rather than the first authoritative form. Secondly, Foxon moves the whole matter of typography from the margins towards the centre of the critical discussion of a Pope text. A varying additional emphasis is effected by italics and capitals, the latter often appealing to the habit of thinking of abstract qualities as personifications —

> Adieu to Virtue, if you're once a Slave . . .

Both 'Virtue' and 'Slave' refer to moral conditions, but the latter is here closer to a human figure, so that the link between the two capitalised nouns enhances the standing of the abstract noun as a human form, to whom one might have to say 'goodbye'. Foxon's argument that Pope, Gay and others moved towards the choice of a plain text as the years went by, does seem cogent in Pope's case with regard to some kinds of edition. But the work of Foxon and McLaverty has prompted more recent scholars to suggest that throughout his life Pope may have chosen different typographies for different kinds of edition of his works.[10] It is certainly now the case that no entirely adequate critical account of a major Pope poem can afford to overlook the 'accidentals' of its major editions during the poet's life. To mention but one often neglected aspect, the decorations which appeared with Pope's texts on some occasions deserve attention. In the quarto *Works* of 1735, for example, a decoration containing the Scottish royal motto: 'Nemo me impune lacessit' occurs three times, once after the Arguments to the Books, once after Bk. I and once after Bk. II. Scottish thistles as well as asses' heads appear in the repeated decoration. Again, in the 1735 *Works*, Pope's Epistle *To Dr. Arbuthnot* concludes with an heraldic decoration properly recording the arms of his parents' families, the Popes and the Turners. This was obviously appropriate to a poem which, in its concluding sections, paid tribute to the poet's

---

[10]See, for example, Tania Rideout, 'The Reasoning Eye: Alexander Pope's Typographic Vision in the *Essay on Man*', *Journal of the Warburg and Courtauld Institutes*, 55 (1992), pp. 249–62.

parents. A more salient point, perhaps, arises when one surveys the first editions of the individual poems which make up Pope's *Imitations of Horace*. Since Vol. IV of the Twickenham Edition it has been assumed that the *ideal* (if not always the most practical) way of printing the *Imitations* was to set Horace's Latin on the facing page, with the system of raised letters, and capitalised and italicised words, carrying the reader's eye backwards and forwards between the Latin and the English texts. Pope himself does set precedents for this, but it should also be noted that the first editions of some individual poems in the *Imitations of Horace* — for example, the rich and subtle Epistle *To Augustus* (Hor. *Ep.* II. i) — was not originally printed in this way. As with certain of Pope's later collected editions, the references to Horace's text was confined to quotations of paragraph beginnings in footnotes. There is room here for more than one editorial view. But it is not evident that Pope invariably required Horace's text on the facing page for all his *Imitations of Horace*.[11]

3

If we now turn from textual study of Pope's poetry to the first circle of contextual consideration, the poet's letters call for consideration. As early as G. S. Rousseau's 1972 survey, many Pope letters not in George Sherburn's 1956 *Correspondence of Alexander Pope* had been published. Most notably, the very appearance of Sherburn's five volumes had prompted the discovery in the Downshire MSS of the further letters, chiefly to Sir William Trumbull, published by Sherburn in *RES* in 1958,[12] while a single letter of exceptional quality and interest, to Martha Blount, Aug. 1734, the 'Netley Abbey Letter', had been published by Rousseau himself in 1966.[13] Forty-six further letters of Pope, previously unpublished, or unpublished in this form, were brought out by Maynard Mack in his volume, *Collected in Himself: Essays Critical, Biographical, and Bibliographical on Pope and Some of His Contemporaries* (1982), gathering together some work published

[11]See *The First Epistle of the Second Book of Horace, Imitated* (London, 1737) (Griffith 458/467; Foxon p. 881).

[12]George Sherburn, 'Letters of Alexander Pope, chiefly to Sir William Trumbull', *Review of English Studies*, 9 (1958), pp. 388–406.

[13]George Rousseau, 'A New Pope Letter', *Philological Quarterly*, XLV, II (April, 1966), pp. 409–418.

earlier by others, and also many letters to and about Pope of great interest. In 1985 Pat Rogers published a helpful list, 'Not in Sherburn', recording the attribution of new letters to Pope since 1956: at least one new letter of Pope has come to light and been published since.[14]

Much more work remains to be done on Pope's letters. In the first place, it seems probable that further work on his contemporaries will uncover further correspondence. There are, further, issues of importance which need to be reconsidered. Ever since C. W. Dilke's discovery of the Caryll transcripts of Pope's letters to John, Lord Caryll, this source has been assumed to be of rock-like primary significance. It naturally appears so because it was from these letters, in many cases, that Pope produced letters addressed to other people for his printed *Correspondence*. The transcripts certainly revealed Pope's procedure in composing his letters for publication, but one may feel less certain that they must be a complete record of what Pope originally wrote. For example, a sexually frank letter of Pope to another and younger member of the Caryll family has survived, which it is inconceivable that Lord Caryll (had he known it) would have asked a female member of his family to transcribe. One may also reflect that, if Pope ever included incautious religious or political remarks in his letters to Caryll, Caryll was too familiar with the dangers of the world in which he lived to allow them to be copied. Dilke's discovery, and its impact on Pope's Victorian editors, has had a further influence on the twentieth-century approach to Pope's letters. Attention has been diverted from the collections of Pope's correspondence printed in his lifetime, as not quite 'the real thing', as an embarrassing or dishonest contrivance on the poet's part. Leaving the ethics of re-composing letters on one side, however, it is clear that Pope's correspondence as reconstituted, selected and arranged by the poet himself, with letters grouped by the correspondents, to whom they were addressed, a very different reading experience from what we get from the chronological sequence of Sherburn, is Pope's only major work not to have been edited in the twentieth century. The one scholar who has shown interest in the correspondence Pope printed as such, Paul Hammond,[15] was able only to illustrate what might be done by this approach. The editing and introducing of

---

[14]This is one of Pope's (probably early) undated notes to the Earl of Burlington. It is in the Greater London Record Office (Middlesex Records), Acc. 1128/185/27, and is now published in Howard Erskine-Hill, 'Pope and Burlington', in Toby Barnard and Jane Clark, eds. *Lord Burlington: Architecture, Art and Life* (London, 1995), pp. 219–20.

[15]Paul Hammond, ed. *Selected Prose of Alexander Pope* (Cambridge, 1987), pp. 232–89.

Pope's own version of his correspondence remains a major task for some future scholar.

4

The question of Pope's letters leads naturally on to biographical study. It is, I think, clear, that the most important work on Pope to appear since George Rousseau's 1972 survey, is Maynard Mack's *Alexander Pope: A Life* (1985). Before confronting this brilliant book, however, it is worth reflecting on the peculiar challenges which face the biographer of Pope. It is to say no more than the obvious if one points out that many of the most important people in Pope's biography have warranted biographical attention in their own right — or would warrant it. Thus, to take some obvious examples, Joseph Addison, Ralph Allen, John Arbuthnot, Francis Atterbury, George Berkeley, Henry St. John, Viscount Bolingbroke, John Gay, John Hervey, Baron Ickworth, Lady Mary Worthley Montagu, Jonathan Swift, Sir William Trumbull, William Warburton, William Wycherley, are all people whom the reader might wish — to say the least — to know something about without wishing to know about Pope. On the other hand, no balanced biography of any of these important eighteenth-century figures could be produced which did not pay attention to the relation between its subject and Pope. Pope, certainly, was a man to whom periods of retirement, solitude, lonely reflection were essential; but he was, on the other hand, a person of extraordinary social and public awareness. His genius, almost, was his responsiveness to other people. This is the formidable difficulty for the biographer of Pope, more so in Pope's case, in fact, than in that of Swift. Yet it must be said that one of the disappointments of reading the rich, extended, and well-written three-volume biography of Swift by the late Irvin Ehrenpreis (1962–83) is that it very largely extracts Swift from his pattern of relationships, even some of the salient and famous ones of his life, such as those with Bolingbroke and Pope. Archbishop William King emerges well from the pages of Ehrenpreis but, despite numerous references, Swift's other friendships are not studied in depth, at least not in the later years, so that it is difficult to see the deeper currents of his later life. This can of course be made good in the case of such figures as Pope and Bolingbroke, themselves the subjects of excellent modern studies.[16] It is not the case with a significant lesser figure such as Charles Ford. Yet one may expect that this exasperating Irish friend of Swift could throw much light on the Dean if one were to study him in his own right. Such a suggestion may seem the mere counsel of despair. How can the biographer of any complex major figure possibly attend to the by-road lives of even the more personally important of his or her friends and acquaintances? But what looks like a by-road to the retrospective biographer may have looked like a main road to the subject of the biography. In any case, there is a modern form, that of multiple biography, which is well able to tackle exactly this problem: the relation between a 'major' subject and a pattern of 'minor' contemporaries.

So far as the career of Alexander Pope is concerned, the advantages of multiple biography were first demonstrated by James Lees-Milne in his study, *Earls of Creation: Five Great Patrons of Eighteenth-Century Art* (1962), not mentioned by G. S. Rousseau in his 1972 survey, though acknowledged by Pat Rogers in the same volume.[17] Lees-Milne may not have conceived of his ground-breaking volume as multiple biography bearing specifically on Pope, though Pope moves through the lives he recounts, influencing and influenced. The next stage in this particular development came with Howard Erskine-Hill's book, *The Social Milieu of Alexander Pope: Lives, Example and the Poetic Response* (1975). Pope was here owned as the central subject; multiple biography as the intended method. To function well, this form demands of its practitioners a dual fidelity: first, to the 'minor' lives recounted, as significant for their own sake; secondly, to the way such lives studied for their own sake can contribute to the 'major' life likely to be the organising centre of consciousness of the book. Seven chapters of this work were devoted to contemporary lives, before the final chapters attempted to draw the threads together to constitute a new portrait of Pope in the context of his time. This approach to Pope was next adopted by Valerie Rumbold in her admirable study, *Women's Place in Pope's World* (1989). Partly responding to the Popeian precedents in multiple biography, and partly to the growing interest in women's writing and women's lives, Valerie Rumbold produced a book which looked more fully and deeply than any had before at the lives and background of Edith Turner (Pope's mother), Martha and Teresa

---

[16]See H. T. Dickinson, *Bolingbroke* (London, 1970).
[17]Pat Rogers, 'Pope and the Social Scene', in Peter Dixon, ed. *Alexander Pope*, p. 113; see also pp. 145, 162–3.

Blount, the Duchess of Buckingham and the Duchess of Marlborough, Mary Caesar and the Countess of Suffolk (including also Lady Mary Wortley Montagu whom Robert Halsband had earlier made his specific study).[18] Here too was a work which acknowledged 'the importance of individual lives' (p. xvi) while keeping steadily in view, not only the life and literary achievement of Pope, but also the issue of gender in eighteenth-century society and literature. The value of multiple biography at the present time is far from exhausted — indeed it has but recently been demonstrated, and is likely to have exceptional potential in the seventeenth and eighteenth centuries when the political and artistic public was, arguably, more in touch with itself than in later periods. In Pope's case, we must look forward to the time when, for example, his friend William Fortescue, a mediator, perhaps, between the poet and Sir Robert Walpole; or the Third Earl of Burlington, or Mr. Hugh Bethel, or the Richardsons, or Anne Arbuthnot, are better known in the context of their age.

The perceptions of multiple biography are, naturally, also to be found in orthodox biography. The reader of Pope's poems and letters might take for granted that, throughout his life, Pope had been a warm supporter of his brilliant literary friend, John Gay. David Nokes, however, the new biographer of Gay, sees the relationship from a different angle.[19] His essay in the present volume, 'The Ambitious Pursuit: Pope, Gay and the Life of Writing' cogently argues that Pope's attitude to his friend Gay was — what wonder! — a somewhat more mixed matter. That there was rivalry within friendship, and conspiracy within homage, in the eighteenth century, need surprise no one, any more than it would if it were found, for example, within the world of Henry James or of Virginia Woolf. This kind of perception, in fact, is the hallmark of the best biographical practice. The common capaciousness of modern biography, is not, according to the best practice, used to achieve a detailed, circumstantial, identification of the reader, through the biographer, with the subject. Rather, the capaciousness of modern biography should be used to balance viewpoint with viewpoint, to poise the moral scales, and to see the ways in which the subject sometimes swam against the tides of his age — as in this volume I argue Pope did on the issue of slavery — and sometimes saw ways in

---

[18]In 'The Jacobite Vision of Mary Caesar', in Isobel Grundy and Susan Wiseman, eds. *Women, Writing, History, 1640–1740* (London, 1992), pp. 178–233, Dr. Rumbold has published a further study of the least well-known figure in *Women's Place in Pope's World*.
[19]David Nokes, *John Gay: A Profession of Friendship, A Critical Biography* (Oxford, 1995).

which those tides could yet express something of the biographical subject. As Pope put it, in a carefully fashioned autobiographical passage: he would

> Sometimes a Patriot, active in debate,
> Mix with the World, and battle for the State,
> Sometimes, with Aristippus, or St. Paul,
> Indulge my Candor, and grow all to all;
> Back to my native Moderation slide,
> And win my way by yielding to the tyde.
>
> (*Ep*. I. i. 27–34; T. E. IV. 281)

It is with this issue above all in mind that we should approach Maynard Mack's biography, *Alexander Pope: A Life* (1985) which may in retrospect prove the most important work to have been published about Alexander Pope in the twentieth century.

Mack embarked on his critical biography of Pope towards the end of an academic career devoted to Pope, but also to Shakespeare, and as in Mack's Introduction to the Twickenham Edition of *An Essay on Man* (1950), the reader is made aware of a rich confluence of Renaissance currents, themselves bearing classical knowledge and ideas, which find expression in the attitudes and works of Pope. This has the effect of seeing Pope in a long perspective, a wide cultural space, and successfully avoids some of the more closed-in biographical approaches deriving from specialisation in the eighteenth century alone. The value of Mack's intellectual range is well illustrated by the short but immensely suggestive section in which he discusses Pope and Montaigne. Here a particular biographical fact, that Pope's copy of Cotton's translation of Montaigne has survived with Pope's annotations (*c.* 1706) not only demonstrates a link between Pope and Renaissance learning, but shows a shared introspective habit of mind, a trend towards self-portrayal, as that learning nourished and directed the intelligence. Connections between Pope's early reading of Montaigne and his later poetry are lightly touched in by Mack: for example, the book-burdened ass on the title-page of the 1729 *Dunciad*, and that moment in the imitation of the *First Satire of the Second Book of Horace* where Tories call Pope Whig, and Whigs a Tory, and where, indeed, Pope pays specific homage to Montaigne (ll. 51–2).[20]

Where a balance of judgement on Pope is concerned, Mack states the issues plainly. 'Without concealing his warts, I have consciously

[20]Maynard Mack, *Alexander Pope: A Life* (London, 1985), pp. 82–3.

avoided magnifying them ... where there are extenuating circumstances to be considered ... I have thought it proper to consider them.
Pope's worst faults were grievous, but so are the faults of most of
us. ... If the results of the effort in my case are dismissed as special
pleading, so be it. There are few poets who cannot use an advocate'
(p. viii). Warts and faults are to be revealed, but the final emphasis
will be that of a counsel for the defence. These explicit statements
seem to me to convey the most reasonable approach for a modern
biographer. It may be put to the proof, perhaps, with the case of Pope's
conspiracy to retrieve his letters from his great, and greatly admired,
friend Swift. Here Pope appears at his most disingenuous and manipulative, working upon Swift through his Irish connections, while
professing a noble candour to Swift himself. Here indeed may be
found an unedifying episode in Pope's life, the alert, duplicitous poet
conspiring, apparently, to get the better of the great, decaying, Dean.
Mack does not mince words about all this. Pope left, he says, 'no stone
unturned, no lie untold' to gain his end. 'Pope's conduct in this episode
was discreditable by any standard' (pp. 670–1). There is then no white-
washing here. Are there extenuating circumstances to be considered?
Not in the way one might expect. That is to say, there is no effort to
explain why Pope had become circumspect, cunning, manipulative,
mendacious, in this particular affair. Such an explanation could have
been mounted, and would, probably, have made some difference to
our modern view, though it might also have smacked of that special
pleading which Mack admits as a possible charge against himself only
in the last resort. What Mack actually does in his narrative of this
episode is a master stroke of biographical art. On very good empirical
grounds he shows how probable it was that Swift already knew what
Pope was trying to do.[21] Within their sincere admiration for one
another, he suggests, each knew pretty well what were the aims of the
other. When, in response to Pope's quite plausible representations that
his letters to Swift could, were they to fall into the wrong hands, be
damaging, and Swift first says that all Pope's letters to him are safe
at the Deanery, but later that he has discovered a 'Chasm' in the
correspondence, 1717–22 (the period leading up to the Atterbury Plot),
Swift is almost certainly teasing Pope. When we remember how many
friends each writer had who were considered treasonous, at some time
or other, by the Hanoverian authorities, a 'Chasm' in the correspon-

[21]*Pope: A Life*, pp. 666–71.

dence could mean one of two things: first, that incriminating letters had somehow been obtained by the government, in which case their writer might fall into trouble not stopping short of execution; or, alternatively, the 'Chasm' could mean that a sequence of dangerous letters had already been recognised and destroyed. Swift is teasing Pope in not making clear which was the case. We may conclude that, if teasing over such an issue seems a little cruel, Pope's manipulative duplicity had earned the punishment. Beyond all this, what Mack's picture presents, is two affectionate, competitive, subtle, worldly, writers, each well-accustomed to the ways in which authors could deal with publishers, sparring with one another in a contest which each thoroughly understood. While Mack is still prepared to condemn Pope's procedure on straightforward moral grounds — and is surely right to do so — still his intelligent and well-supported hypothesis as to exactly what Swift understood in these proceedings, draws the sting out of Pope's conduct. The case made is more than an extenuation.

Alexander Pope: A Life appeared between the two works of multiple biography mentioned above. If the first, possibly, contributed anything positive to an *opus* long in the making, it may also have bequeathed temptations and difficulties. Mack speaks of 'fascinating material' 'jettisoned along the way in order to keep some degree of proportion . . . enough material to supply almost any number of other biographical studies' (p. viii). This is credible indeed, and it would be absurd to complain that more has not been said about many of Pope's fascinating contemporaries and friends. Indeed the scholar who manages to connect Mack's main text with its related endnotes (awkwardly separated by a bad convention of publishing) will discover hidden riches: for example, the long, tightrope-walking religious history of Pope's maternal forbears, or Blount of Blagdon's important initiative to reconcile Roman Catholic worship with the taking of an oath to the *de facto* Protestant king (pp. 3–4, 820–21; 407–9, 886).[22] If we turn from figures like these to those who already enjoy a prominent place in eighteenth-century history, such as Joseph Addison or Francis Atterbury, we find that we are offered full and satisfying discussions. If anything might be added, it might be something to explain Addison's surprising sense of his own vulnerability as a great Whig and Hanoverian, and also of the great Tory and Jacobite Atterbury's sense of

---

[22]These connections exemplify Mack's constant and relevant use of the work of other scholars, even when he might have been forgiven for not having been aware of the more specialised items cited.

crisis and danger after the death of Anne. Why were Addison and his circle so nervous and competitive over the Homer project of the young *parvenu*, Pope? How could that staunch Anglican, Atterbury, turn to the exiled, *de jure*, Roman Catholic, James III, to defend the established church? Each man clearly felt under a severe threat in the second decade of the century, and the explanation clearly lies within the political history of the time. It is here essential not to fix a particular political character to the time. It was not a stable, Whig, era after the death of Anne. Men like Addison and Walpole in the seventeen-teens felt their ambitious Whig project for the estate to be precarious; indeed men such as Atterbury, contemplating the restoration of Charles II, could not really believe that the *de Jure* king would not come into his own again: everything depended on how, and with what undertakings, the return was managed.

These are deep political and historical issues, but there can be little doubt that they bear on Pope's sense of his identity and role within the state. Our historical picture of the first half of the eighteenth century is changing in various ways at the present time. Mack treats the Hanover versus Stuart conflict with much knowledge and tact, but it may be that these and other political issues warrant more saliency in future eighteenth-century biography.

A final word on *Alexander Pope: A Life* should pay tribute to its illustrations. Pope himself, as an amateur painter and a man acutely sensitive to the visual arts, was an intensely visual person, who kept portraits of many of his friends on the walls of his Twickenham villa. The extraordinarily rich visual material (even to the Studio of Kneller portrait of Betterton and the copy of it executed by Pope himself) is a feature of this excellent work. The study of Pope's interest in the visual arts has continued to be a feature in the period under survey. Mack was able to draw on Morris Brownell, *Alexander Pope and the Arts of Georgian England* (Oxford, 1978), a substantial and detailed piece of research. This line of work was continued by Peter Martin, in his *Pursuing Innocent Pleasures: The Gardening World of Alexander Pope* (London, 1984).

5

Changes in taste, and what many will feel to be an overproduction of academic books, during the last twenty-five years, have ensured that

few critical works on Pope have become so well-known as, say, R.
A. Brower's *Alexander Pope: the Poetry of Allusion* (1959), Aubrey
Williams's *Pope's Dunciad: A Study of its Meaning* (1955) or Maynard
Mack's *The Garden and the City: Retirement and Politics in the Later
Poetry of Pope* (1969). These books have stood the test and will remain
academic classics, which is not, of course to say that they may not be
questioned and controverted. Later works, however, had they been
published earlier in the century, would have been likely to have
achieved comparable fame: D. B. Morris, *Alexander Pope: The Genius
of Sense* (1984), David Fairer, *Pope's Imagination* (1984), Leopold
Damrosch, Jr., *The Imaginative World of Alexander Pope* (1987) and
Howard Weinbrot, *Pope and the Traditions of Formal Verse Satire*
(1982). Each of these builds visibly upon its predecessors, but has its
own revisionist programme, or its own selective emphasis.

A group of books has further explored the relations between Pope's
poetry and the literature of Greece and Rome. A major controversy
occurred about the resonances of the name 'Augustus' and the eighteenth-century meanings of 'Augustan', in which Howard Weinbrot, in
his book *Augustus Caesar in 'Augustan' England* (1978), proposed the
salient hypothesis that in the earlier eighteenth century the *princeps*
Augustus and the era of Augustan Rome were disliked, or detested —
at any rate had strongly negative associations. In fact there has been a
Tacitean, anti-Augustan tradition in English writing since the end of
the reign of Elizabeth I; this was certainly not forgotten, and may even
have become more widely shared, in the age of Pope. On the other
hand, Weinbrot pressed his half of the truth relentlessly on, quantifying
instances of attitude, rather than responding to the complexities of
poems. Pope emerges from his argument with the irony of his Epistle
To Augustus abolished — since on Weinbrot's view Pope was equally
hostile to Augustus and to George Augustus, George II of Great
Britain. Again, on this view, Pope's *Imitations of Horace* are satires on
Horace, a court poet of Augustus. The relative crudity of this analysis,
emphasising the Pope who goes out on the satirical attack as indeed
he often does, but neglecting the personal, autobiographical, introspective and humorous ways in which Pope responds to Horace's example,
prompted the responding argument of Howard Erskine-Hill in the
eighteenth-century chapters of his book, *The Augustan Idea in English
Literature* (1983). This controversy was quite productive. Neither side
was entirely in the right. The earlier eighteenth century may be seen
to have held a debate about the Augustan Age, in so far as negative

and positive views of that classical era were certainly held by educated contemporaries, and sometimes by individual writers (though usually on different occasions and with different rhetorical ends in mind). On the other hand, the view that in the eighteenth century there was a steady move away from a monarchical, pro-Augustan, vision towards a republican, pro-Tacitean, vision, is hard to sustain. In the mind of Pope the positive vision of the Augustan Age was indispensable to his literary practice though it is also clear that he was aware of the Tacitean view.[23] The issue remains one of great interest, and in the discussion of what the eighteenth century meant by the word 'Augustan', word and world, or word and world-view, are in close connection.

Early in the period under survey, H. A. Mason's *To Homer through Pope: An Introduction to Homer's Iliad and Pope's Translation* (1972) explored afresh the critical and cultural issues of translation from an heroic to an unheroic era. Several themes raised here receive fuller consideration in Claude Rawson's learned and sharply critical discussions of eighteenth-century mock-heroic, including his essay in the present volume, 'Heroic Notes: Pope's Epic Idiom Revisited'. In 1983 Steven Shankman published *Pope's 'Iliad': Homer in the Age of Passion*, a precursor to the same author's edition of Pope's *Iliad* version for Penguin Books, thus supplying the late twentieth-century reader with a poem in popular form which was often published in popular form in the eighteenth century. The latest book to discuss Pope and Homer, however, is that of Carolyn D. Williams, *Pope, Homer and Manliness* (1993), which is also perhaps the best of the various gender-focused critical studies of Pope to have appeared in recent years. (I exclude from this comparison Valerie Rumbold's *Women's Place in Pope's World* which I have already mentioned under the category of biography.)

The best recent work, however, to make detailed critical comparison between poetic texts of Pope and those of a major classical predecessor is surely Frank Stack's *Pope and Horace: Studies in Imitation* (1985). Other books should be mentioned in the same connection; Jacob Fuchs, *Reading Pope's Imitations of Horace* (1989)

---

[23]Joseph Spence, *Anecdotes*, ed. J. M. Osborn, I. 229–30, on Virgil, Augustus and the Roman Republic. The balance of Pope's thought on Augustus may have been misunderstood, at least partly, because the Index to Sherburn's Edition of *The Correspondence of Alexander Pope* has a defective entry on Augustus. See, for example, II. 455 and 503 for unlisted allusions to Augustus; above all, see III. 420, a deliberated, formal, letter to Dr. Arbuthnot, printed after his death, in which Pope deploys a positive image of Augustus (also unlisted).

and J. F. C. Plowden, *Pope on Classic Ground* (1983), the latter raising a quite new literary relationship in his discussion of Manilius's *Astronomica*, Thomas Creech's verse translation of this, and Pope's borrowings from Creech.[24]

More attention, probably, has in recent years been devoted to the exploration of Pope's poems in relation to their own time. Pat Rogers is the first name that should be mentioned here, not only for his first book, *Grub Street: Studies in a Sub-Culture* (1972), but for numerous richly suggestive essays in *Eighteenth-Century Encounters: Studies in Literature and Society in the Age of Walpole* (1985), *Essays on Pope* (1993), and in several other collections. His work is investigative rather than argumentative: not usually pressing a particular academic programme, its disinterestedness is a form of generosity to the interests of others. Another who revealed an unexpected aspect of Pope's world, and crossed swords with Rogers in doing so, is the late E. P. Thompson, in the notable Appendix to his book, *Whigs and Hunters: The Origins of the Black Act* (1975). A well-conceived approach to Pope and his poetic contemporaries is executed by Thomas Woodman's *Politeness and Poetry in the Age of Pope* (London, 1989), which brings together social and literary issues with particular success.

In the work of Claude Rawson, the concept of 'Pope's world' is less social and topographical than in Rogers, but is ever more rangingly and richly literary. Originally known for his studies of Swift and Fielding, Rawson has maintained a valuable scepticism towards the several totalising and predatory concepts under which scholars have attempted to line up eighteenth-century writing and thought. This makes Rawson an especially well-qualified critic to encounter Augustan mock-epic, that most volatile and surprising of literary forms. In 'Heroic Notes: Pope's Epic Idiom revisited' Rawson, while fully responsive to the comic subtleties of Pope's poetic practice, finds occasion to substantiate further a larger finding, already adumbrated in his recent book, *Satire and Sentiment, 1660–1830* (1994): the 'astonishing reticence about bloodshed and war' in the 'major Augustan mock-heroics'. The mock-heroic is thus revealed as a civilian — though by no means civil — comedy of war, its roots reaching back to the Humanist comedy of Erasmus and Rabelais, and the humane ethics of Montaigne.

An aversion to over-orderly schemes, so good a feature of Rawson's work, finds some support from a book on Pope published in 1977:

---

[24]Plowden, *Pope on Classic Ground*, pp. 130, 166.

This has revealed an alternative Britain, focused on the exiled dynasty, which, for many during Pope's lifetime, constituted the probable future. Such an altered view of the period was always bound to affect our picture of Pope more than of his main literary contemporaries, if only because of Pope's Roman Catholic origins, and his many connections with those active at some time or another in the Jacobite movement. Literary scholarship on Pope made some contribution to this new movement in historiography. *The Social Milieu of Alexander Pope* (1975) touched on some of the salient issues, as did three later essays by the same author.[29] On the other side of the Atlantic, John M. Aden's study, *Pope's Once and Future Kings: Satire and Politics in the Early Career* (1978), added independently to a new view of Pope's earlier years. These developments, it may be, gave a sharper Popeian focus to the work of another scholar, whose route to the earlier eighteenth century was originally from the late Frances Yates's studies in Renaissance mysticism. Douglas Brooks-Davies's *Pope's Dunciad and the Queen of Night: A Study in Emotional Jacobitism* (1985), amidst much recondite learning more applicable to the eighteenth century than one might at first suppose, suggests the helpful distinction between hard political commitment to the Jacobite cause, and a structure of feeling partly shaped by Jacobite culture. Two further books, neither devoted wholly to Pope, have recently followed up the new Jacobite lines of exploration. They are: Murray G. H. Pittock, *Poetry and Jacobite Politics in Eighteenth-Century Britain and Ireland* (1994) and Howard Erskine-Hill, *Poetry of Opposition and Revolution: Dryden to Wordsworth* (1996).

The rediscovery of Jacobitism has made a large difference to the modern study of Pope, and indeed to several of his literary contempor-

---

Ideology and Conspiracy: Aspects of Jacobitism, 1609–1759 (Edinburgh, 1982), *By Force or By Default? The Revolution of 1688–1689* (Edinburgh, 1989); and, edited with Jeremy Black, *The Jacobite Challenge* (Edinburgh, 1988). Several historians have followed or independently chosen her directies. Among those whose work is most relevant to Pope are Daniel Szechi, *Jacobitism and Tory Politics, 1710–14* (Edinburgh, 1984), J. C. D. Clark, *English Society, 1688–1832: Ideology, social structure and political practice during the ancien régime* (Cambridge, 1985) and Paul Kléber Monod, *Jacobitism and the English People, 1688–1788* (Cambridge, 1989).

[29]'Alexander Pope: The Political Poet in His Time', *Eighteenth-Century Studies*, 15; 2 (Winter 1981–82), pp. 123–48; 'Literature and the Jacobite Cause: Was There a Rhetoric of Jacobitism?' in Eveline Cruicksbanks, ed. *Ideology and Conspiracy: Aspects of Jacobitism, 1689–1759* (1982), pp. 49–69; and 'Pope and Civil Conflict', in Eiichi Hara, Hiroshi Ozawa, and Peter Robinson, eds. *Enlightened Groves: Essays in Honour of Professor Zenzo Suzuki* (Shohakusa, Tokyo, 1996), pp. 90–114.

aries. The seam is very far from being exhausted and many young scholars, on both sides of the Atlantic, are currently working on aspects of Jacobitism relevant to the writers of Pope's time. The new development does, however, remain controversial; many historians and literary scholars remain unconvinced by its findings, while in some quarters readers have been too ready to jump to the simple conclusion that Pope 'was a Jacobite'. On that issue it may be said that the jury is still out. That as a result of the new Jacobite scholarship more is now known about Pope and the world in which he moved is a claim that may safely be made.

This is the point to mention the many interesting collections of essays on Pope, or on Pope among others, by several hands, which have been published towards the end of the period under survey. These collections well display the directions of current interests, and thus afford a perspective in which to see salient trends. These are: Maynard Mack and James A. Winn, eds. *Recent Essays on Pope* (1980); Claude Rawson, ed. *English Satire and the Satiric Tradition* (1984); Leopold Damrosch, ed. *New Eighteenth-Century Essays* (1988). The anniversary year of 1988 saw the inception of three new collections on Pope: Colin Nicholson, ed. *Alexander Pope: Essays for the Tercentenary* (1988); G. S. Rousseau and Pat Rogers, eds. *The Enduring Legacy: Alexander Pope Tercentenary Essays* (1988); and David Fairer, ed. *Pope: New Contexts* (1990). The editor of the last of these consciously hunted new approaches, so that even the original offerings of more traditional young scholars, at the original Binfield symposium on which the book was based, were firmly excluded. Taken together, the three tercentenary volumes achieved an excellent representation of recent work on Pope. Perhaps Colin Nicholson found the best balance. In 1994 the two hundred and fiftieth anniversary of Pope's death was marked by a Warton Lecture and a Pope Symposium in the British Academy. The present volume is the long-deferred result of that symposium. Here, too, a balance has been sought between new and established scholars.[30]

In the critical section of this survey, we have considered Pope in relation to his past, Pope in relation to his own world, and there remains briefly to mention Pope and his own future. Early in our period John Barnard published his invaluable edition of *Pope: The Critical Heritage* (1973). Near the end was published *Pope's Literary*

---

[30]A recent collection on one of Pope's most distinguished friends is Toby Barnard and Jane Clark, eds. *Lord Burlington: Architecture, Art and Life* (London, 1995).

Legacy: The Book-Trade Correspondence of William Warburton and John Knapton, with other letters and documents, 1744–1780, ed. Donald W. Nichol (1992). This significant and substantial work contributes much to that picture of Pope and publishing history which David Foxon and James McLaverty have so interestingly drawn, and which contributes so much to the critical understanding of Pope's art. Pope's critical influence on later eighteenth-century poetry — aside from the old tale of the Romantic reaction — is, surprisingly, a subject little explored. Here the final contribution of the present volume, Thomas Keymer's brilliant essay, 'Reception, and *The Rape of the Lock*, and Richardson', in its discovery of an eighteenth-century poem of exceptional interest, and in its discussion of the fascinating literary relationship between Pope the poet and Richardson the novelist, brings the present volume to a distinguished conclusion.

6

Almost at the beginning of the twentieth-century period of interest in Alexander Pope, Geoffrey Tillotson published his admirable monograph, *On the Poetry of Pope* (1938). It offered nearly all that the first-comer to Pope required: a critical exposition of the chief formal features of his art, with one notable exception, there being a rather spare discussion only of Pope's use of rhyme. Some critics, American and British, followed up this particular topic, but Tillotson, with his second critical book, *Pope and Human Nature* (1958) executed a decisive turn, from the craft and art of Pope strictly considered, to the views and ideas of Pope, the content of his writing. The great subsequent growth of interest in Pope in his context, Pope and his world, might be traced to that decision of Tillotson, though doubtless there were other factors which affected the direction of studies on Pope at that time. The time does now seem to have come to attempt to redress the recent imbalance: not to reject the study of Pope in his world, far from it, but to attempt once more that most difficult thing of all in literary scholarship and criticism: to bring contextual knowledge to bear sharply upon verbal artistry: without relegating Pope's world to turn again to his word and art. It was with this in mind that, looking for a subject on Pope for the 1994 Warton Lecture on Poetry, I chose perhaps the greatest human issue of Pope's world, slavery, and sought to trace the word in his works from its literal meaning as Pope went out on a limb to challenge contemporary practice, through various metaphorical usages, until it touched the poet's own career in his undergoing of the bondage and art of rhyme.

Proceedings of the British Academy, **91**, 27–53

Pope and Slavery

HOWARD ERSKINE-HILL

I am certainly desirous to run from my Country, if you'll run from yours, and study Popery and Slavery abroad a while, to reconcile ourselves to the Church & State we may find at home on our return. (Pope to the Earl of Marchmont, 22 June 1740; *Correspondence*, IV. 250)

1

IN 1790 THE POET Alexander Radishchev, called 'The First Russian Radical', printed his *Journey from St. Petersburg to Moscow*, criticising the condition of the serfs under Catherine the Great, and dedicating it without permission to his friend, the poet A. M. Kutuzov. Kutuzov, alarmed with reason at this dedication, recounts how on an earlier occasion he had remonstrated with Radishchev, quoting to him in English Pope's translation of Homer's *Iliad*, Bk. I, the lines of Calchas to Achilles on the perils of telling unwelcome truths to kings:

> For I must speak what Wisdom would conceal,
> And Truths invidious [to] the Great reveal.
> Bold is the task! when Subjects grown too wise
> Instruct a Monarch where his Error lies;
> For tho' we deem the short-liv'd fury past
> Be sure, the Mighty will revenge at last.
>
> (I. 101–6)[1]

[1] In my reference to Radishchev I am indebted to Professor Monica Partridge and to Professor A. G. Cross. The lines quoted from Pope's *Iliad* translation by A. M. Kutuzov are I. 101–6; T. E. VIII. 92. The allusion is briefly discussed in David Marshal Lang, *The First Russian Radical 1749–1802* (London, 1959), pp. 198–201. What appears to have happened is that Kutuzov originally quoted the passage from Pope's Homer to Radishchev in response to the latter's dedication to him of *The Life of Fedor Ushakov*, itself a politically controversial work. Radishchev followed this up by the further dedication to Kutuzov of his *Journey from*

Interesting as a Russian response to Pope's work, Kutuzov's invocation of these lines brings home to us the relevance of Homer's lines, as handled by Pope, to the real dangers of offending an eighteenth-century prince, not to say a benevolent despot of the Enlightenment (Radishchev was sent to Siberia) but there is something yet further interesting in Kutuzov's account. Pope's version of *Iliad* I uses the word 'slave' and makes slavery, in various senses of the term, a theme in this part of his translation. Yet the Greek hardly seems to demand the modern word 'slave'. Homer's word δμως for a slave taken in war (cf. *Odyssey* I. 398) or for a slave generally (cf. *Odyssey*, VI. 69–71) would have been appropriate at several points in the Book but is not in fact used. The word δουλον is known not to have been used in Homer (though see *Odyssey*, XVII, 320–23). Kutuzov's warning quotation was drawn from a text which addressed some of Radishchev's concerns in a way which Homer's *Iliad*, Bk. I, did not.

In the great project of his Homer translation Pope not only had the best advice to turn the original Greek, but was a scholar of the seventeenth-century English translators. Thomas Warton, whom this lecture commemorates, tells us that he had in his possession Pope's copy of Chapman's Homer (the *Iliad*) with his underlinings and comments.[2] As Pope knew, none of the full-length seventeenth-century translators of Homer had resorted to the words 'slave' or 'slavery' in *Iliad* I, but the immediate cause of his different practice is undoubtedly to be found in the version of *Iliad* I which Dryden included in his *Fables* in 1700. In setting forth the fatal quarrel of Achilles and Agamemnon, Dryden was more lavish in his use of the word 'slave' than Pope. Thus the 'Captive-Maid' Chryseis is referred to as 'the fair Slave' by Calchas to Agamemnon (I. 44, 146) and as a 'Slave' twice by the King in his

---

St. Petersburg to Moscow (1790). In his letter to E. I. Golischeva-Kutuzova, 6/17 December 1790, Kutuzov recounts how he has quoted the passage from Pope's Homer in warning response to Radishchev's earlier book, and denies that he has seen the *Journey*. He says that the same fate as that of Radischev awaits him, should he return to Russia (Barskov, *Perepiska*, pp. 65–6). Lang notes that Radishchev was a member of the 'English Club at St. Petersburg' (p. 85) and so would, in all probability, have appreciated the application of the Homeric passage and its literary context as Pope presented them. It may just be worth noting that Kutuzov was a prominent Freemason, and that Pope had some connection with Masonry, as Maynard Mack records in *Alexander Pope: A Life* (London, 1985), pp. 437–440, though it seems unlikely that Kutuzov would have known such a detail.

[2]Thomas Warton, *The History of English Poetry, From the Close of the Eleventh to the Commencement of the Eighteenth Century... A New Edition Carefully Revised...*, 4 vols. (London, 1824), IV. 271–2. 'A diligent observer will easily discern,' Warton noted, 'that Pope was no careless reader of his rude predecessor.'

reply (I. 165, 180). Angrily disputing Agamemnon's decision to seize his own prize, Briseis, Achilles accuses the King of treating his 'Friends' 'like abject Slaves' (I. 228) while the narrator himself, in Dryden, suggests that Agamemnon regards his supporters as 'sceptered Slaves' (I. 258). After Nestor's attempted reconciliation Achilles returns to the verbal attack. 'Command thy Slaves', he rages, 'My freeborn Soul disdains/A Tyrant's Curb' (I. 415–6). Later Achilles, recounting to his goddess-mother Thetis what has happened, calls Chryseis 'the sacred Slave' (I. 534).[3] Dryden has thus rung several changes on the word. From the quasi-literal sense as applying to women taken captive as spoils of war, he moves into metaphor with the accusations of Achilles, attaining the further reaches of the metaphorical with 'sceptered Slaves', to come to rest on the more contemplative usage: 'sacred Slave.'

There is method here but it is not Pope's. While Dryden distributes the word widely Pope concentrates it in the mouth of Achilles, leaving a single literal reference for Nestor, who calls Chryseis 'beauteous Slave' (I. 362), while before and after this speech a metaphorical use conveys the pitch of Achilles' anger:

> Tyrant, I well deserve thy galling Chain,
> To live thy Slave, and still to serve in vain
>
> (I. 388–89)[4]

If Pope ever considered following in detail Dryden's use of the word 'slave' in *Iliad* I, his Homer MS in the British Library shows no trace of it. His revisions do show him strengthening the bond of opposites between slavery and tyranny, heightening Achilles' accusations against Agamemnon, and (for example) rejecting the word 'servile' for 'slavish' at line 306.[5] Dryden creates an irony in which a quarrel about slaves leads to one accusing the other of treating him like a slave. Pope mounts a stronger attack on Agamemnon as a tyrant, in Achilles' view. Each, though in different measure, makes the reader think about the relation between literal and metaphorical senses of the word 'slave'.

If we look at other recent translations of *Iliad* I only, we find the sometime Jacobite Arthur Mainwaring using the word 'slave' once as

[3]*The Poems of John Dryden*, ed. James Kinsley, 4 vols. (Oxford, 1958), IV. 1585, 1587, 1588, 1589, 1590, 1594, 1597.
[4]T. E. VII. 106.
[5]BL Add. MSS 4807, ff. 20ʳ and ᵛ, 21ʳ, 23ᵗ and 24ʳ.

he reworks Dryden's 'sceptred Slaves' to help him point the accusation of Achilles against Agamemnon: 'Vile are the slaves who thy dull Presence throng'[6], while Pope's early rival in translating Homer, Thomas Tickell, in 1715, uses the word three times: once in Achilles' accusation against Agamemnon, once in Agamemnon's counter-accusation against Achilles, and once in allusion to Briseis in Achilles' explanation to Thetis.[7] Tickell seems to have been at the opposite end of the political spectrum from Dryden, but, after Dryden's precedent, translators of different political view evidently found the word 'slave' irresistible for this part of the *Iliad*. There is hardly enough evidence on which to hazard a political generalisation, but it may seem that those towards the Tory/Jacobite end of the spectrum (Dryden, Pope, perhaps Mainwaring) are more hostile to Agamemnon as king and leader of a warlike league, levelling against him the charge of treating his supporters like slaves. They are all closer to the viewpoint of Achilles. Only the Whig Tickell has Agamemnon return the charge upon Achilles.

If Dryden's version of *Iliad* I provides a short-term explanation of why the word and idea of slavery were conspicuous in Pope's version of the early *Iliad*, this merely pushes the problem back for fifteen years. A fuller explanation must take a more extensive view. The words 'slave' and 'slavery' had long been part of the English political lexicon. Thus Sir Richard Hutton in the Ship Money case of King Charles I had averred: 'The people of England are subjects, not slaves; freemen not villeins; and are not to be taxed de alto et basso and at will. . . .'[8] The same term was used on the other side of this dispute. In 1648, when the parliamentary cause might seem to have triumphed, the Leveller William Walwyn summed up all the civil wars as 'a pulling down of one Tyrant, to set up another, and instead of

[6]Arthur Mainwaring, 'Part of Homer's *Iliad*, Book I', in Tonson's *Miscellanies*, V (London, 1704), p. 472.

[7]Thomas Tickell, *The First Book of Homer's Iliad* (London, 1715): 1. 'A Tyrant Lord o'er Slaves to Earth debas'd;' (p. 16); 2. 'And hopes for Slaves, I trust, he ne'er shall find.' (p. 20); 3. 'And bore *Briseis* thence, my beauteous Slave,' (p. 26). Pope thoroughly annotated his copy of Tickell's book, and finds some objection to the first two lines quoted, as he does to a large number of lines. Maynard Mack tentatively suggests that 'Tyrant Lord' was found insufficiently strong to render Homer's Greek: 'δημοβόρος βασιλεύς' and that Pope considered 'Slaves' in the second example 'obsolete or affected' (Maynard Mack, *Collected in Himself*, pp. 452, 450).

[8]Rushworth, *Historical Collections*, II, part ii, Appendix p. 176, quoted in Conrad Russell, *Unrevolutionary England, 1603–1642* (London, 1990), p. 142.

Liberty, heaping upon ourselves a greater Slavery then that we fought against'.[9]

King Charles I in his *Eikon Basilike* was made to complain how it was 'the badge and method of Slavery by savage Rudeness and importunate obtrusions of Violence to have the mist of his [own alleged] Error and Passion dispelled': words which supplied Samuel Johnson with his only illustration of the word 'slavery' in the first edition of his *Dictionary*.[10] Dryden in his *Absalom and Achitophel* wrote how:

> ... *Israel*'s Monarch, after Heaven's own heart,
> His vigorous warmth did, variously, impart
> To wives and slaves. ...

(ll. 7–9)

following up this literal reference by a satirical and metaphorical one to rebellious subjects of the King who

> ... led their wild desires to Woods and Caves
> And thought that all but Savages were Slaves.

(ll. 55–6)[11]

a procedure with the word similar to that which he would employ in his version of *Iliad*, I.

Two other instances of the political use of the slavery metaphor have a special salience in later seventeenth-century England. The first is surprisingly little known:

> I was born free, & desire to continue so, and tho I have adventured my life very frankly on severall occasions for the good & honor of my Country, & am as free to do it again (and wch I hope I shall do as old as I am, to redeem it from [the] slavery it is like to fall under) yet I think it not convenient to expose my self to be secured as not to be at liberty to effect it. ...

These words are those of King James II in the declaration he drew up before withdrawing to France in 1688, and subsequently published.[12] The second is well known:

---

[9]Howard Erskine-Hill and Graham Storey, eds. *Revolutionary Prose of the English Civil War* (Cambridge, 1983), p. 94.

[10]King Charles I and John Gauden, *Eikon Basilike. The Portraicture of His Sacred Majestie in His Solitudes and Sufferings* (London, 1648 [OS], 1727 Edition), p. 28; see too Philip Malone Griffith, 'Samuel Johnson and King Charles the Martyr', *The Age of Johnson*, II. 259.

[11]*The Poems of John Dryden*, ed. James Kinsley, I. 218.

[12]BL Add. MSS 28252, f. 55. This hitherto unnoticed MS of James II's Declaration is discussed in Howard Erskine-Hill, 'John, First Lord Caryll of Durford, and the Caryll Papers', in Eveline Cruickshanks and Edward Corp, eds. *The Stuart Court in Exile and the Jacobites* (London, 1995), pp. 78–81.

> Slavery is so vile and miserable an Estate of Man, and so directly opposite
> to the generous Temper and Courage of our Nation; that 'tis hardly to be
> conceived, that an *Englishman*, much less a *Gentleman*, should plead for't.[13]

These are the opening words of Locke's *Two Treatises of Government*
(published 1689 but composed earlier, probably in support of the
Shaftesbury faction in the Exclusion Crisis of 1679–81). More, perhaps,
than in the debates of the mid-seventeenth-century civil wars, the word
'slavery' was invoked by both sides in the 1688 Revolution and after;
indeed in the 1690s it is part of that network of public argument which
opens out into allegations of tyranny, accusations and invocations of
military conquest, a renewed contention about patriarchal and contrac-
tual theories of the origin of government and, amidst it all, the image
of rape, a sexual as well as a military term, deployed in pamphlet and
poem. It is this kind of polemic that Dryden would draw on, from his
own Jacobite viewpoint, when in his version of *Iliad* I he wrote:

> Command thy Slaves: My freeborn Soul disdains
> A Tyrant's Curb; and restiff breaks the Reins.
> Take this along; that no Dispute shall rise
> (Though mine the Woman) for my ravish'd Prize:
>
> (ll. 415–8)

and thus used the Homeric quarrel to illuminate the political rights and
wrongs of Williamite England.

2

If my road from Radishchev to Renaissance slavery should seem
unduly prolonged, the reason is in my evidence itself: namely the ease
and frequency with which the word 'slave' was used metaphorically in
political polemic, without direct mention of slavery. In 1576 Jean Bodin,
well aware of new slavery in the Americas, surveyed the great
and grievous subject in the history of the world, and concluded
that 'although servitude in these latter times was left off, for about
three or foure hundred yeares, yet is it now againe approved...'[14]

---

[13]John Locke, *Two Treatises of Government*, ed. Peter Laslett (Cambridge, 1960; rev. 1963;
Signet Classics, 1965), p. 175, also 75–9.
[14]Jean Bodin, *Six Livres de la République* (1576), Bk. I, ch. V; tr. Richard Knolles (London,
1606), pp. 34 (for the quotation), 39, 40, and 43 (bearing especially on new enslavement by
Portugal and Spain). Towards the end of this notable chapter Bodin affirms his own view:

The debate about Indian slavery, Bartolomé de las Casas' representations to the Spanish crown, and his later, unpublished, recognition of objections to African slavery, occurred early in the Iberian conquest of the West Indies.[15] Bodin, while perceiving the power of the new economic demand and supply in slaves, and while characteristically noting a mass of precedents and arguments, nevertheless explicitly opposes the institution. His *Six Livres de la République* was well known in seventeenth-century England; Locke had it in his library; so had Jonathan Swift but one can hardly pretend that this feature of Bodin's great work was influential on English political thought, least of all, perhaps, on the 'progressive' Locke.[16] But a renewed awareness of slavery, and knowledge of the expanding slave trade between West Africa and the Americas, surely lent power and sensationalism to the modern word 'slave': a word which nevertheless pre-dates the first voyage of Columbus by about two centuries, and seems to derive from the servitude of Slavs from Dalmatia and the Black Sea area, in and through Venice.[17] The new rise of slavery in the Renaissance perhaps supplies the longer-term explanation of why 'slave' and 'slavery' spill over from political polemic into translations of parts of Homer where the Greek does not seem to warrant the words. Imaginative literature in English is early aware of slavery: both Shakespeare's Venetian dramas, significantly enough, allude to it, Shylock to remind the Duke what it means to possess another person (IV. i. 90–100); Othello, the black Moor, to refer to the risk of his having been conquered in war and 'sold to slavery' (I. iii. 138). Of course Shakespeare is also aware of what was happening in the

---

'there is nothing that doth more discourage and ouerthrow, (and if I may so say) bastardise a good and noble mind, than seruitude . . . if it be true that reason and the law of God is alwaies and euerie where to take place, and that it was not shut vp only within the bounds of Palestine: why should not that law so profitably and so wisely made by God himselfe, concerning slaverie & libertie, stand in force, rather than that which was by man's wisedom deuised?' (p. 46).

[15]David Brion Davis, *The Problem of Slavery in Western Culture* (New York, 1966; rept. Oxford, 1988), pp. 166, 169–70.

[16]For Locke's knowledge of Bodin's *Six Livres*, see Locke, *Two Treaties*, ed. Laslett, p. 151. For Swift's view, see Jonathan Swift, *Miscellaneous and Autobiographical Pieces, Fragments and Marginalia*, ed. Herbert Davis (Oxford, 1969), pp. 244–47. Swift possessed the 1579, French, edition of the book, and dated his short character of Bodin, pasted in the volume, as 2 April 1725. Among other chapters, Bodin's chapter against slavery (I. V) escaped Swift's generally hostile annotation.

[17]David Brion Davis, *The Problem of Slavery*, pp. 111–12; *Slavery and Human Progress* (Oxford, 1984), p. 156.

New World and has Prospero repeatedly call Caliban slave (*The Tempest*, I. ii. 308, 313, 319, 344, 351).[18]

A century or more after Bodin's book and Shakespeare's plays, with the new slavery established, and the slave trade an expanding and vastly profitable concern, Pope too was well aware of what was done in the world. His reference to the exposure of 'the poor naked Indians' to 'our guns', in a letter of 5 Dec. 1712 to his friend John Caryll when his poem *Windsor-Forest* was in its final stages of expansion and revision, shows his knowledge of the condition of the native Indians of the New World as the victims of conquest. Further, by this same time, the much-debated provisions of the Treaty of Utrecht, which so many hoped would end the wars brought on Britain by that militaristic monarch, the Prince of Orange, included the great sweetener designed to reconcile bellicose Whigs with the Tory peace: the Asiento Clause. This would allow British participation in the slave trade between West Africa and the Spanish Indies, on terms similar to those recently enjoyed by the fortunate French.[19]

To read the Asiento Clause — itself a document of 42 articles — is to see exemplified what might be regarded as a kind of baseline for Swift's *Modest Proposal*. Report of it had a great impact in 1712; many regarded it as a triumph of Tory diplomacy and it figured in one of Queen Anne's most famous speeches from the throne: '. . . the Part which We have born in the Prosecution of this War, entitling Us to have some Distinction in the Terms of Peace, I have insisted and obtained, That the Asiento or Contract for furnishing the *Spanish West-Indies* with Negroes, shall be made with Us for the Term of Thirty Years, in the same manner as it hath been enjoyed by the *French* for Ten Years past.'[20] The Treaty itself would be more explicit, 'the English

---

[18]*Oxford English Dictionary*, Sense 1 (AD, 1290); Johnson's *Dictionary* 2 vols. (London, 1755), II: 'Slave'.); David Brion Davis, *The Problem of Slavery*, pp. 41–2. See also *Johnson on Shakespeare*, ed. Arthur Sherbo (New Haven;), VII. 227. In one of these instances, Johnson praises Theobald for taking the lines from Miranda and giving them to Prospero (*Johnson on Shakespeare*, VII. 124). Prospero also calls Ariel a slave, I. ii. 272, but the whole exchange between Prospero and Ariel in this scene seems to show that Prospero regarded him as an indentured servant: a slave, as it were, for a fixed term (ll. 243–301). Line references are to the New Oxford one-volume edition.

[19]*The Correspondence of Alexander Pope*, ed. George Sherburn, 5 vols. (Oxford, 1956), I. 162.

[20]The Queen's Speech *in Parliament*, the 6th *of* June, 1712; *A Collection of All Her Majesty's Speeches, Messages, &c. From Her Happy Accession to the Throne, To The Twenty First of June 1712* (London, 1712), p. 46.

Company's obliging itself to supply the Spanish West-Indies with Black Slaves for the Term of Thirty Years. . . .'[21]

Windsor-Forest, often regarded as a kind of English Georgic, is a poem of a wider variety of effect, skilfully related through an exceptional mastery of the art of transition and metamorphosis. It opens a vision of the past and a vision of the future, linked conceptually by the themes of warfare and hunting, but spatially and temporally by the Thames, river of English history. The subject of slavery is first introduced in Pope's vision of the past, dominated as it is by Norman Nimrods, hunter-conquerors:

> Cities laid waste, they storm'd the Dens and Caves
> (For wiser Brutes were backward to be Slaves). . . .
>
> (ll. 49–50)

Pope is here turning Dryden's couplet on slavery in *Absalom and Achitophel* (ll. 55–6). Here the Norman ruler 'makes his trembling slaves the Royal Game' (ll. 64–5) (note the wide range of the word 'Game') and Pope paints a scene of desolation which begins perhaps (such is the nature of the poem's subtle historical transitions) to gather more recent association:

> The levell'd Towns with Weeds lie cover'd o'er,
> The hollow Winds thro' naked Temples roar;
> Round broken columns clasping Ivy twin'd;
> O'er Heaps of Ruin stalk'd the stately Hind;
> The Fox obscene to gaping Tombs retires,
> And savage Howlings fill the sacred Quires.
>
> (ll. 66–72)

These lines seem to recall the wanderings of the Roman Catholic Hind in 'kingdoms, once Her own', in Dryden's *Hind and the Panther* (I. 26);[22] once the poem was well-established, Pope would add as a footnote to this part further lines, allegedly rejected, which seemed to associate William III as conqueror and 'foreign master' with William I and II (T. E. I. 159). Again, in the poem's tribute to Charles I, 'sacred *Charles*', (l. 319) lines on the mid-seventeenth-century civil wars elide into lines on wars begun by William III, as Queen Anne, 'great ANNA' says — 'Let Discord cease!/She said, the World obey'd, and all was

[21] *The Compleat History of the Treaty of Utrecht* . . . 2 vols. (London, 1715), I. 55.
[22] T. E. I. 156; Dr. Michael O'Loughlin has pointed out to me Pope's probable allusion here to the Hind in Dryden's *The Hind and the Panther*, emblematic of the Roman Catholic Church. If he is right (as I believe) the 'Heaps of Ruin' and the 'sacred Quires' take on Reformation as well as Norman associations.

Peace!' (ll. 327–8). In this part of his poem, Pope has connected the word 'slaves' with those who, in times long past, were the prey of hunter-kings, and also, perhaps, those who were dispossessed and displaced at the Reformation and thereafter. Queen Anne's declaration of peace, however, occasions in the poem Pope's vision of a golden-age future for the whole world, a messianic vision invoking Virgil's Fourth Eclogue and Pope's own recent bid to unite in imitation that famous work with the prophecies of Isaiah.[23] Here Pope certainly celebrates a worldwide mercantile and missionary rôle for Britain. Here too, however, at the very historical moment when Britain proposed specifically to engage in the slave trade on an enlarged scale, Pope's idealistic poetic vision totally repudiates slavery:

> Oh stretch thy Reign, fair *Peace*! from Shore to Shore,
> Till Conquest cease, and Slav'ry be no more:
> Till the freed *Indians* in their native Groves
> Reap their own Fruits, and woo their Sable Loves,
> *Peru* once more a Race of Kings behold,
> And other *Mexico*'s be roof'd with Gold.
>
> (ll. 407–12; T. E. I. 192)

The word 'Conquest', within the structures of the poem, links the myth of slavery under the Norman yoke, European slavery, with real modern slavery.

There is no possibility of Pope's being ignorant of the Treaty of Utrecht: apart from the Queen's speech, and the battery of welcoming or warning pamphlets, he was on personal terms with some of the very people who were negotiating it and defending it: Prior, St. John, Swift, Robert Harley himself. Further, while critics have quibbled about the use of the word 'Sable' (these 'are not Negroes', T. E. I. 192), it seems likely that it was chosen with the particular purpose of bringing black slavery to mind. True, 'sable' could at this time signify a hue between tawny and black, and the Twickenham editors therefore think Pope is writing about Indian slaves only. But tawny and black seem to have been the recognized colours of New World slavery; the black slave trade was in the news; and Johnson's *Dictionary* would supply a list of instances of 'sable' meaning black, many of them poetic examples prior to Pope.[24] I am reinforced in my view by Pat Rogers, who has

---

[23]T. E. I. 112–22.

[24]See Morgan Godwyn, *The Negro's and Indians Advocate, Suing for Admission into the Church.* . . . (London, 1680), who refers to '*the Tawneys and Blacks*', i.e. Indian and Negro slaves (p. 4). Johnson, *Dictionary*, 2 vols. (London, 1755), under 'Sable'.

demonstrated the emblematic and heraldic idiom of *Windsor-Forest*.[25] Pope is not attempting to use colour realistically, but with a richly contrastive, stylised, signification. At this level the word 'sable' may be thought to have an ennobling function.[26] Neither is Pope observing human behaviour realistically. Love between liberated Indian and African slaves is a feature of an imagined messianic age of gold, such as a poet alone might delineate.

Here I don't want to over-idealise Pope. In December 1716 he was apparently ready to invest in stocks of the South Sea Company (to whom the opportunities of the Asiento were chiefly assigned), and did so in 1720, when the Company was obviously a gambler's opportunity rather than a trading venture. In each case he seems to have been sharing his 'Venture' with his needy friends Martha and Teresa Blount. In later life he alludes quite openly to how much he might have been worth when the South-Sea stocks were at their height.[27] But against this mistaken conduct must be set Pope's salient and surprising denunciation of slavery in his poem. David Foxon's bibliography of *English Verse, 1701–50*,[28] lists all the Treaty of Utrecht poems known to him in 1975. My research in these, and in others which have sub-

[25]Pat Rogers, '*Windsor-Forest*, Britannia and river poetry', *Essays on Pope* (Cambridge, 1993), esp. pp. 68–9.

[26]By this I mean that the noble associations of an heraldic term and colour are bestowed upon slaves. It may also be relevant to recall the subtitle of Aphra Behn's popular novel, *Oroonoko, or The Royal Slave* (1678), which Pope seems to remember in drafting his version of *Iliad* I, BL Add. Mss. 4807, l. 245. C. F. *Iliad*, I. 362; T. E. VII. 105.

[27]Alexander Pope, *Correspondence*, ed. Sherburn, I. 379; II. 33–4; 'To Mr. Bethel' (The Second Satire of the Second Book of Horace, Imitated), ll. 133–40; T. E. IV. 65–6.

[28]David Foxon, *English Verse, 1701–1750*, 2 vols. (Cambridge, 1975), II. 296 and item references there listed. Foxon lists 74 Treaty of Utrecht poems. I have read all but four of these, this remainder not having been available or traceable during the two years when I worked on this subject. In some cases the reclassification of small, anonymous items has been a problem. Foxon's list includes a number of Latin poems, which have also been read. In the course of consulting these poems, I have encountered a large further number of poems which, if not all formal Treaty of Utrecht poems, do comment seriously on the Treaty. Again, I have found no other poem which denounces slavery in the literal sense. It is of course possible that a poem denouncing slavery may come to light. Further, it could be argued that references to South-Sea trade are, in the particular context of the Treaty years, allusions to the slave trade. If so, many of these allusions must be construed as approving references. The difference from *Windsor-Forest* is in such cases even greater. What in the end is most notable, however, is that when so many Whig writers wished to find all possible arguments to oppose the Treaty and the peace, none, apparently, did so by attacking the Asiento Clause and opposing the slave trade. I am grateful to Professor H. T. Dickinson for drawing my attention to B. M.'s *The Planter's Charity*. I owe to Dr. D. K. Money, who has made a special study of university volumes of celebratory poems in learned languages, my knowledge of Maynard's poem.

sequently come to light, has discovered no other English poem commenting on the Treaty or Peace which squarely confronts, let alone opposes, slavery in the New World. An earlier poem, indeed, B. M.'s *The Planter's Charity* (1704), urged the baptism of black slaves while supporting slavery, and shows that the subject could be presented in English poetry in the reign of Anne. A Latin poem on the Treaty of Utrecht, *Assiento, sive commercium Hispanicum* (1713), by J. Maynard of St. John's College, Oxford, unhesitatingly supports the slavery of African negroes by the British and the Spanish. By comparison with these two explicit poems, *Windsor-Forest* appears more remarkable still. In other prominent English poems on the Peace, slavery is indeed commonly mentioned but it is always what we might term metaphorical: for example, a way of referring to the Dutch or the French under their several governments. If we look at the poems of the more salient talents of the time, the Jacobite Bevil Higgons, the Scriblerian Thomas Parnell, the Addisonian Whig Thomas Tickell and the time-server Edward Young, two, the most politically opposed of the four, consider slavery. In his poem, *On the Prospect of the Peace* (1713), Tickell celebrates the European discovery of the New World, prophesies that 'savage *Indians*' will soon 'swear by ANNA's Name' but, in his extended passage on slavery, makes no reference to Africans or Indians. Tickell's 'filial Subject' sunk into 'a Slave' is part of a post-Lockeian polemic against the designs of Louis XIV.[29] Higgons, for his part, compares Harley to a Columbus discovering a new world, this time a world of peace. He too talks of slavery, and here the slaves are Britons:

> *Britons*, no more like Slaves, be bought and sold,
> To daub their Leaders shining Vests with Gold....

This is an attack on Britain during William's and Anne's wars: in one edition a footnote gives a clear factual definition of 'Slaves' (men pressed for military service and then sold by the officers of one regiment to those of another) but there is little doubt that slavery is really meant as a metaphor for the condition of Britons after the usurpations of William and Mary, and Anne.[30] Against the background of these

---

[29]Thomas Tickell, *On the Prospect of the Peace* (London, 1713; 4th edn.), pp. 15, 5.
[30]Bevil Higgons, *A Poem on the Glorious Peace of Utrecht: Inscrib'd in the Year 1713, To the Right Honourable Robert Late Earl of Oxford and Earl Mortimer* . . . [now re-dedicated to Edward, Earl of Oxford] (London, 1731), p. 12. The explanatory footnote may belong to this edition only.

poems *Windsor-Forest* begins to look remarkable. In her shallow study, *Alexander Pope* (1985), Laura Brown argues that the 'slave monopoly' 'is the liberty and concord' which the poem 'specifically defends'.[31] Strange, then, that it should be explicitly excluded from what is defended! The critic in quest of ideological double-think would do better to follow the lead of David Brion Davis and turn to Locke.[32] For, while in Pope's text references to European (and perhaps metaphorical) slavery reinforce the challenge to slavery in the New World, there is something uneasy about Locke's triumphal deployment of the metaphor of slavery against his patriarchalist opponent, when supported by well-informed and apparently uncritical references to slavery in the West Indies.

Pope's response to New-World slavery is not confined to the conclusion of *Windsor-Forest*. In a poem less suffused with hope, more with resignation to things as they are, the poet returns to the theme and recalls his own earlier lines. The 'poor Indian', in *An Essay on Man* (1733–34), untaught by theology or science, can still imagine a humble heaven beyond the hill:

> Some safer world in depth of woods embrac'd,
> Some happier island in the watry waste
> Where slaves once more their native land behold,
> No fiends torment, no Christians thirst for gold!
> To Be, contents his natural desire,
> He asks no Angel's wing, no Seraph's fire;
> But thinks, admitted to that equal sky,
> His faithful dog shall bear him company.

> (I. 104–112)

Notice the words 'once more' (l. 106) which suggest that Pope is still thinking about transported slaves, as well as Indians: not African Americans but Indian Africans, it seems. Notice too the 'behold'/'gold' couplet (cf. *Windsor-Forest*, ll. 411–12) which no longer conveys a reversal of fortune and a restoration of right, but a humbler and more widely human wish. Pope's tender tone is very different from his sources, here,[33] but to say that Pope is moving in the direction of sentimentalism would, I think, be a shallow judgement. We have only to consider the realms of thought behind some of Pope's simplest

[31]Laura Brown, *Alexander Pope* (Oxford, 1985), p. 40.
[32]First Treatise, Section 130; *Two Treatises of Government*, ed. Peter Laslett, p. 276.
[33]T. E. III–i, pp. 27–8 (Louis Hennepin's *Continuation of the New Discovery* (English translation, 1698) is especially contemptuous of the Indians' ideas of immortality, including the immortality of animals.

words, to come to an opposite conclusion: 'that equal sky' or, more profound, 'To Be, contents his natural desire . . .'; Pope here sees one of the most orthodox of Christian hopes through the eyes of a slave.

3

In his *Patriarcha* (composed in the 1630s, published in 1680), Sir Robert Filmer foresaw that 'Many will be ready to say that it is a slavish and dangerous condition to be subject to the will of any one man who is not subject to the laws' (XXVI).[34] He had earlier declared that 'the greatest liberty in the world . . . is for a people to live under a monarch . . . all other shows or pretexts of liberty are but several degrees of slavery. . . .' (I. p. 53). Locke took up the challenge of these remarks; the question is what is the precise status of such words as 'slave' and 'slavery' in their exchange. In the foregoing discussion, I have been sufficiently of a Cratylist trend as to see the literal sense of the word 'slave', one who is bought and sold out of any right, as the primary and most powerful sense of the word. Secondary senses, which might, for example, suggest that the English under Charles I or Cromwell were slaves, I have taken as senses transferred or metaphorical. The trick of Locke's derisive polemic, with 'Slavery' its very first word, is to make the reader unable to know from the start whether Locke is writing literally or metaphorically. On this view, Locke gets full advantage of the literal power of the word without meaning it literally. Filmer's remark, however, admits to the possibility of 'degrees of slavery', and one wonders whether the OED should not have admitted some primary senses of the word, short of the sense which would properly apply to a transported and sold slave such as Aphra Behn's Oroonoko, or Homer's Eumâeus. To take an example nearer home, may there be a literal sense in which a subject of an absolute king, such as Louis XIV was held to be, or James II was supposed to wish to become, was a slave?

Any historian of transported slaves from West Africa would, I think, regard this possibility with derision. Yet in those times the semantic and social boundaries were less clear-cut than they seem today. At the poetic level the Catholic Irish of the mid-seventeenth

---

[34]Sir Robert Filmer, *Patriarcha . . . and Other Political Works*, ed. Peter Laslett (Oxford, 1949), p. 105.

century thought that many of their number had been transported into slavery on the West-Indian islands, after defeat in the Cromwellian wars.[35] Other uses of the word 'slave' give us pause. When James II anticipated that England would fall into slavery after 1688, he of course meant that it would yield its rights and laws to the invasion of the Prince of Orange. In his famous speech in the last Parliament of Scotland, in 1707, the Earl of Belhaven wound up his peroration with the words: ' *"now we are slaves for ever!"* '[36] Are we to take such statements as mere empty rhetoric? Not if we wish to take Locke's *Two Treatises* seriously. Pope himself would use the word slave in a Lockeian sense, in *An Essay on Man*, III, where superstition and tyranny 'Gods of Conqu'rors, Slaves of Subjects made' (III. 245–8).[37] It must further be said that, while the condition of the eighteenth-century English and Scots was in no way comparable with that of enslaved Indians or transported Africans, real changes did take place in 1689 and 1707. In England the legal hereditary monarchy was relegated under the threat of arms; Scotland did lose its ancient Parliament. Additional senses of the word 'slave' should perhaps include those displaced from status and power after revolutions in the state. Even where the use of 'slave' was primarily rhetorical, it was not, by that token, empty rhetoric.

This, I believe, may be demonstrated by looking forward to the articles against Russian serfdom published by the great reformer, Alexander Herzen, in 1852. Not only did Herzen ally the condition of Russian serfs with American slaves: his arguments as to how in the seventeenth and eighteenth centuries Russian peasants became white slaves uncannily recall those lines of Tickell and Pope which describe

[35]For recent historians of the slavery of transported blacks, see Winthrop D. Jordan, *White Over Black* (Chapel Hill, 1968); Edwin S. Morgan, *American Slavery, American Freedom: The Ordeal of Colonial Virginia* (New York, 1975); and Leon A. Higginbotham, Jr., *In the Matter of Color: Race and the American Legal Process in the Colonial Period* (New York, 1978). Of the seventeenth-century Catholic Irish, it has been said that their condition 'smacked of the hunted slave and not the indentured servant': see Éamonn Ó Ciardha, 'Woodherne, Tories and Rapparees in Ulster and North Connought in the Seventeenth Century' (unpublished ed MA dissertation, University College, Dublin, 1991), p. 74. In this connection one might note *Ireland's Declaration* (Dublin, 1649), (13 March): 'The continual slavery we have groaned under for these Nineteen years . . .', though Ó Ciardha is using the word in a stronger sense than is the seventeenth-century tract.

[36]*The Treasury of British Eloquence*, compiled and arranged by Robert Cochrane (Edinburgh, 1885), p. 102.

[37]On the political issues explored in *An Essay on Man*, III, see Howard Erskine-Hill, 'Pope on the Origin of Society', in G. S. Rousseau and Pat Rogers, eds. *The Enduring Legacy: Alexander Pope Tercentenary Essays* (Cambridge, 1988), pp. 79–93.

how the 'filial Subject,' sinks into a slave, or how 'Slaves of Subjects' were made.[38] A serious scholar will not therefore easily dismiss language of this kind, not even that anthem composed by James Thomson, set by Arne, and sung at Clivedon in the Masque of *Alfred* in 1740 for the edification of Frederick, Prince of Wales: 'Britons never will be slaves.'[39]

All this should be remembered as we turn from those places in his poetry where Pope speaks of slavery itself to those where he uses the word 'slave' as, at least, a substantial metaphor. I don't mean to discuss the full range of the word in Pope's poetry, but it runs, for example, from a stylised form of 'goodbye': 'Your Slave' (T. E. vi. 140, l. 4), through various sexual, psychological and moral uses, such as Eloisa's self-accusation that she is not 'the spouse of God' but 'slave of love and man' (ll. 177–8); or the true seeker after divine wisdom who is 'Slave to no sect' (*An Essay on Man*, IV. 331);[40] to several notably aggressive or defiant uses in the Horatian poems, often having a pointed relation with Horace's text. In the Sixth Epistle of the first Book, Horace suggests that if we want popularity and influence,

[38]I am greatly in debt here to Professor Monica Partridge, an authority on Alexander Herzen and England, not only for her monograph, *Alexander Herzen, 1812–1870* (Paris, for Unesco, 1984), but for her guidance on the three articles on Russian Serfdom written by Herzen for the English journal *The Leader*, and which were published there in an English translation on 5, 12 and 19 November 1853 (see the USSR Academy of Sciences Edition of *The Collected Works of Herzen*, Vol. XII (Moscow, 1957), pp. 77–33, for further details). Under Western Eyes (to invoke the title of Joseph Conrad's novel) Herzen's account of the growth of serfdom in Russia is astonishing, and Herzen the internationalist is aware of this: 'Serfdom was established, step by step, at the beginning of the seventeenth century and attained full development under the "philosophical" reign of Catherine II. This seems inconceivable and it will take many years for Europe to be made to comprehend how Russian serfdom developed. Its origin and development form so exceptional and unparalleled a history that it almost defies belief. . . . How . . . is it possible to believe that one half of a population of the same nationality, endowed with rare physical and intellectual faculties, could have been reduced to slavery not by war, not by conquest, not by revolution but just by a series of special *ordinances*, by immoral concessions, by infamous claims?' (I gratefully acknowledge Monica Partridge's slight redrafting based on a Russian version also given in the Soviet Academy's *Collected Works*, XII. 34–61 since there are occasional inadequacies in the English rendering as published in *The Leader*, due to the translator's lack of familiarity with the subject matter, and to his florid style. Herzen's original original French version does not appear to have survived).

It is interesting to observe both Bodin and Herzen, in their very different periods, writing of the development of a new slavery. With Bodin before the age of Pope, and Herzen after, we have a kind of frame to warn us against drawing too hard a line between literal and metaphorical senses of the word 'slave' in the period between.

[39]James Thomson, *Poems*, ed. J. Logie Robertson (Oxford, 1908), p. 422.

[40]T. E. II. 334; T. E. III–I. 160.

Mercemur *servum, qui dictet nomina, laevum*
Qui fodicet latus et cogat transpondera dextram
Porrigere . . .

(ll. 50–52; T. E. IV. 242)

Horace is just saying: pay a servant (*nomenclator*) to keep a list of names. Pope translates 'servum' faithfully: 'Then hire a Slave', he suggests, but of course such advice means something quite different in a society where slavery was instituted, from where it is not. Pope's verbal fidelity to Horace here has a new, sharp and moral effect, outrageously compounded by the latter part of the line: 'or (if you will a Lord)' (*Ep*. I. vi. 99).[41] This anticipates other lines of the later 1730s where Pope assails the aristocracy under Walpole:

See, all our Nobles begging to be Slaves.

(*Ep. Sat*. I. 163)[42]

A much-noticed divergence of Pope from Horace, in word and emotion, occurs in his first imitation (*Sat*. II. i), the famous passage

[41]T. E. IV. 243. It is of great interest that this poem, which sparks into verbal and moral life in its sharp juxtaposition of a slave-holding with a non-slaveholding society, was addressed to William Murray who, later in his career, as Lord Mansfield and Chief Justice of the King's Bench, was to hear two cases concerning the legality of owning a slave in England. These were brought on by the Anglican philanthropist Granville Sharp, the author of a series of eloquent pamphlets against the growing practice of importing slaves and holding them as such in England. In dealing with these cases he cannot but have remembered the epistle addressed to him as a young man by the most famous poet of his day. C. H. S. Fifoot, in his assessment of Murray's career, *Lord Mansfield* (Oxford, 1936), sees Mansfield's achievement as having, with scrupulousness and subtlety, amended positive law by natural law, precedent by principle (Ch. VII). Yet he is rather dismissive of Mansfield's record on the two slavery cases, *Lewis's Case* and *Sommersett's Case*, on the grounds that he sought, or seemed to seek, to evade the great issue that they raised (pp. 41–2). This seems cogent on Lewis's case, though the possibility that Mansfield was looking for the strongest possible ground for a definitive judgement should be considered. When, in *Sommersett's Case*, the 'owner' refused to take Mansfield's clear hint that he should release his 'slave', Mansfield surely found his ground and made his stand: 'The state of slavery is of such a nature, that it is incapable of being introduced on any reasons, moral or political, but only by positive law, which preserves its force long after the reasons, the occasion, and the time itself from which it was created, is erased from memory. It is so odious that nothing can be suffered to support it, but positive law. Whatever inconveniences, therefore, may follow from the decision, I cannot say that this case is allowed or approved by the law of England; and therefore the black must be discharged' (C. P. Lascelles, *Granville Sharp and the Freedom of Slaves in England* (New York, 1928; repr. 1969), p. 33. This was on 22 June 1772.) On Lord Mansfield and slavery, see also L. A. Higginbotham, Jr., *In the Matter of Color*. Both Lascelles and Higginbotham take a more positive view than Fifoot of Mansfield on *Sommersett's Case*.

I am most grateful to to my colleague, Dr. David Husain, of Pembroke College, Cambridge, for first drawing my attention to Granville Sharp and *Sommersett's Case*.
[42]T. E. IV. 309.

where his use of the first-person singular is realigned in relation to poetic precedent, and intensified by a non-Horatian repudiation of slavery: he is: 'Unplac'd, un-pension'd, no Man's Heir, or Slave . . .' (l. 116). Pope almost certainly recalls Donne's Satyre IV, which he was about to imitate. Donne, writing probably in the decade of *The Merchant of Venice*, had asked: 'Shall I, nones slave/Of high-borne or rais'd men, feare frownes' (ll. 162–3); Pope's version would keep the general sense without using the word 'slave': he used it for his imitation of Horace, Horace with a difference.[43] In the second of the two dialogues which eventually became the 'Epilogue to the Satires', the interlocutor of the satirist is made to say, in a tone between patronage and accusation: 'You're strangely proud' while the other person, the poet, Pope, bursts forth:

> So proud, I am no Slave: ⎫
> So impudent, I own myself no Knave: ⎬
> So odd, my Country's Ruin makes me grave. ⎭
> Yes, I am proud; I must be proud to see
> Men not afraid of God, afraid of me . . .
>
> (ll. 205–9 T. E. IV. 324)

In the debates of the 1970s and 1980s about whether Pope was closer to Horace or Juvenal in his 1730s satires, this satiric repudiation of slavery hardly arose as an issue.[44] Horace might quietly acknowledge that his father had been a freedman — a point to which I shall return — and each of the three Roman satirists alludes to slaves and slavery, as we might expect. None saw the need to say he was no slave. The peculiar moral resonance such a declaration has for Pope stems from the fact that he is writing out of and to a society in which slavery is not instituted, but which knows very well its significance in the modern world.

In Pope's case there may be another reason. I have quoted James II's declaration on his retreat to France alluding to the 'Slavery' his 'Country' was now 'like to fall under'. This was a view explored in *Windsor-Forest* through its subtle elision of ancient conquest with modern, earlier civil war with recent European war. Late in Pope's life, however, it was less easy to think of a Britain conquered than one

---

[43]T. E. IV. 17; 42–3.
[44]T. E. IV. 324. See Howard D. Weinbrot, *Augustus Caesar in 'Augustan' England: The Decline of a Classical Norm* (Princeton, 1978) and Howard Erskine-Hill, *The Augustan Idea in English Literature* (London, 1983). See also, the more recent Jacob Fuchs, *Reading Pope's Imitations of Horace* (1989).

sunk in self-induced decline. This is exemplified in the strange poem
Pope sent to *The Gentlemen's Magazine* in 1740 (taking the idea of
voluntary servitude, perhaps, from *Paradise Lost*, XII. 220):

> Yes, 'tis the time, I cry'd, impose the chain!
>   Destin'd and due to wretches self-enslaved!
> But when I saw such Charity remain,
>   I half could wish this people might be saved...
>   *(On the Benefactions in the late Frost, 1740)*[45]

The poem is partly, of course, a product of the culture of opposition
to Walpole, George I and George II, skilfully orchestrated by Pope's
friend Bolingbroke. Bolingbroke sought to draw in Jacobite attitudes
for not necessarily Jacobite ends: he was *politique*, and so ultimately,
perhaps, was Pope. But each came from a different ethos. Pope's
repudiation of 'slavery' is the affirmation of one whose community
and values had been drastically marginalised by the events of 1689, and
again by those of 1714. Like Dryden in the 1690s, Pope probably hoped
for a restoration, but as the years rolled by and the House of Brunswick
hung on, it became a point of honour to say: 'So proud I am no Slave'.

4

In his *Journey from St. Petersburg to Moscow* Radishchev includes
passages from his own *Ode to Liberty*, in which he speaks of himself
as a slave praising freedom.[46] Slaves may have wisdom, while slavery
does not. One of the literary figures who expressed this perception for
Pope is Eumâeus in Homer's *Odyssey*. Eumâeus, it may be remembered,
had been son of a king, betrayed into slavery to grow up a swineherd
and faithful servant to his long-lost master Odysseus (XV. 403–484;
XIV. 55–147). One of the first parts of the Odyssey Pope translated,
'The Arrival of Ulysses in Ithica' (1713), dealing as it does with the
return of a lost monarch to his native land, is likely to have had some
Jacobite poignancy for Pope.[47] The role of Eumâeus in the later books
of the *Odyssey* (I draw only on those Pope originally translated) retains
some of these associations. Thus Pope calls Eumâeus 'he, of ancient
faith' (XIV. 30) without specific warrant from the Greek; he expands

[45]T. E. VI. 389.
[46]Lang, *The First Russian Radical*, p. 173.
[47]Howard Erskine-Hill, *Poetry of Opposition and Revolution* (Oxford, 1996), pp. 62–3.

on Eumâeus' words when he makes him call himself 'A man opprest, dependant, yet a Man' (XIV. 70), and this line was most deliberately shaped, for the Homer MS shows that it originally ran: 'A wretch opprest . . .', which makes a large difference.[48] The working drafts show the emergence of Eumâeus's line: 'No profit springs beneath usurping pow'rs' (XV. 404) with the last two words as a clear afterthought.[49] There is much politically suggestive eighteenth-century phrasing, hereabouts, in MS and print, but the paradox Pope needed was straightforwardly provided by Homer, whose text speaks of Eumâeus as both slave and leader of men (XIV. 53–61, 80–82; XV. 389) and who puts into Eumâeus' mouth the judgement on slavery which the Homer MS suggests Pope was able to translate directly and with minimal amendment (the occasion is the moving moment when the slave explains to Odysseus the reason for the neglect of the faithful dog Argos):

> Jove fix'd it certain, that whatever day
> Makes man a slave, takes half his worth away.   (XVII. 392–3)[50]

This is the testimony of the slave who plays so important a part in the restoration of Ulysses. Broome is struck by it, quoting among other authors Longinus ('servitude . . . is a kind of prison . . .' (T. E. X. 151).

Yet the action of the *Odyssey* vindicates Eumâeus as one who plays a wise and prosperous part, and there is, correspondingly, a serious metaphorical sense in which Pope felt himself to know the nature of bondage, as an ultimately prosperous condition. This turns, partly on Pope's long poetic labours, especially in the translation of Homer, partly on a tradition of conceit with which a series of poets represented the nature of rhyme. Thus Samuel Daniel, noting rhyme to be 'farre more laborious than loose measures', says that 'if our labours haue wrought out a manumission from bondage, and that we goe at libertie, notwithstanding these ties, we are no longer the slaues of Rhyme, but we make it a most excellent instrument to serve us.'[51] This political wit was turned back upon the defence of rhyme by Milton, when in his

---

[48]BL Add. MSS 4809, f. 128ʳ. The balance of the line, as amended, affirms Eumâeus's irreducible humanity, despite the oppression of servitude.

[49]BL Add. MSS 4809, f. 148.

[50]T. E. X. 150–51. BL Add. MSS. 4809, f. 166ʳ andᵛ: ' . . . (for Jove ordains,) the Day/That makes a slave, takes half his worth away.' On slavery in the ancient World see T. E. J. Wiedemann, *Slavery, Greece and Rome*, i, New Surveys in the Classics, 19 (Oxford, 1987; rev. 1992).

[51]Samuel Daniel, *Complete Works*, ed. A. B. Grosart, 4 vols. (London, 1896); reissued New York, 1963), IV. 45.

note on The Verse of *Paradise Lost* he sought to give his blank verse a libertarian association: 'ancient liberty', as he put it, 'recover'd to Heroic Poem from the troublesom and modern bondage of Rimeing.' In appreciative response Marvell developed the conceit by introducing the comic and familiar image of the packhorse:

> Well mightst thou scorn thy readers to allure
> With tinkling chime, of thy own sense secure;
> While the town-Bayes writes all the while and spells,
> And like a pack-horse tires without his bells:[52]

which Pope, certain to have known these exchanges, recalls on three occasions in varied tones of self-mockery. 'I really make no other use of poetry now, than horses do of the bells that gingle about their ears ... only to travel on a little more merrily' (to Caryll, 20 Sept. 1713); 'I cannot but think these things very idle; as idle, as if a Beast of Burden shou'd go on jingling his Bells, without bearing any thing valuable about him, or ever serving his Master' (to Edward Blount, 27 June, 1723).[53] The packhorse is a beast of burden; Pope writes elsewhere of 'A Pension, or such Harness for a slave' (*To Bolingbroke*, l.87), slaves and beasts of burden being connected in his mind. Such remarks about rhyme are perhaps part of Pope's poetic psychology. The self-depreciating tone acknowledges both the burden of writing and the imputed criticism of rhyme as childlike, cheerful, ludic:

> Farewell then Verse, and Love, and ev'ry Toy,
> The rhymes and rattles of the Man or Boy:
> What right, what true, what fit, we justly call,
> Let this be all my care—for this is All.
>
> (*To Bolingbroke*, ll. 17–20)[54]

The subject of rhyme may be followed up in Pope's critical writings, in verse and prose,[55] but it will not appear that Pope ever produced an adequate defence of it, not even a defence of his own practice. The root of the right defence is buried beneath his self-depreciation, and stems not only from custom and demand but probably also from historical and ideological values which hardly could be produced in easy, genteel, conversation with men such as Joseph Spence. Sir William Temple had written in his essay 'Of Poetry' that 'the first Ryme that

---

[52]John Milton, *Poems*, ed. John Carey and Alastair Fowler (London, 1968), p. 456.
[53]Pope, *Correspondence*, ed. Sherburn, I. 330; II. 177. See also II. 209.
[54]T. E. IV. 285; 279–81.
[55]For example in Joseph Spence, *Anecdotes of Books and Men*, ed. J. M. Osborn, 2 vols. (Oxford, 1966), I. 173 (item 395).

ever I read in *Latin*' were 'the Verses ascribed to *Adrian*' 'at his Death':
'Animula vagula, blandula. . . .' Temple said that 'the old Spirit of
Poetry being lost . . ., this new Ghost began to appear in its room even
about that Age . . .'[56] and Pope was strangely intrigued by this short,
apparently rhyming Latin poem, filled with diminutives, the Emperor
supposedly addressing his own soul on his death.[57] Pope defended the
lines as showing, not 'Gaiety' and 'levity' but tenderness and 'concern',
and argued that they evinced a nascent belief in the immortality of the
soul in the mind of a heathen. He both translated the poem and
produced a converted Christian version of it, the latter greatly revised
between 1730 and 1736.[58] Hardly any small poems of Pope are such
studied examples of consonance; Pope took the feminine diminutives
as making an exceptional demand on his resources in rhyme. Thus
(from his translation):

> Whither, ah whither art thou flying!
> To what dark undiscover'd shore?
> Thou seem'st all trembling, shiv'ring, dying,
> And wit and humour are no more.

> *(Corr.* I. 178)

Pope has turned to regularly rhyming stanzas, as he does in his converted version, 'The Dying Christian to his Soul'. Here, especially, we
see the resources of rhyme, not just as added melody, or the knack of
making aphorisms memorable (more or less banal defences of rhyme
in Pope), but rather as a pattern of recognition and response. Thus
'Oh, the pain, the bliss of dying!' is in response to the line where Pope
tries to capture in English internal rhyme the effect of the Latin
diminutives: 'Trembling, hoping, ling'ring, flying'. And thus Pope
develops a second voice in the poem: 'Hark! they whisper; Angels say,/
Sister Spirit, come away.'[59] This poem, at least is likely to be placed far

[56]Sir William Temple, *Essays on Ancient and Modern Learning and on Poetry*, ed. J. E.
Spingarn (Oxford, 1909), p. 62.
[57]Pope, *Correspondence*, ed. Sherburn, I. 149–50 and 178–9. Pope's versions of the Latin
poem are entangled in the complex history of his letters, and the earliest text of each poem
to survive is found at the *last* of the above references, his letter to John Caryll of 12 June
1713. The first reference is a letter to Steele, 7 November 1712, which the latter printed in
Spectator 532, 10 November 1712, but without any poem by Pope (none may yet have been
written). The second reference is to a letter to Steele, December 1712, which survives only
from Pope's printed *Correspondence* (1737) and may be fabricated. For the remaining textual
history of both of Pope's poems, see T. E. VI. 91–5. Pope thought about Hadrian's poem,
and his own Christian parallel to it, off and on, for a quarter of a century.
[58]T. E. VI. 91–2.
[59]T. E. VI. 94.

out on the range of religious sentimentalism by the modern reader, but I cite it here for several reasons. First, the discussion of rhyme has often seemed sterile because it has been treated as an emptily formal device, whereas for Pope it seems to have had a richly associative train of thought, just as blank verse did for Milton. Secondly, and in particular, we cannot but notice the association, in Pope's discussion of the Adrian verses, of rhyme with a dawning Christian vision. Not accidentally, perhaps, Pope writes elsewhere of the same association:

> Where mix'd with Slaves the groaning Martyr toil'd.
>   (*To Mr. Addison*, l.6)[60]

So he imagines the sites of the Roman Empire. Thirdly, and arising from all this, the notion of rhyme as recognition and response, seems a promising way of seeing the bondage of Pope's rhyme in a new light.

The time surely has come for a reconsideration of Pope's art of rhyme. Gillian Beer has just published some excellently perceptive remarks on rhyme in Pope's great imitation of Horace's Epistle to Florus, but the most brilliant discussion of rhyme, in recent years, is, in my opinion, Peter McDonald's essay, 'Rhyme and Determination in Hopkins and Edward Thomas', *Essays in Criticism*, XLIII, 3 (July 1993), whose treatment of the subject is consistently carried out in relation to the presentation of the poetic self. Most germane to my present purpose, however, is McDonald's treatment of rhyme as a paradox of 'submission and mastery' (p. 229, 234, 243).[61] Thinking about Pope more generally, it is many years since we had a good book on the formal features of Pope's poetry, considered in the light of his concerns. The last was certainly Geoffrey Tillotson's *On the Poetry of Pope* (1938).

But here I have some further observations to make about the bondage of rhyme, before coming to my conclusions.

The Temple of Fame (1715), a poem of Pope not often considered, has some brilliant effects. 'What you' (Fame cries to the idle), 'What you (she cry'd) unlearn'd in Arts to please, / Slaves to yourselves, and ev'n fatigued with Ease . . .': in the light of the contrast the rhyme enforces, the art to please becomes the life of action, and the saliency

---

[60]T. E. VI. 202.
[61]Gillian Beer, 'Rhyming as comedy: body, ghost, and banquet', in Michael Cordner, Peter Holland and John Kerrigan, eds. *English Comedy* (Cambridge, 1994), esp. pp. 191–2, but the whole essay is quizzical and suggestive. Peter McDonald, 'Rhyme and Determination in Hopkins and Edward Thomas', *Essays in Criticism*, XLIII, 3 (July 1993), pp. 229, 234, 243.

rhyme gives 'ease' sets up the paradox of the first and final words: the slavery of ease (ll. 396–7). Fame gets further petitioners:

> Last, those who boast of mighty Mischiefs done
> Enslave their Country, or usurp a Throne;
> Or who their Glory's dire Foundation laid
> On Sovereign's ruin'd, or on Friends betray'd;
> Calm, thinking Villains, whom no Faiths could fix,
> Of crooked Counsels and dark Politics;
> Of these a gloomy Tribe surround the Throne, . . .

(ll. 406–12)[62]

Welcome enough to Jacobites, one would imagine, early in 1715, these lines enact some well-qualified responses. There is no reason to doubt a deliberate half-rhyme 'done'/'Throne', in which dissonance conveys shock: no routine mischief. Notice the contrast in surface-sense between 'laid' and 'betray'd', and the responding bond in underlying meaning: treachery from the root in each case. Notice too the disturbing rhyme of the emphatic and familiar word 'fix' with the more recessive 'politics' where the stress-pattern of the second rhyming word falls away (we know how Pope said the word from other poems)[63] and the verse consciously and appropriately fails to achieve the sure symmetry at which heroic couplets seem to aim. So with the justice of politics.

An earlier passage in the same poem reminds us that in Pope's hands rhyming couplets do not fall into a set of barely connected aphorisms like beads on a string. Notice the management of the narrative simile here:

> Thick as the Bees, that with the Spring renew
> Their flow'ry Toils, and sip the fragrant Dew,
> When the wing'd Colonies first tempt the Sky,
> O'er dusky Fields and shaded Waters fly,
> Or settling, seize the Sweets the Blossoms yield,
> And a low Murmur runs along the Field.
> Millions of suppliant Crowds the Shrine attend,
> And all Degrees before the Goddess bend;
> The Poor, the Rich, the Valiant, and the Sage,
> And boasting Youth, and Narrative old-Age.
> Their Pleas were diff'rent, their Request the same:
> For Good and Bad alike are fond of Fame.
> Some she disgrac'd, and some with Honours crown'd;

---

[62]T. E. II. 282–3.
[63]See *To Arbuthnot*, l. 321; T. E. IV. 119.

> Unlike Successes equal Merits found.
> Thus her blind Sister, fickle *Fortune* reigns,
> And undiscerning, scatters Crowns and Chains.
>
> (ll. 282–97)[64]

Notice the trajectory enacted by the rhymes from 'renew' to 'fly' to 'field' and how this movement is combined with the movement of the sound which 'runs along the Field': narrative words. Notice at the end, not only the contrastive rhyme of 'reigns' and 'Chains', but how these highlit words stand in relation to others not necessarily part of the end-rhyme scheme: 'crown'd' in relation to 'Crowns' and 'reigns' and in relation to the ostensibly unrelated, scattered, 'Crowns and Chains.' Syntax makes some words salient, rhyme others; the two schemes subtly counterpoint or coincide with one another.

Following the theme of the slavery of rhyme I turn finally to a later poem, lacking the bravura of *The Temple of Fame*, but with a subtler familiarity and greater depth: Pope's imitation of Horace's Epistle to Florus. Here Pope pays tribute to his father, though Horace said nothing of his father in the Latin poem. But Horace's tribute to his freedman father in *Sat.* I. vi was so celebrated, and the imitative practice which recalled texts, other than the one being formally translated, so common, that Pope surely meant his reader to recall here that Horace's father had been a slave. This seems to align Horace's father who becomes free from actual slavery, with Pope's father who remains inwardly free though a kind of internal exile (something like Seneca's paradox) after the invasion of the Prince of Orange. Both Papists (in Pope's understated pun) manage to survive misfortune and injustice:

> And me, the Muses help'd to undergo it;
> Convict a Papist He, and I a Poet.
> But (thanks to *Homer*) since I live and thrive,
> Indebted to no Prince or Peer alive . . .
>
> (ll. 66–9)[65]

The humorously forced rhyme of the first couplet equates poetry with a suffering that will finally empower rather than constrain: notice then the plain, prosperous, rhyme ('thrive'/'Alive') in the following couplet: a milder way for Pope to say he is no man's slave.

---

[64]T. E. II. 279. G. F. C. Plowden notes, in his valuable study *Pope on Classic Ground* (Athens, Ohio, 1983), that the last line is in debt to an inverted line by Thomas Creech in his translation of Manilius's *Astronomica* (pp. 130, 166).
[65]T. E. IV. 169.

In the remarkable lines that follow the spoils of conquest and history are succeeded by those of time itself:

> This subtle Thief of life, this paltry Time,
> What will it leave me, if it snatch my rhime?
> If ev'ry wheel of that unweary'd Mill
> That turn'd ten thousand verses, now stands still.

(ll. 76–9)[66]

Having been told of the larger deprivations of history and age, we might expect 'rhime' not 'Time' to be termed 'paltry' here. Instead rhyme is esteemed as the poet's last resource. Rather the charge that rhyming is mechanical and laborious is taken up by 'that unweary'd Mill' (an image not in Horace) which at once deprecates yet pays tribute to rhyme as a strength. Since 'subtle Thief of life' echoes a sonnet of Milton (VII, l. 1) one wonders whether labour at the mill with slaves might not also be recalled. The punning word 'turn'd' must here refer to the turning of rhymes but, since Pope has just been talking about Homer, also means: 'translated', a sense he has used elsewhere.[67] There is, possibly, a further meaning, for the turning of the slave in the act of manumission, described by Persius whom Pope was re-reading at this time, and probably alluded to by Daniel, catches that repeated labour and release which rhyme meant for Pope.[68]

Those who remember the subtle, circumspect, courageous, intelligent and stunningly accomplished poet, the two hundred and fiftieth anniversary of whose death we mark at the end of this month, regard him chiefly perhaps as a satirist. Satire, of course, is a major feature of

---

[66]T. E. IV. 171.

[67]John Milton, *Poems*, ed. Carey and Fowler, p. 147; *Samson Agonistes*, l. 41, p. 348; 'Ten thousand', a round figure.

[68]Daniel, *Complete Works*, ed. Grosart, IV. 45; Persius, V, ll. 73–82. To speak of the turning of a line, or, as Ben Jonson did, of Shakespeare's 'well-turnéd and true-filéd lines' (l. 68 of 'To the memory of . . . Master William Shakespeare') was to make a kind of Latin/English pun, since a line was a verse, and the word verse came from the noun *versus*, a row, a line, a furrow, a verse (cf. Spenser, *The Faerie Queene*, VI. ix. 1, ll. 1–4) and from the verb *verto, verti, versum*, to turn. As verse came to be more commonly rhymed than not, turning a verse came to suggest turning a rhyme, though this may have been a post-Pope usage. O. E. D. attributes the first instance of 'turning a couplet' to Washington Irving (1850) referring to Goldsmith (X. 487: Sense II, 5 (b)). Daniel wrote of 'reducing' verse 'in *girum*, and a iust forme', which implied turning a turn into a complete circle, the just or perfect figure. Against Persius's scornful account of the manumission which made a slave free ('heu steriles veri, quibus una Quiritem/vertigo facit') one might set Psalm 126, *In convertendo*, verse 1: 'When the Lord turned again the captivity of Sion . . .'.

his work, and the idea of slavery supplied him with an extreme and
dramatic way of writing about the state of Britain:

> Adieu to Virtue if you're once a Slave:
> Send her to Court, you send her to her Grave.
>
> (*To Bolingbroke*, ll. 118–19)[69]

But Pope challenged the practice of slavery itself in non-satirical lines,
and there is an extended yet serious sense in which he both repudiated
the application of the word to himself and yet identified with slavery.
In turning from world to word we find that the idea of slavery allows
us to see Pope from several related angles, and allows us to turn from
positions publicly proclaimed to his more personal self-presentations
as labourer, craftsman and artist in words.

[69]T. E. IV. 287.

PLATE 1

Honoraliss Dominæ. D Margaritæ Comitissæ
de Orrory Tabulam hanc L MDD D IO Ld. i3.

Pallas Athene and Odysseus on the coast of Ithica, plate from John Ogilby's translation of the *Odyssey* (1665), probably known to Pope as a child.

PLATE 2

The frontispiece from *Pope Alexander's Supremacy and Infallibility Examin'd* (1729), an attack responding to Pope's *Dunciad Variorum*, published in that year. By permission of the British Library.

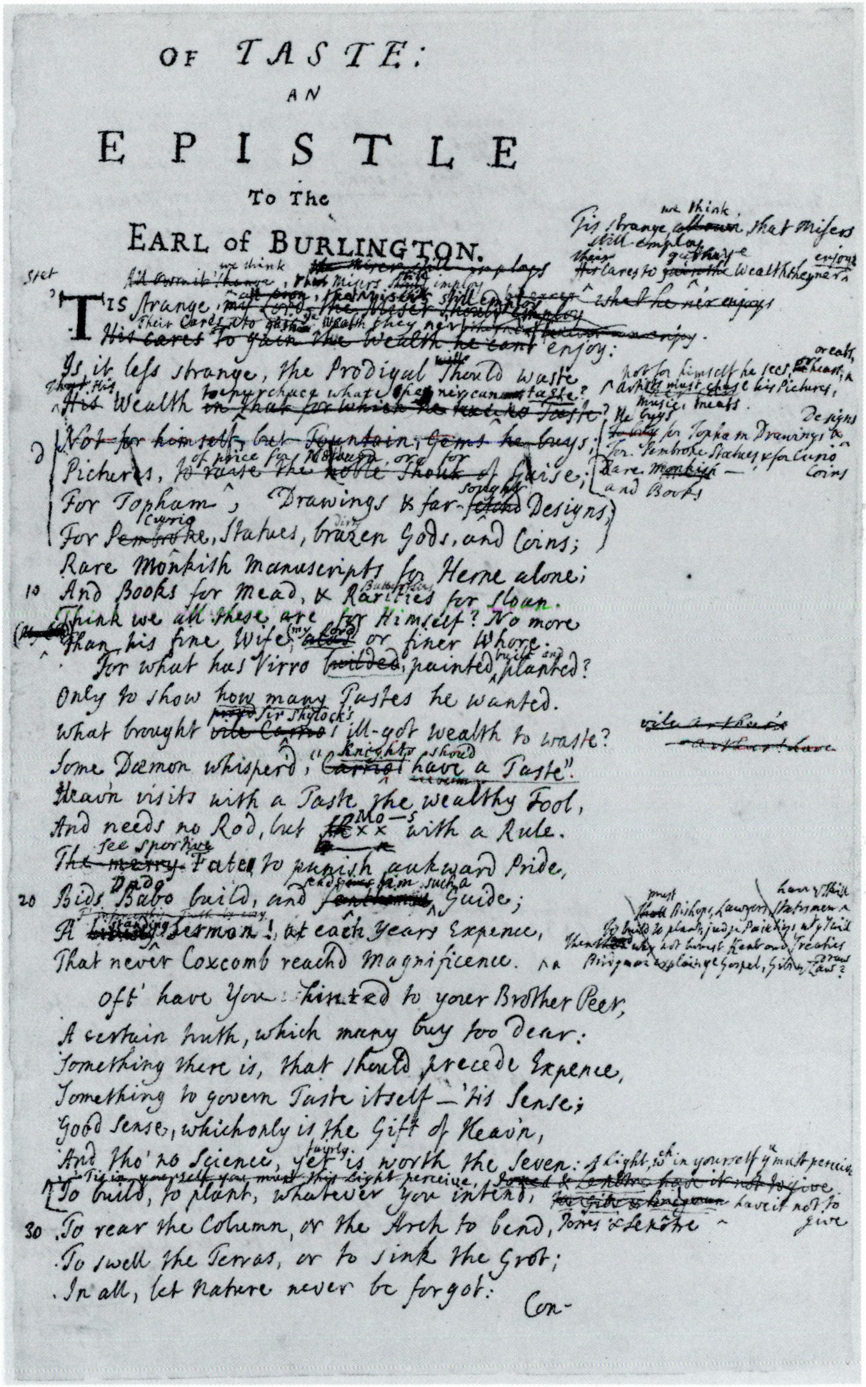

PLATE 3

OF *TASTE*:

AN

EPISTLE

TO THE

EARL of BURLINGTON.

'TIS strange, the Miser should his Cares employ
To gain those Riches he can ne'er enjoy:

Is it less strange, the Prodigal should waste
His Wealth to purchase what he ne'er can taste?
Not for himself, but Fountains, Gems he buys;
Pictures, to raise the noble Thought of Guise;
For Topham, Drawings & far-fetch'd Designs;
For Pembroke, Statues, brazen Gods, and Coins;
Rare Monkish Manuscripts for Herne alone;
And Books for Mead, & Rarities for Sloan.
Think we all these are for Himself? No more
Than his fine Wife, or finer Whore.
For what has Virro painted, planted?
Only to show how many Tastes he wanted.
What brought Sir Shylock's ill-got Wealth to waste?
Some Dæmon whisper'd, "have a Taste"
Heav'n visits with a Taste the wealthy Fool,
And needs no Rod, but with a Rule.
The Fates to punish aukward Pride,
Bids Babo build, and such a Guide;
A Sermon!, at each Year's Expence,
That never Coxcomb reach'd Magnificence.

Oft' have You hinted to your Brother Peer,
A certain truth, which many buy too dear:
Something there is, that should precede Expence,
Something to govern Taste itself—'tis Sense;
Good Sense, which only is the Gift of Heav'n,
And tho' no Science, yet is worth the Seven:
To build, to plant, whatever you intend,
To rear the Column, or the Arch to bend,
To swell the Terras, or to sink the Grot;
In all, let Nature never be forgot.

Con-

The autograph leaf of the opening of Pope's Epistle *To Burlington*. By permission of the Pierpont Morgan Library, New York, MA 36.

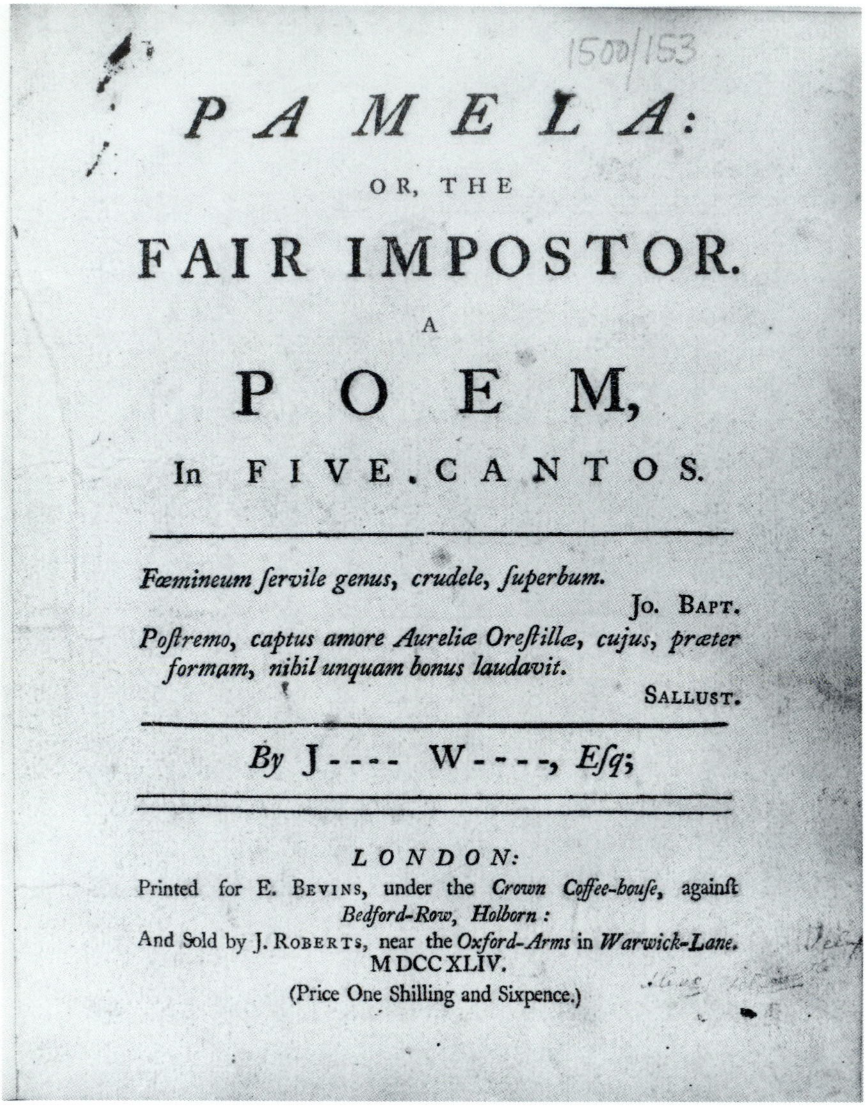

PLATE 4

PAMELA:

OR, THE

FAIR IMPOSTOR.

A

POEM,

In FIVE.CANTOS.

Fœmineum servile genus, crudele, superbum.

Jo. BAPT.

Postremo, captus amore Aureliæ Orestillæ, cujus, præter formam, nihil unquam bonus laudavit.

SALLUST.

By J ---- W ----, *Esq;*

LONDON:

Printed for E. BEVINS, under the *Crown Coffee-house*, against *Bedford-Row, Holborn*:
And Sold by J. ROBERTS, near the *Oxford-Arms* in *Warwick-Lane.*
M DCC XLIV.

(Price One Shilling and Sixpence.)

The titlepage of *Pamela: Or, The Fair Imposter. A Poem, in Five Cantos* (1744). By permission of the British Library.

Proceedings of the British Academy, **91**, 55–68

Pope's Homer:
The Shadow of Friendship

HESTER JONES

AT THE BEGINNING of his poem 'To Mr. Pope', Thomas Parnell admires
Pope's skill at combining 'music' and 'affection' in his poems. He says:

> To praise, and still with just respect to praise
> A Bard triumphant in immortal bays,
> The Learn'd to show, the Sensible commend,
> Yet still preserve the province of the Friend,
> What life, what vigour, must the lines require?
> What Music tune them, what affection fire?
> —O might thy Genius in my bosom shine!
> Thou shouldst not fail of numbers worthy thine

Pope's translation of Homer, Parnell goes on to say, provides a perfect
example of animating friendship; the epic poet has languished 'long
unknown, /Like monarchs sparkling on a distant throne', but now
Pope's redeeming and befriending language has brought the work to
life.[1] I shall suggest in this essay, that Pope's Homer, and in particular
his *Odyssey* translation, displays, as Parnell's poem hints, a constant
regard for friendship in a variety of contexts, even at moments where
Homer's original poem seems to be describing a somewhat different
relation. I shall also suggest that Pope's prominent emphasis on friendship, among poets as well as among the characters in Homer, had a
precedent in the prose epic of Archbishop Fénelon, *The Adventures of
Telemachus*. Further, that Pope's work looks to friendship as a relation
which may bridge the dualistic opposition between passion and mind,
an opposition which is sometimes said to characterise the Augustan
period: in the friendship Pope articulates, tender feeling is given ani-

[1] '"To Mr. Pope', ll. 1–8, *The Collected Poems of Thomas Parnell*, ed. Claude Rawson and F.
P. Lock (Newark, London and Toronto, 1989), p. 119.

mation and direction by poetic vision. Again, Pope found a precedent in Fénelon, who was regarded as 'the most amiable philosopher that ever Europe produced', and particularly admired for what William Langhorne described as his 'affluence of imagination'[2]; according to the Chevalier Ramsay, Fénelon treats the reader with friendly candour, and 'lets him into his own Heart'[3]. Pope's characters in his translation of Homer have, like Fénelon's, their own heart and their own mind; they are unsubdued by passion, but capable of a more elevated friendship. I shall also suggest that this regard for wise friendship led Pope, like his epic hero Ulysses, to adopt the goddess Athena as his Mentor, a choice which has broad implications for many of his poems.

Parnell's gesture of friendship towards Pope is answered and extended in Pope's gesture of saving friendship towards Homer; or so Parnell's *Essay on Homer* would suggest. According to Spence, Pope, grudgingly, said of the *Essay*: 'Tis still stiff, and was written much stiffer', but the *Essay* was nonetheless published, after extensive 'correcting' by Pope, and it opens with a sentence which deserves consideration, since it seems to serve as a kind of manifesto for the translation as a whole:

> There is something in the Mind of Man, which goes beyond bare curiosity, and even carries us on to a Shadow of Friendship with those great Genius's whom we have known to excell in former Ages.[4]

First of all, then, Pope, with Parnell's help, was doing something new in the *Essay on Homer*, something which is in line with the translation's persistent interest in interpersonal friendship. Translation is always to some extent a collaborative enterprise: the translator must negotiate between his own audience and the ancient original. A crafty translator, however, may use his translation as a means of integrating past, present and future. Such an activity has heroic, even epic, potential; the poet, like the crafty Ulysses, the man of the present, escapes the Cyclops of the past to move into the open seas of the future.

On the other hand, the evident Augustan quality of Pope's trans-

[2]William Langhorne, *The Correspondence of Theodosius and Constantia, from their first acquaintance to the departure of Theodosius* (London, 1765), p. 45.

[3]Andrew Michael Ramsay, 'Discours de la poesie épique, et de l'excellence du poème de Télémaque', *Les aventures de Télémaque* ([?] Rotterdam, 1717) quoted from *The Adventures of Telemachus, the Son of Ulysses [. . .] Done from the new edition just printed at Paris [. . .]*, by Mr. Ozell, 3rd ed. 2 vols. (London, 1720), p. xli.

[4]Alexander Pope, 'An *Essay* on the Life, Writings *and* Learning of Homer', *Homer's Iliad and Odyssey*, ed. Maynard Mack, The Twickenham Edition of the Works of Alexander Pope, Vols. VII–X (London and New York, 1967), VII. 26 and n.

lation may suggest a somewhat guileless translator, wedded to the criteria of his time. Dr. Johnson, however, replied to the well-known objection that Pope's Homer was not Homerical, by saying: 'elegance is surely to be desired if it be not gained at the expense of dignity. A hero would wish to be loved as well as to be reverenced.'[5] Johnson, that is, defends an Augustan translation by making the wish for love as well as reverence the attribute of a secondary culture. Parnell's *Essay on Homer* makes these two movements — of reverence and of friendship — common to both ancient and modern cultures, and even, simultaneous: the latter a natural consequence of the former.

The combination of reverence and affection is epitomised in the phrase 'shadow of friendship'; the distant genius casts a long shadow over the younger poet, who in turn responds by waiting on the older with a dogged attentiveness. The translator both is, and is drawn into, a 'shadow of friendship'. Both Pope and Homer are shadows: Homer because he is dead, though great; Pope because he is living, but small; and this reciprocal action generates a friendship, one 'compounded' of admiration, respect, affection and, most importantly, the desire for wisdom.

Pope's searching extension of friendship to the Father of Poetry perhaps anticipates, yet does not quite pre-empt, the move to 'desacramentalize' Homer, as Howard Clarke has called it, performed by later critics such as Thomas Blackwell and Robert Wood.[6] It also distinguishes his approach from that of Joseph Addison in his *A Discourse on Ancient and Modern Languages*. There Addison, like Parnell, regrets the distance of ancient writing, and like him uses an image which longingly imagines the possibility of extending human friendship to distant writers, for the ancients

> appear to us in the Splendour and Formality of Strangers. We are not intimately enough acquainted with them, and never met with their Expressions but in Print, and that too on a serious Occasion.[7]

Pope's bolder and more intimate approach may also be distinguished from his earlier rival in translation, John Dryden. Pope often protests

[5]Samuel Johnson, *Lives of the English Poets*, World's Classics ed., 2 vols. (Oxford, 1929), II. 336.
[6]Howard Clarke, *Homer's Readers: A Historical Introduction to the 'Iliad' and the 'Odyssey'* (Newark, NJ, 1981). See Robert Wood, *An Essay on the Original Genius and Writings of Homer* (London, 1767), p. 298 and Thomas Blackwell, *An Enquiry into the Life and Writings of Homer* (London, 1735), pp. 301–2.
[7]Joseph Addison, *A Discourse on Ancient and Modern Languages* (Dublin, 1739), p. 23.

deficiency before 'that great man'[8] as he calls him, yet his application of the metaphor of friendship to Homer actually contributes something new to a subject Dryden had also considered.

Pope's translation rarely struggles to establish a literary pedigree. Dryden, however, writes in the *Preface to the Fables, Ancient and Modern*, that poets have 'our lineal Descents and Clans, as well as other Families' and he traces his own pedigree, along the 'threads and connexions' of discourse and of thought, through Chaucer and Boccaccio and Spenser. Such a linear, familial understanding of how poetic tradition is founded applies too to poets' creations, so that, for example, 'Dido cannot be denied to be the poetical daughter of Calypso'.[9] The role of poet, like the essential character shared by Dido and Calypso, descends on the worthy heir like a crown. Dryden is, according to this view, at the end of a long line of such worthy figures.

Pope's metaphor of friendship, however, as applied to his own relation to Homer, is both more fluidly animate — poetic relations are always subject to alteration — and also more private. Modestly, it maintains a discreet distance from the original. But, more stridently, it also claims that the acts of reading and writing can acquire living, responsive, human properties, so that the ancient shade may, through the animating vision of the translator, even become a friend.

Now, as Douglas Stewart has observed, there are few instances of real friendship in the *Iliad*. Pope, though, converts other relationships, such as those between Briseis and Patroclus, between Hector and Andromache, and between Glaucus and Sarpedon, into ones which obey all the rules of friendship: the individuals have a high regard for freedom and autonomy; they are mutually responsive; their affection is given distance and dignity by soulful reflection, and they place their relation above the demands of role or of duty. Dryden's Andromache, for example, is primarily a dutiful wife; Pope's, a wisely detached, though affectionate, friend.[10]

The *Odyssey*, however, allowed Pope a freer rein as far as the pursuit of friendship was concerned. The poem is *often* read as an allegorical expression of the soul's journey to spiritual enlightenment; a recent study, by Jean Houston, *The Hero and the Goddess*, actually describes this journey as a 'crazy friendship' in which divine and human

[8]Pope, *Iliad*, Book 6, l. 462 n, T. E. VII. 349.
[9]John Dryden, *Poems*, ed. by James Kinsley, 4 vols. (Oxford, 1958), IV, pp. 1445–6, 1448.
[10]Douglas J. Stewart, *The Disguised Guest: Rank, Role and Identity in the Odyssey* (Lewisburgh, PA, 1976).

worlds assist each other in their shared voyage of transformation. The impresario of this venture is the goddess Athena, who becomes, in Houston's phrase, Odysseus' Great Friend. Pope was always alert to the rivalrous claims of word and world, of narrative and allegory, and, consequently, he writes a collaborative, if not friendly, translation which puts such a Platonic quest in solidly social terms. In his translation, the self, Ulysses, the 'godlike man', finds a way to divine wisdom through the co-operative exchanges of earthly friendships.[11]

One example of this emphasis on the redeeming power of friendship may be seen in Book 11, which was in fact translated by Fenton, but nonetheless bears the mark of Pope's own vision. Visiting the dead, Ulysses is asked to remember Elpenor. John Ogilby's version, which constituted Pope's first experience of Homer, appeals to domestic loyalty. The dead man begs:

> By thy dear Wife, thy Son, and aged Sire[12]

and Cowper's later translation also speaks of family ties:

> But now, by those whom thou hast left at home,
> By thy Penelope, and by thy sire
> The gentle nourisher of thy infant growth,
> And by thy only son Telemachus,
> I make my suit to thee.[13]

But Pope / Fenton refers specifically to the 'soft tye and sacred name of friend', and asks 'there call to mind thy poor departed friend.'[14] Friendship, furthermore, takes the place of hierarchical service; Cowper's shade, by contrast, describes himself as 'mariner of thine'.[15]

Friendship, in Pope's translation, is also extended to, and sometimes invoked by, the female temptresses whom Ulysses encounters. So Calypso boasts:

> It was my crime to pity, and to save [. . .]
> Hither this Man of miseries I led,
> Receiv'd the friendless, and the hungry fed;[16]

[11]Jean Houston, *The Hero and the Goddess* (London, 1992), pp. 300–320.
[12]John Ogilby, *Homer his Odysses translated* (London, 1669), Book 11, l. 62, p. 145.
[13]William Cowper, *The Odyssey of Homer translated into English Blank Verse* (London, 1791), Book 11, ll. 75–9, p. 248.
[14]Pope, *Odyssey*, Book 11, ll. 82, 88, T. E. IX. 385.
[15]Cowper, *Odyssey*, Book 11, l. 92, p. 248.
[16]Pope, *Odyssey*, Book 5, ll. 166, 171–2, T. E. IX. 180.

Calypso also addresses Ulysses actually as a friend, in the following lines:

> This shows thee, friend, by old experience taught,
> And learn'd in all the wiles of human thought.
> How prone to doubt, how cautious are the wise?[17]

Book 6, again not initially translated by Pope, but nonetheless bearing his mark, describes Ulysses' arrival on Phaecia, and his meeting with the royal princess, Nausicaa. Many readers have wondered whether there were not romantic potential in this encounter, but Pope made his views on the subject quite clear in a lengthy note. I shall quote it in full, since it clearly illustrates Pope's keenness to play down the role of passion in the life of the man of Ulyssean wisdom:

> *Eustathius* and *Dacier* are both of opinion, that *Nausicaa* had conceiv'd a passion for *Ulysses*: I think this passage is an evidence that she rather admir'd and esteem'd, than lov'd him; for it is contrary to the nature of that passion to give directions for the departure of the person belov'd, but rather to invent excuses to prolong his stay. 'Tis true *Nausicaa* had wish'd in the foregoing parts of this book, that she might have *Ulysses* for her husband, or such an husband as *Ulysses*, but this only shews that she admir'd his accomplishments, nor could she have added *such a spouse as he*, at all, if her affections had been engag'd and fix'd upon *Ulysses* only. This likewise takes off the objection of a too great fondness in *Nausicaa*; for it might have appear'd too great a fondness to have fall'n in love at the first with an absolute stranger.[18]

It is significant that Pope uses this passage to argue in favour of a form of converse, based on admiration and esteem, which does not depend exclusively on marital, or even extramarital designs, but which is, rather, content to stay as friendship. Though Pope acknowledges the possibility of romantic interest in the first instance, he is eager to chart the progression by which these interests are transformed into a more distanced relation, but one nonetheless which is animated by a mutual regard.

While many interpretations of the poem view Ulysses' adventures as a series of preparations for the final great scene of homecoming, Pope's translation makes the encounter between Ulysses and Athena in Book 13 a cardinal moment, and an archetype for the meetings radiating around it. Pope put this encounter into the 1717 *Miscellany*: this chosen moment is emblematic of the whole poem, and gives a key

[17]*Ibid.*, ll. 235–7, p. 182.
[18]Pope, *Odyssey*, Book 6, l. 347 n, T. E. IX. 228–9.

to Pope's understanding of it.[19] A reading which emphasises this central encounter, divides the poem into two halves and enhances its bifocal Janus-like aspect: the first half culminates in the apprehension of wisdom and understanding; the second begins to put that wisdom into practice. The apprehension of wisdom and the experience of enlightenment is, then, the goal of the *Odyssey*'s voyage of friendship. It was also Pope's portrayal of this aspect of the poem which many contemporary readers particularly admired.

Parnell was referring to this quality when he said the translation 'reveals the work to light'. Pope reaches the heart of the *Odyssey* and makes its meaning plain. Such contemporary praise is of importance because so many readers have shared the opposite view, most eloquently expressed by Maynard Mack in his introduction to the Twickenham edition of Pope's Homer. Mack writes that:

> Homer's directness and simplicity in treating the responses of men and women to each other come figured, in Pope's translation, through a fine silk screen of baroque *sensiblerie*.[20]

The use of the French term suggests that something alien and obfuscating has been placed between original and reader. But the term 'screen' perhaps underestimates the dynamic, responsive nature of Pope's treatment of enlightenment. A remark made by Joseph Spence in connection with *Odyssey* Book 10 in *An Essay on Pope's Odyssey* clarifies Pope's endeavour in this respect:

> It is a power almost unknown even to Poetry before, and the Criticks have not as yet found out any Name for it. The extraordinary Beauty I mean, is that *Insight* which the Poet gives his readers into *Circe's Mind*: We look into her Soul, and see the Ideas pass there in a Train. [...] Her Mind acts with Tumult and Rapidity, but at the same time with a series and gradual Collection of Truths, at first unknown. Everyone may perceive the Tumult, and the *successive Enlightenings* of her Mind. We are led into a full View of the shifting of her thoughts; and behold the various openings of them in her Soul [...] Circe's very Thoughts are made visible to us; they are set full in our Eyes, and we see the different degrees, as it were of light, breaking in upon her Soul.[21]

If there is a 'screen' dividing men and women from each other in

---

[19]Alexander Pope, 'The Episode of Sarpedon, Translated from the *Twelfth* and *Sixteenth* Books of *Homer's Iliads*', *Pastoral Poetry and An Essay on Criticism*, E. Audra and Aubrey Williams, Twickenham Edition, I (London and New Haven, 1961), pp. 447–64.

[20]Maynard Mack, 'Introduction', Pope, *Iliad*, T. E. VII. li.

[21]Joseph Spence, *An Essay on Pope's Odyssey* (London, 1726), pp. 58–9.

Pope's translation, it is a screen, paradoxically, of 'light breaking in upon the soul'. In this respect, Pope follows the lead of Archbishop Fénelon in his moralistic prose epic, *The Adventures of Telemachus*, whose style Pope apparently disparaged, but nonetheless read 'with pleasure'.[22] This work makes the journey to spiritual enlightenment the central interest; further, its focus is divided between the young hero Telemachus and his elderly wise friend, Mentor, in fact the goddess Athena in disguise. It is their friendship, and the wisdom imparted through it, which really interests Fénelon, and, with a further extension of friendly concern, he, I think like Pope, endows female characters such as Calypso, with an inwardness, dignity and intelligence lacking in other treatments of the same theme — for example, in John Hughes's comic opera, *Calypso and Telemachus*.[23] Fénelon's replacement of the single solitary hero with the pair of friends, makes an important point which Pope, I would suggest, absorbed: the pursuit of wisdom (such as the epic hero is engaged in) and the practice of friendship, go hand in hand.

Pope's concern to locate wisdom in social friendship also determines the goddess that he chooses to regard as his Mentor. Francis Thompson, in *Pope: A Renegade Poet* has written: 'if Dryden was the Mars of English Satire, Pope was the Venus'.[24] However, in his minor poem, 'On receiving from the Right Hon. the Lady Frances Shirley a standish and two pens', Pope suggests otherwise:

> Yes, I beheld th' Athenian Queen
>   Descend in all her sober charms;
> 'And take (she said, and smil'd serene)
>   'Take at this hand celestial arms . . .'[25]

Pope is concerned, in the translation and in his own poems, to prove himself, like Ulysses, a disciple of Athena, the giver of just, celestial arms, and the bearer of 'sober charms'. There are several reasons why Pope might have found Athena a congenial Muse. One reason is indirectly suggested by Dr. Johnson, who remarked: 'In the Letters both of Swift and Pope there appears such narrowness of mind, as makes them insensible of any excellence that has not some affinity with

[22]Joseph Spence, *Observations, Anecdotes, and Characters of Books and Men*, ed. James M. Osborn, 2 vols. (Oxford, 1966), I, p. 222.
[23]John Hughes, *Calypso and Telemachus* (London, 1712).
[24]Francis Thompson, *Pope: A Renegade Poet and other Essays* (Boston, 1910), p. 197.
[25]Pope, *Minor Poems*, ed. Norman Ault and John Butt, Twickenham Edition, VI (London and New Haven, 1954; repr. with corrections, 1964), p. 378.

their own'.[26] Johnson here makes the recognition of affinity equivalent to 'narrowness', equivalent, in fact, to the narrowness of self-love. However, for Pope, as for many poets, the recognition of affinity, of likeness between things, is the source of self-knowledge and the means to both charity and wisdom. Athena, not Venus, is the goddess of likenesses, of similarity in difference.

This may be linked to Athena's own history: she is, in fact, not one goddess, but two. One Athena is severe, helmeted, and girdled, with a firm stride and protective shield, the unvanquished virgin warrior, a female goddess who nonetheless seems to uphold 'patriarchal' values. A few examples of this attitude may suffice here: Pomey's *Pantheon*, for example, in 1698 described Minerva as a 'virago in armour' whose stern looks 'threaten violence'. This image fused with the myth of Britannia, as in John Durant Breval's *Henry and Minerva* (1739), a poem which celebrates the birth of classicism in the sixteenth century and attributes it to a happy alliance of Minerva and Henry the Eighth. The myth of the motherless goddess contributed in some seventeenth-century texts to the ungenerous belief that, as Anthony Ross put it, 'women are hinderers, not furtherers of wisdom and learning'.[27]

There is another Athena, however, who lived as an Earth Goddess on the island of Crete, and who protected the rights of her female suppliants. As Jean Houston has suggested in *The Hero and the Goddess*, when the northern Greeks took over the Minoan mother-goddess they necessarily suppressed this matriarchal association, assimilating her instead into the city-based myth of the virgin-daughter. Such an assimilation may be compared with suppression in Marian cults of the revolutionary Mary who spoke the Magnificat.[28]

Athena, therefore, represents a fusion between male and female principles; a fusion which more often bears witness to a process of erasure and appropriation, than to the confident acceptance of divergent ideas and loyalties. However, Athena's patronage of male and female craft ideally gestures towards an image of breadth and open-ended expansiveness; and such a combination appealed, I think, to Pope. In his translations, he goes some way towards reinstating the

[26]Johnson, *Lives of the English Poets*, II, p. 316.
[27]François Antoine Pomey, *The Pantheon* (London, 1694), p. 108; Anthony Ross, *Mystagogus Poeticus or the Muses' Interpreter* (London, 1648), p. 282.
[28]Houston, *Hero and Goddess*, p. 42. See also Marina Warner, *Monuments and Maidens* (London, 1985).

fluid, animate, multiple, dynamic goddess, in place of the statuesque, spear-brandishing warrior of which Pomey's *Pantheon* and Anthony Ross's *Muses' Interpreter*, speak.

To understand still better why Pope might have been drawn to Athena, the goddess of wisdom, of craft and, Walter Otto has suggested, of friendship too,[29] we need to turn for a moment to two nineteenth-century disciples of Athena, W. E. Gladstone, and John Ruskin. Gladstone's *Studies on Homer* takes pains to point out Athena's unique role among the Greek gods, and in particular the paradoxical relation she represents between purity and worldly action. This paradox returns in Gladstone's discussion of Athena's ambiguous status among the gods: though she never, as he puts it, submits to dishonour, yet she is not 'above condescension to deceit'. Her multiple forms express divine approval of the variety of creation; yet, at the same time, her care for Ulysses is:

> a contact so close and intimate, a care so sleepless and so tender, embracing alike the course of events without, and the state of mind within; so affectionate in relation to the person, yet so entirely without the least partiality and caprice; so personal, yet so far from what Holy Scripture calls, with the highest perfection of phrase, respect of persons[30]

Such an image of constant, attentive presence recommended itself to John Ruskin too; in the *Queen of the Air*, he interprets such constant presence as referring to what he calls the 'ruling power of the air' — air which nourishes, strengthens, and is essential to many forms of practical art. This infinitely changeable, yet infinitely constant aspect of Athena, which Gladstone and Ruskin recognised, is also truer to the spirit of Athena in Homer's *Odyssey* than certain commentators, whom I have mentioned, realised.[31] W. J. B. Stanford has written in *The Ulysses Theme* of the poem's evolutionary character: and its evolution, furthermore, is one which is promoted and represented by Athena herself. Stanford also reminds us that Homer's portrayal of the relationship between Athena and Ulysses is unique, since it is neither simply erotic in its nature nor specifically practical in its function. So, as Stanford puts it, 'a special relationship between a divinity and a mortal

---

[29]Walter F. Otto, *The Homeric Gods: The Spiritual Significance of Greek Religion*, trans. Moses Hadas (London, 1955), p. 54.
[30]W. E. Gladstone, *Studies on Homer and the Homeric Age*, 3 vols. (Oxford, 1858), II, p. 122.
[31]John Ruskin, *The Queen of the Air* (London, 1869), pp. 56, 69.

needed a special explanation', and that explanation came in Book 13 of the *Odyssey*.[32]

At the core of this book is a single experience: the discovery of affinity amidst apparent difference. Such an experience, too, informs Pope's translation. As usual, Pope uses a pair of characters to point up individual distinctiveness. An aside in the 'Postscript' to the *Odyssey* similarly suggests that we should read it for 'its own nature and design' and not with 'an eye to the Iliad'; Pope habitually 'brings things into pairs', then directs one's attention to the distinctive, individual elements that constitute them.[33]

Pope's version of the encounter between Athena and Ulysses, consequently, loses some of its charming ease, but gains instead a not uncalled for emphasis on the element of surprising compatibility, of friendly equivalence, between hero and goddess. Each borrows the attributes of the other's kind: Ulysses is a 'godlike' man, Athena a 'blue-ey'd maid'. While Ulysses tells his tale of woe, she 'began / With pleasing smiles to view the godlike man'. This response suggests that even the gods can be charmed, though the susceptibility implied by 'pleasing smiles' is tempered by the cooler, more distant 'began / To view'. Further, Pope omits the detail given in the original that Athena 'fondles' the hero, as if he wished to place the friendly nature of the relationship beyond question.[34]

This indeed suggests that, in Pope's view, the process of deification is a mutually dependent one: Athena's human appreciation of Ulysses facilitates his repossession of godlike, or rather, Pope suggests, kinglike, status. Ulysses' infinite capacity for dissimulation, however, also acts as a trigger for Athena's own transformation into the 'divinely bright', heavenly daughter of Jove. Yet even after this apotheosis, she is only, according to Pope, 'divinely' bright; her brightness still retains qualities which may be perceived by mortal eyes. And furthermore, she speaks in terms which not only Ulysses, but Pope too, would have understood.

On the one hand she is, Pope says:

> Like a fair virgin in her beauty's bloom,
> Skill'd in th' illustrious labours of the loom.[35]

With their heavy alliteration and rather leaden rhythm, the lines point

[32]W. J. B. Stanford, *The Ulysses Theme* (Oxford, 1963), p. 30.
[33]Pope, 'Postscript' to the *Odyssey*, T. E.X. 386.
[34]Pope, *Odyssey*, Book 13, ll. 327–8, T. E.X. 23.
[35]*Ibid.*, ll. 329, 331–2, p. 23.

up the archaic nature of the simile. But when a moment later Athena
speaks herself, her terms are thoroughly contemporary:

> O still the same *Ulysses*! she rejoin'd,
> In useful craft successfully refin'd!
> Artful in speech, in action, and in mind!
> Suffic'd it not, that thy long labours past
> Secure thou seest thy native shore at last?
> But this to me? who, like thy self excell
> In arts of counsel, and dissembling well.
> To me, whose wit exceeds the pow'rs divine,
> No less than mortals are surpass'd by thine.
> Know'st thou not me? who made thy life my care,
> Thro' ten years wand'ring, and thro' ten years war;[36]

Ulysses, Athena reminds us, represents a union of 'counsel', and artful-
ness. 'Counsel' is a useful word in this connection, since it contains both
the sense of prudent privacy (self-possessed is probably the modern
equivalent) and also of open conversation or debate. As Gladstone
pointed out in his *Studies on Homer*, Athena is exceptionally mobile
among the gods, in terms of the numbers of mortals and immortals
that she talks to, but she is also exceptionally good at self-effacement,
at disappearing and delegating.[37] Pope, collaborating with Broome and
Fenton in such a way that individual voices are lost in the service of
the 'whole' translation, would have responded with alacrity to Athena's
versatile person.

Versatility requires a person to possess both inwardness and force
of will. Gladstone, on the one hand, chooses to emphasize Athena's
executive powers; Jupiter cannot operate without her practical assistance among mortals. Modern commentators, such as Anne Baring and
Jules Cashford in *The Myth of the Goddess*, have stressed the opposite:
Athena's 'self-disciplined awareness' and her powers of inward reflection.[38] Pope, by contrast with both these approaches, and also properly,
I think, combines the process of private thought and its realisation in
worldly action, in the phrase 'arts of counsel'.

Similarly, George de Forest Lord has commented that Pope's style,
compared with that of Chapman's *Odyssey*, tends to elevate its subject
matter and treat the speeches in a 'uniformly elegant' manner, consequently eliminating the local, accidental or individual differences which

---

[36]*Ibid.*, ll. 333–43, pp. 23–4.
[37]Gladstone, *Studies on Homer*, pp. 133–6.
[38]Anne Baring and Jules Cashford, *The Myth of the Goddess* (London, 1992), pp. 332–345.

animate Homer's original poem.[39] In the original, Athena actually acknowledges Ulysses' self-interested guile, yet, contrarily, condones it, because she admits to similar faults in herself. Pope's version, it is true, smooths over these faults, and presents them in favourable terms, as 'useful craft'. Pope emphasises equivalent excelling: both Athena and Ulysses are more crafty than other people and other gods. The recognition of another master-craftsman — such as Homer, in Pope's case — becomes the means by which the excelling hero can be adjusted to his non-heroic world.

Such a transition from friendly recognition to a reaccommodation in the social world, furthermore, marks many passages in Pope's *Odyssey*, and many, though not all, involve female characters, whom Pope remodels in the form of the goddess Athena. The most striking example in his own poems, however, of Pope's explicit self-dedication to Athena comes at the end of the *Epistle to a Lady*. The poem performs an Odyssean journey around the 'characters of women', relocating its series of female characters in the conceit of a gallery. Miss Blount, whose words we have heard at the beginning of the poem, returns to the poet's vision after a period of absence. She is adorned with 'the Moon's more sober light' (and 'sober' is a word Pope associates with Athena) and 'Serene in Virgin Modesty she shines, / And unobserv'd the glaring Orb declines.'[40] Athena, too, is often 'unobserv'd'; she is also the giver of good temper or restraint, and, most importantly, she sustains a constant character beneath an array of diverse disguises.

In the encounter scene in Book 13, Ulysses exclaims 'He who discerns thee must be truly wise, / So seldom view'd, and ever in disguise', to which, a little later, Athena replies, 'How prone to doubt, how cautious are the wise! / Who, vers'd in fortune, fear the flattering show, / And taste not half the bliss the Gods bestow.'[41] Of the characters of women, Pope makes a similar point about their paradoxical variety and consistency, and in the course of the poem, Pope displays his own wisdom in perceiving and expressing the character of the true woman, the poem's lady, who is, like Athena herself, subject to many disguises, both divine and yet also visible to mortal eyes. The Lady is, like

[39] George de Forest Lord, *Homeric Renaissance: The 'Odyssey' of George Chapman* (London, 1956), p. 207.
[40] Pope, *Epistle to a Lady*, ll. 249–56, *Epistles to Several Persons (Moral Essays)*, ed. F. W. Bateson, T. E. III. ii (London and New Haven, 1951), p. 70.
[41] Pope, *Odyssey*, Book 13, ll. 375–7, T. E. X. 25.

Athena, independent, 'Mistress of Herself'; Pope even refers to 'those blue eyes', with which he had adorned his Athena, where 'grey' or 'bright' is the more usual translation.[42]

Such an understanding of affinity, of compatibility in an alien world, won Ulysses Athena's constant friendship. And such a generous acknowledgment on the Lady's part of the necessarily separate nature of their paths, won Miss Blount Pope's friendly tribute:

> The gen'rous God, who Wit and Gold refines,
> And ripens Spirits as he ripens Mines,
> Kept Dross for Duchesses, the world shall know it,
> To you gave Sense, Good-Humour, and a Poet.[43]

These are some of Pope's most elegant, and yet also most generously self-deprecating lines; whereas Ulysses and Athena recognised a shared pre-eminence in comparable fields, Pope acknowledges the Lady's superiority in her own field, and makes his own achievement sound as trifling as the gawky rhyme. Imitating her example of self-possession, he refrains from appropriating her charms, although they are also his inspiration. Instead, he pays tribute to her respect for freedom, as essential to friendship as Athena's uncompelled assistance is to the completion of the epic journey.

[42]Ruskin takes pains to point out that the Greeks were concerned not with colour as such, but with degrees of light, the extent to which something is bright or dark. See Ruskin, *Queen of the Air*, pp. 105, 107.
[43]Pope, *Epistle to a Lady*, ll. 289–92, *Epistles*, T. E. III. ii. 74.

Proceedings of the British Academy, **91**, 69–110

Heroic Notes: Epic Idiom, Revision and the Mock-Footnote from the *Rape of the Lock* to the *Dunciad*[1]

CLAUDE RAWSON

1A	For this, e'er *Phœbus* rose, he had implor'd	
	Propitious Heav'n, and ev'ry Pow'r ador'd,	
	But chiefly *Love*—to *Love* an Altar built,	
	Of twelve vast *French* Romances, neatly gilt.	
	There lay the Sword-knot *Sylvia*'s Hands had sown,	55
	With *Flavia*'s Busk that oft had rapp'd his own:	
	A Fan, a Garter, half a Pair of Gloves;	
	And all the Trophies of his former Loves.	
	With tender *Billet-doux* he lights the Pyre,	
	And breaths three am'rous Sighs to raise the Fire.	60
	Then prostrate falls, and begs with ardent Eyes	
	Soon to obtain, and long possess the Prize:	
	The Pow'rs gave Ear, and granted half his Pray'r,	
	The rest, the Winds dispers'd in empty Air.	

Rape of the Locke, 1712, I. 51–64

1B	For this, ere Phœbus rose, he had implor'd	35

[1] In preparing this paper for publication, I was grateful to be able to take account of discussion that followed its delivery at the British Academy on 27 May 1994. Maynard Mack and Howard Erskine-Hill were kind enough to read a subsequent draft, and to do so with the generosity and thoroughness that are characteristic of both. The final version owes much to their comments. Its faults are my own.

Quotations from the *Rape of the Locke* (1712) and the five-canto *Rape of the Lock*, unless otherwise noted, are from the edition by Geoffrey Tillotson, 3rd edn., 1962, and those from the *Dunciad* from that by James Sutherland, 3rd edn., 1963, both in the Twickenham Edition. Page references are, unless otherwise indicated, to these volumes.

Book and line references to the *Dunciad*, unless otherwise noted, are to the four-book (or B) version (1743). The notes to this version, not fully and exactly recoverable in the Twickenham Edition, are cited from Pope, *Poetical Works*, ed. Herbert Davis, intr. Pat Rogers, Oxford, 1978.

Propitious Heav'n, and ev'ry Pow'r ador'd,
But chiefly *Love*—to *Love* an Altar built,
Of twelve vast *French* Romances, neatly gilt.
There lay three Garters, half a Pair of Gloves;
And all the Trophies of his former Loves.   40
With tender *Billet-doux* he lights the Pyre,
And breaths three am'rous Sighs to raise the Fire.
Then prostrate falls, and begs with ardent Eyes
Soon to obtain, and long possess the Prize:
The Pow'rs gave Ear, and granted half his Pray'r,   45
The rest, the Winds dispers'd in empty Air.
                            Rape of the Lock, 4th edn., 1715, II. 35–46

2   But, high above, more solid Learning shone,
           The Classics of an Age that heard of none;
           There Caxton slept, with Wynkyn at his side,
           One clasp'd in wood, and one in strong cow-hide;   150
           There, sav'd by spice, like Mummies, many a year,
           Dry Bodies of Divinity appear:
           De Lyra there a dreadful front extends,
           And here the groaning shelves Philemon bends.
               Of these twelve volumes, twelve of amplest size, 155
           Redeem'd from tapers and defrauded pies,
           Inspir'd he seizes: These an altar raise:
           An hecatomb of pure, unsully'd lays
           That altar crowns: A folio Common-place
           Founds the whole pile, of all his works the base: 160
           Quartos, octavos, shape the less'ning pyre;
           A twisted Birth-day Ode completes the spire.
                                  Dunciad, 1743, I. 147–62

3   But anxious Cares the pensive Nymph opprest,
           And secret Passions labour'd in her Breast.
           Not youthful Kings in Battel seiz'd alive,
           Not scornful Virgins who their Charms survive,
           Not ardent Lovers robb'd of all their Bliss,   5
           Not ancient Ladies when refus'd a Kiss,
           Not Tyrants fierce that unrepenting die,
           Not *Cynthia* when her *Manteau*'s pinn'd awry,
           E'er felt such Rage, Resentment and Despair,
           As Thou, sad Virgin! for thy ravish'd Hair.   10
                            Rape of the Lock, 1714, IV. 1–10

4A   She ey'd the Bard, where supperless he sate,
           And pin'd, unconscious of his rising fate;   110
           Studious he sate, with all his books around,
           Sinking from thought to thought, a vast profound!

Plung'd for his sense, but found no bottom there;
Then writ, and flounder'd on, in mere despair.
He roll'd his eyes that witness'd huge dismay,   115
Where yet unpawn'd, much learned lumber lay,
Volumes, whose size the space exactly fill'd;
Or which fond authors were so good to gild;

Dunciad A, 1729, I. 109–18

4B   Swearing and supperless the Hero sate,   115
Blasphem'd his Gods, the Dice, and damn'd his Fate.
Then gnaw'd his pen, then dash'd it on the ground,
Sinking from thought to thought, a vast profound!
Plung'd for his sense, but found no bottom there,
Yet wrote and flounder'd on, in mere despair.   120
Round him much Embryo, much Abortion lay,
Much future Ode, and abdicated Play;

Dunciad B, 1743, I. 115–22

THE TWO GROUPS of three passages from the *Rape of the Lock* and the *Dunciad*, with which this study is chiefly concerned, represent successive stages in Pope's treatment of epic or heroic material, and illustrate a development, though not one for which I would wish to claim a neatly progressive clarity of outline. The transitions which define this development, in both groups, occur not only from the *Rape of the Lock* to the *Dunciad* but also within successive versions of each poem. The analysis which follows, however, is not primarily concerned with Pope 'at work', with the slow and intimate charting of processes of composition, any more than it is an attempt at what used to be called 'practical criticism', or what passes now for 'close reading', though the reading is in its way intended to be close.

The textual changes within each passage, like the larger changes from one poem to the other and the still larger differences between the two groups, illustrate a series of subtle and exploratory negotiations with the heroic mode. The starting point for these negotiations is a predicament which I have tried to define in some earlier studies, and which was shared in some sense by all good writers of the period whose cultural loyalties were on the traditionalist side of the Ancients-Moderns divide:[2] writers who still thought of the heroic poem as the

---

[2]'Pope's *Waste Land*: Reflections on Mock-Heroic', in *Order from Confusion Sprung: Studies in Eighteenth-Century Literature from Swift to Cowper* (London, 1985), pp. 201–21; and two chapters on 'Mock-Heroic and War' in *Satire and Sentiment 1660–1830* (Cambridge, 1994), pp. 29–129. These chapters contain fuller statements and documentation on several matters to which the present study has had to refer in a more summary form.

apex of poetic achievement, whose effort or ambition was to find a heroic voice that genuinely expressed some live and ardent aspirations, but who had to recognise the impossibility of writing a true unironic epic in their own time. Pope and Dryden both projected epics which they left uncompleted. Both translated the epic masterpieces of Græco-Roman antiquity, and both discovered in high mock-heroic a vehicle for some of their most powerful writing, as though a heroic idiom had ceased to be possible except by proxy or through a filter of irony. In its primary or unironic form, it was no longer available to good poets for the elevated expression of high matter, and the epic genre, for all the reverence it continued to receive, seemed to have become disqualified as a vehicle for unforced grandeurs. In the final version of the *Dunciad* Pope achieved a negative or inverted model which was perhaps the only wholly successful example of an epic in English since *Paradise Lost*, and which was also his own poetic masterpiece. This discussion seeks to define patterns and directions in the long process through which something resembling a high epic idiom was fashioned from a mock-form, or parody, fulfilling in perhaps unexpected ways the potential implicit in Dryden's idea that the majesties of mock-heroic might make of satire a species of heroic poetry in its own right.[3]

Such an idea, fraught with paradox and inevitably subject to constraints and complications, seems to have inspired the practice of poets, including Dryden himself, even before Dryden gave it a resonant critical formulation in 1693. It underlies some of the transformations of mock-heroic from the 1660s to the death of Pope. The present discussion will be concerned with these, as well as with broader aspects of parody, including the phenomena which I describe as unparodying and reparodying, and with some unsuspected transitions within high Augustan satires to modes of expression we more readily associate with prose fiction or with an incipient Romanticism.

The six passages fall into two groups of three. In the first group, two versions (1712, 1715) of the same passage from the *Rape of the Lock* are considered beside the final version of a comparable passage from the *Dunciad* (1743). The second group brings together a passage from the *Rape of the Lock* (1714) and two versions of a counterpart from the *Dunciad* (1729, 1743) which underwent substantial revision. All are, I believe, familiar, and will enable me, at the

---

[3]Dryden, 'Discourse concerning Satire' (1693), *Works of John Dryden. Volume IV; Poems 1693–1696*, ed. A. B. Chambers and William Frost (Berkeley, 1974), pp. 83–4.

outset, to dispose of some bread-and-butter observations on mock-heroic, in a way which may at the same time open up what I think are some less familiar perspectives. Both sets loom large in their respective poems, indeed in successive versions of each. Those from the *Rape of the Lock* exist fully formed in the early version of 1712. In the case of 1A and 1B, indeed, the earlier version is longer by two lines, about fifteen per cent, though the early version as a whole is about two and a half times shorter than the later five-canto version of 1714/1717, with an air of brisk narrative efficiency without frills (or sylphs or gnomes). The two lines come after the 'twelve vast *French* Romances', and were followed by a variant wording of the line about garters and gloves:

> There lay the Sword-knot *Sylvia*'s Hands had sown,
> With *Flavia*'s Busk that oft had rapp'd his own:
> A Fan, a Garter, half a Pair of Gloves;
> And all the Trophies of his former Loves.

(1712; I. 55–8)

These lines remained in the five-canto version of 1714, their removal being effected not in the 'definitive' and further enlarged version of 1717, but in the fourth edition of 1715. The idea is to provide a catalogue of fashionable social detritus, of the kind recently provided in fuller detail in John Hughes's 'Inventory of a Beau' in *Tatler*, 113, 29 December 1709, a list of items for auction after the beau's death, which includes among other things 'Five Billet-Doux, . . . a Silk Garter, a Lock of Hair, and Three broken Fans'.[4] (Swift offers many such lists, which in his case are more often female than male). That Pope shortened his own list in his own longer version suggests some local strategy, in which particularities of social notation — which are not typically skimped in the longer versions — here yield to a more economical, summarising style of point-making. This appears even more clearly in the change from 'A Fan, a Garter, half a Pair of Gloves' to 'There lay three Garters, half a Pair of Gloves', a further reduction in itemising, sufficient to evoke the erotic bric-à-brac of a worldly fop, but homing in with greater concentration on its almost literally half-cock incompleteness. The change seems a throwback to, or a flip expression of, Augustan notions, quite unHomeric, that the epic is inhospitable to details of ordinary life and that heroic outlines should be kept simple.

One effect, as the social particularities become fewer and more

[4] Cited *Rape of the Lock*, p. 161 n.; see *Tatler*, ed. Donald F. Bond, 3 vols. (Oxford, 1987), II. 178–9.

recessive, is that the *sottisier* of epic evocation emerges more sharply in the foreground: the mock-Miltonic enjambment, the sacrificial altar, the twelve objects of sacrifice (a number with both Homeric and Biblical precedents not reported in either Tillotson's commentary or Sutherland's notes to the corresponding passage in the *Dunciad*),[5] the three sighs, and the gods granting half the prayer, the other half being dispersed to the winds. It's as though Pope were at this point intent on establishing the mock-epic business with a textbook simplicity and completeness — a kind of summarising analogue to the extensive exemplifications of Swift's *Battle of the Books*, as some capsule anthologising of idiomatic usage in the *Rape of the Lock* (an example might be Sir Plume's sputtering outburst in IV. 127–30) is the brief counterpart to the Flaubertian cataloguing of Swift's *Complete Collection of Genteel and Ingenious Conversation*.

That some such impulse was tacitly at work is perhaps also confirmed by a different analogue, suggested by Tillotson, Palamon's prayer to Venus (or Love) 'in Chaucer's "Knight's Tale", iii'. Pope, I assume, would be more likely to have remembered this in Dryden's version, *Palamon and Arcite*, which appeared twelve years earlier in *Fables* (1700), though he did read Chaucer in the original and, like Dryden, made 'imitations' of some of his poems.[6] 'Tillotson's sense of this analogue seems confined to the fact of the two prayers to Venus (the prayers themselves are not very resembling), and to some scattered details in other parts of the poem (II. 48, V. 13), but Dryden's imitation (and especially its third Book) has a distinct presence in the background of Pope's poem and invites comparison with it. Book III recounts how all three protagonists, Palamon, Emily, and Arcite, pray to the gods (Venus, Diana and Mars, to whom altars are erected by Theseus) before the contest, and where somewhat bolder prefigurations of other parts of the *Rape of the Lock* may be discerned:

[5]For Biblical examples, see Tuvia Bloch, 'Pope's Mock-Epic Altars', *Notes and Queries*, CCXVI (1971), 331; for Homeric examples, see below, pp. 77–8.
[6]Chaucer, *Knight's Tale*, ll. 2221ff. (text and lineation are those of the *Riverside Chaucer*, ed. F. N. Robinson and Larry D. Benson, 3rd ed. (Oxford, 1988), pp. 50ff., and notes, pp. 834ff.); Dryden, *Palamon and Arcite*, III. 124ff., in *Fables*, 1700, pp. 54ff., and *Poems*, ed. James Kinsley (Oxford, 1958), IV. 1503ff., and notes, 2068ff.
   Pope owned a first edition of Dryden's *Fables*, which also printed the Chaucerian originals, including 'The Knight's Tale, As it was Written by Geffrey Chaucer'. Pope owned at least two other Chaucers, one of them from as early as 1701 (Maynard Mack, *Collected in Himself*, Newark, DE, 1982, pp. 401, 410). Although he read Chaucer in the original, it remains probable that those of Chaucer's poems which he was able to read in Dryden's adaptation would retain a special vividness in his mind in that form.

> Now Morn with Rosie Light had streak'd the Sky,
> Up rose the Sun, and up rose *Emily*,
>
> (III. 189–90)

we read, after Palamon's prayer, in a passage which combines elements of Belinda's 'sacred Rites of Pride' and her launching out like the sunrise on the silver Thames. Emily, 'attended by her Maiden Train', worships at '*Cynthia*'s Fane' (the temple of Diana), with 'Incence, and od'rous Gums'. Dryden's matter is here as in Chaucer, and 'Up roos the sonne, and up roos Emelye' (l. 2273) is Chaucer's wording. But Dryden's idiom is ceremoniously periphrastic in the mode to which the term 'poetic diction' became attached, and which is also in these instances the idiom of the *Rape of the Lock*: 'her Maiden Train' replaces Chaucer's 'Hir maydens' and Chaucer has 'encens' but not the somewhat Virgilian flourish of Dryden's 'od'rous Gums' (ll. 2275, 2277).

Dryden articulates in this passage (with a harsher and more extended explicitness than Pope) what is in fact a central intimation of the *Rape of the Lock*, a sense, which the poet makes some pretence of intending to conceal, that (in Dryden's words) 'their chast mysterious Rites / Might turn to Scandal, or obscene Delights' (III. 203–4). Dryden points to pagan mysteries rather than, in Pope's manner, to psycho-sexual undercurrents in the social fabric of his own time. He seems to mean something like those secrets of the good goddess, 'At whose Feasts no Men were to be present', to which he referred in note 20 (to l. 430) of his translation of Juvenal VI. Kinsley says this element was added by Dryden but Chaucer has a more innocent version of it, parading a genial Shandean mock-reticence:

> But hou she dide hir ryte I dar nat telle,
> But it be any thing in general;
> And yet it were a game to heeren al.
> To hym that meneth wel it were no charge;
> But it is good a man been at his large.
>
> (ll. 2284–88)

(J. A. W. Bennett translates this as 'A full account would be delightful, and it would do no harm to the pure-minded; but it's best to let you imagine it for yourselves'.)[7]

When Dryden's gods dispute over which prayers will be granted, Saturn sets out to compose differences. He invokes his vast powers, including a maleficent repertoire of 'Cold shivering Agues, melancholy Care, . . . And Rheumatisms I send to rack the Joints', which are Drydenian particularities surely kindred to Pope's Cave of Spleen, and not spelled out among Chaucer's medical examples except in generalised references to 'maladyes colde' and 'pestilence' (Dryden, III. 381ff.; Chaucer, ll. 2443ff.).[8] As with the 'mysterious Rites', Dryden goes on to propose harsh suggestions from which Pope, in the relatively benign universe of the *Rape of the Lock*, would be likely to draw back, including an underworld of political malfeasance altogether outside the scope of the brainless decorative *jeunesse dorée* of his poem, though it does have a place in Chaucer's high chivalric world:

> When Churls rebel against their Native Prince,
> I am their Hands, and furnish the Pretence;
> And housing in the Lion's hateful Sign,
> Bought Senates, and deserting Troops are mine.
> Mine is the privy Pois'ning, I command
> Unkindly Seasons, and ungrateful Land.
> By me Kings Palaces are push'd to Ground,
> And Miners, crush'd beneath their Mines are found.

> (III. 408–15)

Chaucer (ll. 2453ff.) has some of this, haunting, lurid, and in starker and less elaborated detail ('cherles rebellyng' *tout court*, walls merely falling on the 'mynour', and of course no 'Bought Senates' or 'deserting Troops' recalling 1688), just as the fuller specifications of medical nightmare are largely added by Dryden. From this unlikely Saturnian source, accommodations eventually come, as the phantasmagoric

---

[7]Dryden, *Poems*, ed. Kinsley, IV. 2069 n.; *Knight's Tale*, ed. J. A. W. Bennett (London, 1954), p. 136 n. Both Chaucer (ll. 2293–4) and Dryden (III. 211–2) refer to Statius as an authority on sacrificial procedures, but those references seem to concern the rites actually described, not those that are said to be unmentioned: for two possible antecedents in Statius, see *Thebaid* IV. 443ff. and IX. 570ff., noted in the Riverside commentary to Chaucer, ll. 2273–94 (p. 837). Statius is a source of Chaucer's immediate source, Boccaccio's *Teseida*, VII. lxxff., which does not seem to have a parallel for the secret rites or the Shandean reflection upon them.

[8]Dryden, *Poems*, ed. Kinsley, IV. 1510–1; Chaucer, p. 58. Saturn's paradoxical composition of differences consists of arranging for Arcite to be fatally unseated from his horse, after Palamon has been defeated (ll. 2684ff.; Dryden, III. 699ff.). Thus he wins the battle, but Palamon ends up possessing Emily, so no one is the loser and the rivalry is settled.

doings of the Cave of Spleen in the *Rape of the Lock* are activated by a symmetrically opposite purpose, to compound, not compose, trouble.

The Saturnian repertoire of evils in Dryden is not, like that of Spleen, contained in a Cave, though it includes a 'dark Dungeon' (III. 402; Chaucer's 'derke cote', l. 2457). But Dryden has here expanded the Chaucerian original (the Saturn episode is not in Boccaccio) in a direction which assimilates his account to the sub-genre of the cave of evils, which was becoming a staple of Augustan mock-heroic, though it has ancient originals. Such allegorical 'caves' are an old commonplace, related to epic journeys to the underworld, though the most closely resembling classical analogue to Pope's passage is Ovid's Cave of Envy (*Metamorphoses*, II. 760ff.).[9] Mock-epic analogues include the *antre* of Chicane in *Le Lutrin* (V. 39ff.) and the lairs of Envy, Disease and Death in the *Dispensary* (1699, II. 11ff., IV. 196ff., VI. 90ff.). The major modern epic analogue, which Tillotson does not list, is the Cave of Death in *Paradise Lost*, XI. 466ff. But my immediate point is that if Tillotson was right to bring up the *Knight's Tale* in connection with the Baron's prayer, the passage in the *Rape of the Lock* is stripped clean, in the version Pope is likeliest to have used, of elements which are germane to his own poem, and which are given their head in other parts of it: the rites of pride, the perverse bawdy subtext, the pathology of caves. This is in line with Pope's general tendency, in the passage, to keep things focused on a particular piece of epic business, free of accretions, however pertinent to the larger design.

The parallel passage from the *Dunciad* underwent more changes than that from the *Rape of the Lock*, the most decisive ones having to do, directly or indirectly, with the switch of heroes from Theobald to Cibber in 1743. The evolution of the passage from its prototype in the *Rape of the Lock* and through its subsequent Dunciadic stages traces a momentous transformation in the whole generic character of mock-heroic. It also, I believe, marks a crisis in the status of epic in the European sensibility which is both an end and a beginning. I will look first at the obvious connection between the episodes in both poems, the sacrificial altar of twelve books. Twelve is a highly Homeric number, occurring some five dozen times in Pope's translation, including important sacrificial occasions: 'twelve young Heifers' are offered at Pallas's altar by the Trojan women, *'to entreat her to remove* Diomed *from the Fight'* in *Iliad*, VI; Achilles vows to kill 'twelve, the

9*Rape of the Lock*, p. 183 n.

noblest of the *Trojan* Line' on Patroclus's 'flaming Pyre' in Book XVIII, captures them for the purpose in Book XXI (a 'piece of Cruelty in *Achilles*' which, Pope says, 'has appear'd shocking to many', explainable by Achilles's vindictive ferocity and 'the military Laws of those times', backed by their 'Religion itself' — an expression of anguish about epic which I believe underlies some radical features of the *Dunciad*), and finally executes them to Patroclus's shade in Book XXIII (the 'Argument' says baldly 'Achilles *sacrifices several Animals, and lastly, twelve* Trojan *Captives at the Pile, then sets fire to it*'). In Book XXIV, during his reconciliation scene with Priam and the return of Hector's body, Achilles tactfully reminds him that 'Such Griefs, O King! have other Parents known' instancing the slaying of Niobe's twelve offspring by Apollo and Artemis.[10]

There are various analogues in the *Odyssey*, in which acts of propitiation involve twelve urns of wine, or beasts, and there is a sacrifice of 'twelve black oxen' to 'angry *Neptune*' in Book XIII, plus gifts that also come in twelves.[11] The Old Testament contains important analogues too, as Tuvia Bloch pointed out in 1971. Examples include Numbers 7. 84, 87: 'This *was* the dedication of the altar . . . twelve chargers of silver, twelve silver bowls, twelve spoons of gold . . . All the oxen for the burnt offering *were* twelve bullocks, the rams twelve, the lambs of the first year twelve . . . the kids of the goats for sin offering twelve'; 1 Kings 18. 31–32: 'And Elijah took twelve stones . . . And with the stones he built an altar . . .'; 2 Chronicles 4. 1–4: 'Moreover he made an altar of brass . . . It stood upon twelve oxen . . .'.[12]

These analogues constitute a powerful recognition factor. Sources are not at issue, but the ordonnance of Pope's mock-heroic altars suggests a mainly Homeric orientation, except that they are unsanguinary, and tacitly so. That silence is important because, as I've tried to argue in other places, the tribute to epic proposed in all the major Augustan mock-heroics comes with an astonishing reticence about bloodshed and war, considering that war is the central preoccupation of the primary prototypes and prowess in war the highest value in the

---

[10]Pope, *Iliad*, Argument to VI; VI. 116, 343, 382; XVIII. 394–6; XXI. 34–9 and Pope's note to 35; XXIII. 215, 223, and Argument; XXIV. 780, 755–66 (Twickenham Edition, ed. Maynard Mack and others), VII. 322, 329, 343, 345; VIII. 340, 422–3, 498, 485, 568–9).

[11]Pope, *Odyssey*, II. 394ff.; IV. 858ff.; VIII. 53ff.; XXIV. 321 *et passim*; XIII. 210–11 (T. E., IX. 80, 159, 264; X. 365, 15).

[12]Tuvia Bloch, 'Pope's Mock-Epic Altars', p. 331.

heroic code.[13] In *Le Lutrin* and the *Dispensary*, wars have shrunk
to guild disputes, and missile weaponry to a few books and some
pharmaceutical clutter: a few lines of Homeric bloodshed in the *Dispensary* turn out to be by Blackmore, reciting lines from his own poems
as a character in Garth's, part of the subtext being that only an oafish
and ungifted Modern would think Homeric imitation in his power, or,
in this particular sphere decent to undertake: 'Oft tho' your Stroaks
surprize, you shou'd not choose / A Theme so mighty for a Virgin
Muse'. In Ozell's translation of Boileau's *Lutrin*, the Barber goes
searching for iron weapons, expressly announced as being 'Not like
those Arms of the *dead-doing* Kind' (a line which does not occur in
the original, suggesting that the pudeur I am describing may be a
specifically English one), and which turn out to be, in a favourite mock-
heroic formula later much fancied by Fielding, 'In Vulgar Speech call'd
Nails'.[14] In the *Battle of the Books*, an extended prose *sottisier* of
epic commonplaces, carnage sometimes occurs with a simulacrum of
Homeric realism, but always with the reminder that no blood is spilt
since it's books that are fighting and not men. In the *Rape of the Lock*,
no one dies except in metaphor, in song, or in orgasm.

Fictions of derealisation were radical to this enterprise. The battle
in Canto V is preceded by the reassurance that 'No common
Weapons in their Hands are found, / Like Gods they fight, nor dread

[13]I should perhaps make clear that it is no part of my argument that war is a more remote
or less frequently mentioned experience in this period than in earlier ones, but only that
there seems to have been a pudeur about calling it to mind in contexts where a homage to
the epic is on the agenda. Denial of actual warfare is not suggested: it is an accentuated
awareness of it that, in my judgement, led to embarrassment about its centrality in epic
poems. The feeling that the heroic would be contaminated by reminders of its martial
character is what distinguishes mock-heroic in this period from earlier treatments of epic
material, direct or oblique. Swift's evocations of war are very fierce, but are wholly or largely
outside the range of epic reminder. Both Dryden and Pope were perfectly able to write
about epic warfare, so long as they did it by proxy, in translations of the ancient masters:
their own attempts at epic were never completed. Blackmore's epics, on the other hand,
contain plenty of Homeric gore, but he was without Pope's protective loyalty to Homer, and
his example was seen as one to avoid, a vivid warning that a large heroic poem is only likely,
in that period, to proceed from inferior talent. Fuller evidence for these propositions is
provided in the two chapters on 'Mock-heroic and War', in *Satire and Sentiment 1660–1830*,
cited in n. 2 above.
[14]Garth, *Dispensary* (1699), IV. 232–3, in *Poems on Affairs of State. Volume VI: 1697–1704*,
ed. Frank H. Ellis (New Haven, 1970), p. 104. The poem also has an unsanguinary altar,
prefiguring Pope's, though without the Homeric duodecimal arrangements, III. 77ff., in *POAS*,
VI. 84; *The Lutrin: A Mock-Heroic Poem . . . Render'd into English Verse*, 2nd edn. (London,
1711), p. 24, corresponding to II. 85ff. of the French text, which omits the specific sentiment
of the English line quoted.

a mortal Wound' (V. 43–4). One implication is that the weaponry is
sexual, but the couplet more broadly reflects a pattern in which, when
humans fight, there is no bloodshed, and when there is a presumption
of bloodshed (as in Satan's wound in the War in Heaven, or the severed
sylph in the *Rape of the Lock*, III. 451–2), it is of a spiritous, non-
sanguinary sort, and thus not, in human terms, for real. Swift in the
Battle and Pope in Canto V of the *Rape of the Lock* rang variations
on this resource, which was distantly inspired, as Pope's couplet implies,
by the invulnerability of the gods, who shed ichor not blood and don't
die of wounds. Behind the neutralised wound of Milton's Satan and
the severed sylph lies a benign and momentary maiming of Aphrodite
in *Iliad*, V.[15] Milton's use occurs in a primary epic battle, albeit of a
special sort, in an epic dedicated to downgrading the ethos of war,
hitherto the only argument heroic deemed. It's arguable that his mock-
heroic successors were more protective of the hallowed but problematic
originals than Milton was in the straight version, with its openly incorporated critique: but his War in Heaven pointed the way for more
discreet circumventions of intractable topics, until the *Dunciad* broke
through all such attenuating strategies by going over into total denial.

As the sacrificial altars of books are without bloodshed, the
Dunciad is an epic without war. It has everything else, the full range
of stylistic routines and most of the substantive situations, heroic games,
an underworld visit, an east–west journey, momentous prophecy, but
no blood. The entry for blood in the concordance runs to several
columns from the Homer translations, but almost the only and certainly
the most telling blood-derived phrasing in the *Dunciad* is 'bloodless
swords and maces' (I. 87), preceding the unsanguinary altar of books
by a mere sixty lines.[16] In the light of Pope's anguished Iliadic note
about Achilles's sacrifice of twelve Trojan youths, it seems appropriate
to note that a pair of mock-Homeric aggrandisements, in both *Rape
of the Lock* and *Dunciad*, are sanitised *ab initio*, much as the *Dunciad*
is as a whole, in an oddly inverted or negative manifestation of the
anxiety of influence. That this occurs in a context not significantly
hostile to epic, but offering a classic confrontation of its majestic forms
with a lowered or pretentious modern reality unworthy of them, is the
remarkable thing.

[15]*Iliad*, V. 339ff., 416ff.; and cf. 899ff. For Pope's rendering, see *Iliad*, V. 421–4 and nn., 505,
1009ff., T.E., VII. 287–9, 292, 320–1. For the *Dunciad*'s version of an ichor episode, see II. 92.
[16]Two other occurrences are 'noble blood' (III. 334) and 'Infant's blood' (IV. 142), both of
them references to school floggings.

The *Dunciad*'s way with this confrontation is different from the *Rape of the Lock*'s. The earlier poem's 'twelve vast *French* Romances, neatly gilt' are vast, but also French, and thus elegant and insubstantial. The ballooning fantasia to which their insignificance is subjected falls within the standard mock-heroic scenario of a studiedly inappropriate aggrandisement, inviting deflation. A variation, itself habitual to the genre, sees to it that formal puncturing, of the kind seen, for example, in passage 3, from Canto IV, is withheld. The inflation remains in a sense uncancelled, in one of the more flippant incarnations of Dryden's insight about the majesty of the heroic devolving on the mockery, and if the passage's sober signal is of doings hugely trivial, they come over as at least hugely something.

Such effects would not be available, or not in the same way, in the reverse form of mock-heroic to which the name 'burlesque', as Tillotson informs us, later became attached (both terms were in fact used for both): the form of Scarron's and Cotton's *Virgil Travestied* or of Butler's *Hudibras*, in which high actions are recounted in low language rather than the other way round.[17] Behind the distinction, seemingly a matter of inert technicality, trivially and formalistically obvious, but reverted to by substantial creative minds, from Boileau to Fielding, with a surprisingly obsessive interest, are impulses of decisive importance in the history of European, but perhaps especially English, poetry. Boileau announced his contempt for the low burlesque of Scarron in *Art Poétique* (1674), I. 79ff. It was from the preference, ratified in Boileau's foreword ('Au Lecteur') to the first edition of *Le Lutrin* (1674), for the non-'burlesque' or 'mock-heroic' mode, which he actually called a *new* burlesque, in which clockmakers speak like Dido and Aeneas, that a genre developed which, for a period of some seventy years from *Le Lutrin* to the death of Pope, engaged the highest imaginative skills of some of the best writers, and relegated the honourable alternative tradition of Scarron, Cotton and Butler to relative insignificance. The phenomenon was short-lived, culminating in the *Dunciad*, and impregnated with lingering loyalties to the epic tradition at a moment when this was manifestly no longer viable for good writers in its traditional military version. It led to perceptions that only a Modern like Blackmore would risk the Ancient form, with the kind of results Garth cited verbatim in the *Dispensary*. The mock-form, on the other hand, provided an ironic guard, protecting the author from epic preten-

---

[17]Tillotson, in *Rape of the Lock*, pp. 107–8.

sion, protecting the epic from the taint of homicidal discredit, while retaining aspirations to heroic utterance. Loyalist mock-heroic seems marked by a determination to evade the subject of war, as though to suppress the connection between a revered genre and the deplorable activity habitually celebrated within it. Though both Dryden and Pope planned and failed to complete epics of their own, it was only in poems like *Mac Flecknoe* or the *Dunciad* that they felt able to sustain with poetic conviction an epic voice which bore a strong and live relation to the heroic poems of Graeco-Roman antiquity. These mock-heroic poems made of parody a new thing, transcending the bookish joke with a wholly unprecedented seriousness, and achieving some of the finest and most ambitious poetry of the age. If the form as we know it only existed at this level of distinction in the brief period I referred to, it was in many ways an enabling model for *Ulysses* and the *Waste Land*: the latter, we recall, began as a pastiche of the *Rape of the Lock*, though its sombre intertextualities and its grand sense of a culture in decay are closer to the *Dunciad* than to the nominal source.

The twelve volumes of Cibber's altar in passage 2 are a big change from the flimsy gigantification of the *Rape of the Lock*'s twelve vast French romances. They have a solid enormity, grotesque and massive, which crystallises (or congeals) that tendency towards degradation without diminution which I have been describing as an inverted or negative epic effect. The altar has something of the monumentality of *Mac Flecknoe*'s 'Monument of vanisht minds' (l. 82), especially when one remembers that Dryden's heroic original for this line, Davenant's *Gondibert* (II. v. 36), referred, in a manner innocent of derision, to a library of deceased authors. 'Dry Bodies of Divinity' come not neatly gilt, but 'clasp'd in wood' or 'strong cow-hide', their dim weighty mass enhanced by the roll-call of names, 'The Classics of an Age that heard of none', Goths in Black Letter. Caxton is obtusely pilloried in a note and an appendix, in a style of blinkered 'anti-medievalism' that is a Scriblerian trademark, exhibited without undue scruple for fact: a note on Nicholas de Lyra (d. 1340) confuses him with Nicholas Harpsfeld, who died 235 years later (1575).[18] They form 'A Gothic Library!' of

[18]The main note on Caxton is to this passage, in *Dunciad*, pp. 79–80, keyed to A I. 129. For other notes mentioning or deriding Caxton, see pp. 82, 83, keyed respectively to A I. 162–3, 166, and both also coupling Caxton with Wynkyn, but the first of them contrasting the two with Homer and Chaucer. For a satirical appendix reprinting Caxton's Preface to his translation of Virgil, included only in editions of 1729, see *Dunciad*, pp. 213–6, in an English whose spellings Pope clearly regarded as barbaric and antiquated. See also *Order from Confusion Sprung*, pp. 219–20n. On de Lyra and Harpsfeld, see p. 80, keyed to A I. 133.

Greece and Rome/Well purg'd', and which includes lists of more recent authors, 'worthy Settle, Banks and Broome' (I. 145–6: the modern roll-call differed in 1728 and 1729, listing an assortment of Wesley, Withers, Watts, Quarles and Blome, plus Ogilby the bathetic translator of Homer, whom Johnson said Pope loved to read as a child, and who is common to all versions).[19]

It is a Modernity simultaneously callow and senile, more than once got up in leather bindings. In the Lethean visit in Book III, the hero is taken to

> Where Brown and Mears unbar the gates of Light,
> Demand new bodies, and in Calf's array,
> Rush to the world, impatient for the day.

(III. 28–30)

Pope's annotation of Brown and Mears reads: 'Booksellers, Printers for any body. — The allegory of the souls of the dull coming forth in the form of books, dressed in calf's leather, and being let abroad in vast numbers by Booksellers, is sufficiently intelligible'. 'Calf', in this allegory, evokes doltishness in empty-headed hacks and brain-dead pedants alike. Cibber remonstrated, in the last of his *Letters to Mr. Pope* (*Another Occasional Letter*, 1744), that the switch from Theobald to himself, 'even to the same Books, in his Study' which Pope 'knew would never be looked into' by him, was exceptionally inept in this context.[20] He had a point, of course, and Pope was unlikely to think that Caxton, de Lyra and Philemon Holland were Cibber's staple reading matter. But if the transition seems somewhat unassimilated in personal or biographical terms, the larger suggestion of an amalgam, familiar in Swift's *Tale* and *Battle*, in which the 'freshest Modern', the Bentleian antiquarian, and the race of critics from primeval times, coexist in eternal up-to-dateness, is a certified Popeian as well as Swiftian theme. Wormius and Welsted are one.

The altar itself, 'an hecatomb', but bloodless, the 'unsully'd lays' replacing the twelve pure 'young Heifers, guiltless of the Yoke' of

---

[19]Samuel Wesley and Isaac Watts appear as 'W——y, W——s' in 1728. The full names are supplied in the copy of 1728 (p. 7) 'in which Jonathan Richardson, Jr., transcribed for Pope the readings of manuscript drafts of the poem' (David L. Vander Meulen, *Pope's Dunciad of 1728: A History and Facsimile*, Charlottesville, 1991, p. 41). On Pope and Ogilby, see Spence, *Observations, Anecdotes, and Characters of Books and Men*, ed. J. M. Osborn, 2 vols. (Oxford, 1966), No. 30, I. 14.

[20]J. V. Guerinot, *Pamphlet Attacks on Pope 1711–1744* (London, 1969), p. 317; *Dunciad*, pp. xxxvi–xxxvii.

Homeric sacrifice, is an odd amalgam of innocence and pollution, triviality and enormity, degradation and massiveness.[21] The lays are 'unsully'd' by readers, like Cibber's works some seventy lines on, 'Unstain'd, untouch'd, and yet in maiden sheets' (I. 229), but they're in all other ways shop-soiled, 'Redeem'd from tapers and defrauded pies', close cousins of the 'Martyrs of Pies, and Reliques of the Bum' in Dryden's *Mac Flecknoe* (1. 101) and of even more degraded and indeed unchaste analogues in other Restoration poets. In Oldham's 'Upon the Author of the Play call'd *Sodom*', Oldham thinks it fitter that the putative Rochester's poems should become not the relics but the sexual partners of the bum, as in the 'publick Jakes' they

> bugger wiping Porters when they shite,
> And so thy Book itself turn Sodomite.

> (ll. 49–53)[22]

This is as removed from the world of the *Dunciad* as the sacred rites of Dryden's Emily were from those of Belinda; and removed in a manner paralleled in the Homer translation by Pope's substitution, in *Iliad* XXIV, of 'A Show'r of Ashes o'er [Priam's] Neck and Head' (1. 202) in place of Homeric *kopros*, dung. (But we may recall that in Pope's own chaster time and beyond, Lady Mary Wortley Montagu liked the idea of using the works of Pope and Swift themselves in the *Mac Flecknoe* if not the Oldham manner, and that Chesterfield more genially proposed that his son keep a copy of Horace's *Odes*, so that he might read one poem, and then dispose of it, at each sitting).[23]

The ordering of the altar, building upwards with books of diminishing size, a folio, quartos, octavos, is revealing. It's described as 'less'ning', but lessening upwards, and concludes, massively, in a 'spire', an effect well within that tradition of defiled monumentalism which Dryden established in *Mac Flecknoe* and which is a distinctive feature of English mock-heroic in this period: you don't find it in Boileau, I think, nor in the prototypes, in Tassoni or in the pseudo-Homeric *Battle of the Frogs and Mice*, though touches of it are glimpsed in Thomas Parnell's version of the latter. This effect is present only in the final version, made possible by Cibber's Laureateship, and the poem's switch to Cibber for hero. The grotesquely magnified metamorphosis of the

---

[21]See Pope's *Iliad*, VI. 382, T. E., VII. 345. Sutherland (p. 81 n.) says the purity of heifers on the altar is often stressed.

[22]Oldham, *Poems*, eds. Harold F. Brooks and Raman Selden (Oxford, 1987), pp. 343–4.

[23]See Maynard Mack, *Alexander Pope: A Life* (London, 1985), pp. 555, 561–2; Chesterfield, *Letters*, ed. B. Dobrée, 6 vols. (London, 1932), III. 1066–7 (11 December, O.S., 1747).

cone-shaped poem into a church steeple is a baroque pictorialism of Disneyan plasticity and inventiveness. All earlier editions from 1728 to 1742 read 'And last, a little Ajax tips the spire' (A. I. 142), with a Popeian gloss identifying Ajax, as 'In *duodecimo* [i.e. one size down, or in the upside-down arrangement, up, from octavos], translated from *Sophocles* by *Tibbald*' (the attribution, like the identification of de Lyra, is, according to Sutherland, probably wrong: the translation seems to have been a collective one, perhaps with notes by Theobald, and it's amusing to remember that the *Dunciad* has its origin in the fact that Theobald was a more accurate scholar, and would eventually prove to be a better editor, than Pope).[24]

This is one of the very few substantial and extended changes in the passage, which existed more or less fully formed, with a few verbal differences, in the earliest text of 1728. No marginalia exist for this passage in the copy of 1728 annotated on Pope's instructions by Jonathan Richardson the Younger,[25] though a few sparse notes exist in the same hand in a *Dunciad* of 1736. Both sets of notes are transcribed by Maynard Mack in *The Last and Greatest Art*, and derive from two Popeian manuscripts (known as the Broglio manuscripts) which, as Vander Meulen argues, *both* appear to precede the 1728 printed text. The second, described by Mack as 'the basis of the 1729 text and therefore ... at least as early as 1728', was processed into a 1736 derivative of 1729. Excluding insignificant verbal variations ('some' against 'one', 'there' against 'here', 'those' against 'his'), it seems instructive to examine a cluster of marginalia entered by Richardson. These marginalia record manuscript variants which are in effect 'earlier readings' superseded by the printed texts of 1728 or (in this case) 1729.[26] (Since all *printed* versions are very close to one another, especially in parts of this passage for which manuscript variants exist, I will refer for convenience to the text and lineation of the B-version of 1743, cited above, followed by the 1729 or A-lineation to which the insertions are keyed.)

Thus line 147 (A 127), 'But, high above, more solid Learning shone',

[24]*Dunciad*, p. 81n., and Sutherland's Introduction, pp. xiff. On *Ajax*, see also R. F. Jones, *Lewis Theobald* (New York, 1919), pp. 6–7, 130; on Theobald's work on Shakespeare, see Peter Seary, *Lewis Theobald and the Editing of Shakespeare* (Oxford, 1990).

[25]Vander Meulen, *Pope's Dunciad of 1728*, pp. 7–8 of facsimile.

[26]Vander Meulen, p. 51; *The Last and Greatest Art: Some Unpublished Poetical Manuscripts of Alexander Pope*, transcribed and edited by Maynard Mack (Newark, DE, 1984), pp. 97–100, and 133 (marginalia to Λ I. 127–42).

might once have been 'But far above in Time's old Varnish shone'.[27]
Three lines later, 'One clasp'd in wood, and one in strong cow-hide'
might instead have been 'Some clasp'd in wood' and continued either
as 'and some in strong cow-hide' or as 'or bound in strong cow-hide'.
Under this line, 150 or A 130, *marked with a delta for deletion*,
Richardson recorded 'Twelve Volumes, twelve, of massy weight, &
size', a trial run (or else a prematurely entered variant) for line 155
(A 135), 'Of these twelve volumes, twelve of amplest size', where, in
its proper place another variant, 'of enormous' for 'of amplest', is
recorded. The latter, as it stands, would have been unmetrical, but both
these versions of the line show Pope, at the earliest known stage of
the poem, groping amorphously and tentatively for effects of enormity
whose fullest expression we associate with the final version. That in
the printed texts the effect in this instance tends to be slightly toned
down implies, I think, not a contrary impulse but an exercise of verbal
tact, in the confidence that the point was already made and that further
labouring would be excessive. In the other changes, 'more solid
Learning' vs. 'in Time's old Varnish', thickness and mass replace
antique phoniness, while the dropping of 'bound' in the second half of
line 150 (A 130), 'or bound in strong cow-hide', seems an insignificant
variation, unless the non-survival of the past participle was again
designed to avoid overemphasis. A final substantive variant, 'spices'
against the printed 'tapers' in line 156 (A 136), suggests no particular
pattern other than a wish to avoid repetition of l. 151 (A 131), though
'spices' might also have seemed a shade exotic for the austere dulness
called for by the context. The four lines corresponding to 151–4 (A
131–4) appear to have been added later than the rest and are thus
described by Mack '*Ll. 131–34 are bracketed and marked*: add.' My
main conclusion is that even in the earliest drafts, and even in parts of
the poem which show a tendency to keep effects of enormity in
check, the essential impulse is unmistakably in the direction of an
atmosphere of brooding massiveness, whose culminating expression
was to be arrived at, fifteen years later, in the four-book version of
1743.

* * *

Passages 3 and 4 represent a different kind of continuity between the
Rape of the Lock and the *Dunciad*, a continuity which is also, in some

---

[27]For these manuscript interventions, see *Last and Greatest Art*, p. 133.

ways, a discontinuity. Passage 3 is probably the simplest textbook example of mock-heroic diminution, with the drop into the real in line 10 offered as a structured anticlimax. I suggested in discussing passage 1 that this effect isn't the commonest one, even in the *Rape of the Lock*, where the stylistic inflation is more often kept in business instead of being neutralised by explicit disclosures. The set-piece mimicks smaller-scale, usually one-line, effects of the 'stain her Honour, or her new Brocade' type (II. 107), though this kind of zeugma, one of the most familiar features of the *Rape of the Lock*, sometimes modulates into more attenuated collocations, where the drop is perceived as less dramatic or at least as occurring from less than heroic heights, e.g. 'When Husbands or when Lap-dogs breathe their last' (III. 158). Parallel desimplifications may be observed in the related routine of the incongruous catalogue: 'Men, Monkies, Lap-dogs, Parrots, perish all!' (IV. 120) seems a simple *dégringolade*, decisively established in the second word, but 'Puffs, Powders, Patches, Bibles, Billet-doux' (I. 138) doesn't quite share the same clean vertical geometry.

These are witty, inventive, delightful, but they're also transparently programmed. They have neither the harshness nor the unpredictability of typical Swiftian catalogues, 'a Lawyer, a Pick-pocket, a Colonel, a Fool, . . . a Whoremunger, a Physician, an Evidence' (*Gulliver's Travels*, IV. xii). These too are programmed, though less transparently, an accredited Swiftian routine designed not for clear-cut shocks but more continuous disturbance. The Popeian predictabilities are style-induced, as the ranting anaphora of passage 3 makes inevitable the eventual drop in line 10. Even where the substantive details don't suggest an undisturbed rise-and-fall trajectory (the 'scornful Virgins' and 'ancient Ladies' belong to a different order of elevation from the 'youthful Kings' and 'Tyrants fierce' on either side of them), the driving force of the rhetorical business overrides local complications, inexorably raising the pitch until the expected collapse becomes due.[28]

This rhetorical flight is mock-heroic but probably not strictly mock-epic. It is not unprecedented in English satire, and Pope may have learned it from Oldham:

> Not enter'd Punks from Lust they once have tried,
> Not Fops and Women from Conceit and Pride,
> Not Bawds from Impudence, Cowards from Fear,
> Nor sear'd unfeeling Sinners past Despair,

[28]The passage was substantially in its definitive form in the 1712 version (II. 1–10), though the 'Lovers' and 'Ladies' of the fifth and sixth lines were in the singular.

Are half so hard, and stubborn to reduce,
As a poor Wretch, when once possess'd with Muse.[29]

I'm not proposing this as a source, or allusion: structured ranting of
the kind both Oldham and Pope are mimicking is commonplace. But
it doesn't evoke classical epic, unless perhaps some things from the
rhetorical excesses of the Latin Silver Age. If there's a specific epic
allusion in the lines beginning 'But anxious Cares the pensive Nymph
opprest,/And secret Passions labour'd in her Breast', it's to Dido in
the *Aeneid* (also, oddly, the opening of Book IV): 'But now for some
while the queen had been growing more grievously love-sick,/Feeding
the wound with her life-blood, the fire biting within her'.[30] Dryden's
translation, as Tillotson notes, strengthens the connection. It begins
'But anxious Cares already seiz'd the Queen', but neither Virgil's nor
Dryden's lines have the slightest intimation of an anaphoric set piece,
and I suspect that to readers of Pope (or of Oldham) such passages
would be likeliest to evoke the speechifying of Restoration heroic
tragedy (a genre in which, incidentally, Oldham's satires are steeped).

The heroic play was commonly viewed as a debased expression of
epic aspirations, and became a lightning rod in critiques of the heroic
ethos which sought to protect the hallowed masterpieces of Homer
and Virgil from the opprobrium of military cruelty and thuggish codes
of honour. Censures which Pope expressed with a gingerly anguished
plaintiveness in his notes to the *Iliad* appear with a sharp explicitness
or exuberant derision in dramatic parodies from the *Rehearsal* to the
Tragedy of Tragedies, and the tendency in Augustan mock-heroic
towards a species of generic displacement or transposition, protective
of epic even as it proceeds through parody of epic forms, is something
which deserves to be better recognised. So, in the *Battle of the Books*,
mock-epic is constantly merging into mock-journalism, and among the
'heroic' targets of *Jonathan Wild* historians openly substitute for epic
poets, and historical villains for epic heroes. If the high Augustan mock-
heroic was to remain what it was programmed to be, a tribute to epic
in the only mode now possible to good poets outside the practice of
translation, such devices were among the possible ways of shielding
epic both from the vulnerabilities of its discredited moral codes and
from the corrosions of irony inherent in any mock form. Pope understood as well as Swift that if mock-heroic was to be accepted as

---

[29]Oldham, 'A Satyr: [Spencer's Ghost]', ll. 271–6, *Poems*, p. 246.
[30]*The Eclogues, Georgics and Aeneid of Virgil*, trans. C. Day Lewis (Oxford, 1966), p. 218.

mocking not the heroic but a lowered modern reality, the fall-out from the derision might readily spread to unintended targets, and they doubtless also sensed that the heroic itself could not be, for them, in all honesty, a *wholly unintended* target. Pope's control of ironic modulation enabled him to maintain complex and conflicting sympathies in something like the desired balance, though the tearaway corrosiveness of Swift's irony, as I've argued elsewhere, ensured that (with the single special exception of the *Battle*) he never attempted mock-epic at all.[31]

Passages 4A and 4B, like 3, show the protagonist in distress: Theobald in A, Cibber in B. There is no reason to suppose, as with 1 and 2, that the later passage was written with some thought of the earlier, but they have a theme, or basic situation, in common, and the transition from the *Rape of the Lock* to the *Dunciad* is as instructive as in the two altar passages, though in different ways. What is special to 4B in particular is that it lacks the display of ordonnance so ostentatiously visible in the other passages, including not only 3 but also, up to a point, its own immediate prototype, 4A. It has nothing of the spectacular set-piece simplicity of the anaphoric paragraph, its relentless clarities of structured bathos, or any trace of the quasi-ekphrastic arrangement of the altar pieces, whose formal disposition and architecture simultaneously confer an additional air of design on the verse description itself. The difference is the more striking because, like 2, the altar passage from the *Dunciad*, 4B shows Cibber among literary *disjecta membra*, here more exclusively his own writings, but as the passage continues, taking in other authors, and indeed culminating in the 'Gothic Library! of Greece and Rome/Well purg'd' which immediately precedes passage 2.

Passage 4 in all versions comes before passage 2 and indeed leads straight into it in less than thirty lines. My quotations are, of course, selective, and start and finish in mid-paragraph. The paragraph to which 4 belongs, which immediately precedes passage 2, has a larger rhythm of its own, and an even larger shape or pattern is discernible in the consecutive placing of this paragraph and the two paragraphs constituting passage 2. The paragraph to which 4B belongs is unusually long (40 lines: I. 107–46), and anything can be made to fall into place if the scheme is large enough. But one of my assumptions is that Popeian set pieces typically come in smaller units; and the other passages I

[31]For fuller discussion and documentation of these points, see chs. 3 and 4 of my *Satire and Sentiment 1660–1830*, pp. 29–129.

have discussed are in this regard more characteristic of the normal style not only of the *Rape of the Lock* and the *Dunciad*, but of most of Pope's poems.

4B was not always the form in which this part of the poem was known. In this regard it also largely differs from 1, 2 and 3, and part of the difference again has to do with Cibber's acquisition of the Laureateship and his absorption into the poem as hero, since the 'future Odes', which are among the literal creatures denoted by the imagery of the embryos and abortions at the end, like the steeple-shaped ode of passage 2, evidently refer to this activity. Cibber's Laureate odes were a standard joke of the 1730s.[32] Cibber himself recognised in the *Apology* that 'the very word, *Ode*, I know', triggered derision of his efforts in that line.[33] The word had only occurred once in the whole of *Dunciad* A, which precedes Cibber's Laureateship by a year. In 1728 and 1729 the passage corresponding to the 40-line paragraph which includes 4B (I. 107–46) is almost exactly half the length, or twenty-two lines, in two paragraphs of four and eighteen lines respectively (I. 95–116 in 1728, I. 105–126 in 1729). Passage 4A (I. 99–108 in 1728 and I. 109–18 in 1729) is more or less identical in 1728 and 1729. Of the two annotated copies based on the Broglio MSS, the copy of 1728 has no marginalia for this specific extract. But that of the 1736 version of the 1729 text has some four variants in lines 110, 116 and 117: we learn that 'his rising' was preferred to 'the Birth of' (110), 'much learned lumber' to both 'the Spoils of Sturbridge' and '*Philemon*'s Labours' (116), and 'size' to 'bulk' (117). All three involve a preoccupation with elevation, magnitude, or mass, in a characteristically grotesque effort to evoke a disfigured epic majesty. It is consistent that an image of 'rising' should be preferred to one of birth (though misshapen nativities are a feature of the poem as a whole, and of the 1743 version of this passage, 4B);

[32]See Sutherland's Introduction, *Dunciad*, p. xxxv.
[33]Cibber, *Apology*, ed. B. R. S. Fone (Ann Arbor, 1968), ch. 2, p. 23. He was speaking of a coronation ode he had to write as a schoolboy. The passage shows his pleasure in acknowledging the jeering of others, his vanity and his genial recognition of vanity: 'The very Word, *Ode*, I know, makes you smile already; and so it does me; not only because it still makes so many poor Devils turn Wits upon it, but from a more agreeable Motive; from a Reflexion of how little I then thought that, half a Century afterwards, I shou'd be call'd upon twice a Year, by my Post, to make the same kind of Oblations to an *unexceptionable* Prince, the serene Happiness of whose Reign my halting Rhimes are still unequal to — This, I own, is Vanity without Disguise ...' The ode he then wrote, 'bad as it was, ... serv'd to get the School a Play-day, and to make me not a little vain upon it'. His vanity 'disgusted my Playfellows', which 'serv'd only to increase my Vanity'. But then, 'If I confess my Vanity while a Boy, can it be Vanity, when a Man, to remember it?' (pp. 23–4).

that the solidity of 'lumber' should be preferred to two alternatives that don't self-evidently evoke ponderousness or mass; and that, if there is little to choose between 'size' and 'bulk', the indecision shows Pope in the act of considering alternative ways of evoking magnitude.[34]

The whole sequence in the earlier *Dunciad* is thus more compact, and I believe more conventionally Popeian, and the extract under special scrutiny as 4A, though obviously a prototype for 4B, has a methodical and definitional quality much closer to the other passages. It has nothing like 4B's suggestive mimicry of disintegration and incoherence, its air of deranged plasticity, with dissolving outlines and surreal shapes. 4B's embryos and abortions are only, as we know from the next line, Cibber's unfinished writings, but like the cone-shaped steeple-ode, they are transmogrified into a fantasy landscape, here not so much Disneyan, but evoking, momentarily, some lurid hell-scapes in a tradition whose most familiar pictorial expressions for us are perhaps by Bosch or Breughel. There are no embryos or abortions in 4A, though 'embryon atoms' are found in the description preceding Satan's flight through Chaos in *Paradise Lost* (II. 900) to which both versions allude, and though 4A otherwise places its Miltonic derivations in rather higher profile than 4B.

Comparison indeed suggests an unexpected retreat from, or attenuation of, Miltonising aggrandisement in the later version. The *Dunciad* in all versions is very much in the business of actualising hell on a supercharged scale, both in the landscape of the big city, and in the bottomless spaces of the hero's empty mind, the two being deeply interrelated in that mythologising of Grub Street, real place, country of the mind, and topographical site of cultural disintegration. What Eliot said in 1930 of the Baudelairean city, of Baudelaire's 'use of the sordid life of a great metropolis', and his 'elevation of such imagery to the *first intensity* — presenting it as it is, and yet making it represent something much more than itself', applies all the more suggestively to the *Dunciad* because of the centrality of infernal resonance in the imagination of the city by both poets, as in that of Eliot's own *Waste Land*, with Milton's 'populous city' in the background.[35] The throbbing, polluted majesties of the great city clearly went back, in Eliot's own perception, to some classic effects of Augustan mock-heroic, perhaps equal in their impact on him to those of Baudelaire. Nine years before

[34]Vander Meulen, pp. 6–7 of facsimile; *Last and Greatest Art*, p. 132.
[35]T. S. Eliot, 'Baudelaire', *Selected Essays* (London, 1953), p. 426; *Paradise Lost*, IX. 445ff.

the essay on Baudelaire, he was citing with admiration the Barbican passage from *Mac Flecknoe* (ll. 64ff.), with its 'Scenes of lewd loves, and of polluted joys; / Where their vast Courts the Mother-Strumpets keep', and its 'transformation . . . into poetry' of a well-known passage from Cowley's epic *Davideis* (also adapted to mock-heroic use in Garth's *Dispensary*).[36] We should not, in this connection, forget that the *Waste Land*, itself deeply impregnated with a Baudelairean feeling for 'the sordid life of a great metropolis', actually began life as a pastiche of the *Rape of the Lock*, coloured or overshadowed by Dunciadic and Swiftian tones.[37] That the infernal imagery in the *Dunciad* has a specifically mock-epic character is fully consistent with its 'epic' status (disfigured, so to speak, rather than diminished), since it's no part of the mock-epic strategy to reduce the primary model as distinct from using it, according to Dryden's formula, for elevating the base material to which it is applied. It is equally a truism that the *Dunciad*'s inferno is not a mockery of epic underworlds but an appropriation of Milton's hell to the modern London nightmare.

This nightmare, as in Milton, where hell is both a place and the state of Satan's mind, carried by him which way he flies, is solidly geographical, but also the gaping mental void of the king of Dulness. The mythologising force of the poem depends on its ability to convey the enormity of both. At all events, 'Sinking from thought to thought', and the two ensuing lines, are common to 4A and 4B. They give the hero's bottomless stupidity the dimensions of a journey through Chaos, 'like the progress of the Devil in *Milton*', as Pope's note makes sure we notice in a note to the A version (omitted from B). Rochester had used Milton in a similar way in the 'Satyr against Mankind' to evoke vast mental vacuities, and Pope, as Gilbert Wakefield noted long ago, took part of his wording from Rochester's 'Satyr against Reason and Mankind': 'Stumbling [or "Tumbling"] from thought to thought, falls headlong down' (l. 18).[38]

But the adjacent Miltonic allusion in 4A, 'He roll'd his eyes that witness'd huge dismay', is dropped from 4B, although in the earlier

---

[36]Eliot, 'John Dryden', *Selected Essays*, p. 308; Cowley, *Davideis* (1656), I. 80ff.; *Dispensary* (1699), VI. 96–7 (also IV. 1–4) in *POAS*, VI. 121, 91.

[37]For a fuller account of these connections, see 'The Nightmares of Strephon: Nymphs of the City in the Poems of Swift, Baudelaire, Eliot', and 'Pope's *Waste Land*: Reflections on Mock-Heroic', in *Order from Confusion Sprung*, pp. 154ff., 201ff.

[38]*Dunciad*, p. 77, Pope's note to A I. 115, not repeated in B; *Paradise Lost*, II. 927ff.; on readings of the Rochester line, see *Complete Works*, ed. Frank H. Ellis (London, 1994), pp. 72, 360.

version Pope seems to have wanted the Miltonic source to be even more clearly in the reader's mind than in the case of 'Sinking from thought to thought', and had taken the trouble to quote it (more or less verbatim) in a note: *'Round he throws his [baleful] eyes / That witness'd huge affliction and dismay'*.[39] One can only speculate about the reasons for the later omission, as also for the dropping in B of the note identifying Milton in relation to line 112 of A. Perhaps he was resisting overkill, just as the 1728 and 1729 versions of the altar passage had drawn back from some of the looser effects of enormity in the manuscript drafts reproduced by Jonathan Richardson. Perhaps 'he roll'd his eyes that witness'd huge dismay', with its odd evocation of a discomfited Disneyan giant, was felt to fall short of Miltonic *gravitas*, though elements of baroque visual humour are not foreign to any version of the *Dunciad* — or to *Paradise Lost* itself.

4A comes over as a good sample of the efficient definitional bravura that is a hallmark of Pope's writing in the 1720s and 1730s, with the potential suggestion of patness that sometimes goes with that at its less than best. Pope's 'He roll'd his eyes that witness'd huge dismay' may be compared with Milton's, the square brackets indicating Pope's omissions or changes: '[round] he [throws] his [baleful] eyes / That witnessed huge [affliction and] dismay'. We witness a process of efficient simplification, which is even carried over into the actual citation of Milton in Pope's note, which perpetuates the omission of 'baleful'. Pope would have called it 'correctness', and as often happens, this is cheekily set off against a presumed lack of it in Milton: the gnarled metrical intricacies, the failure to use rhyme because (as Pope supposedly told Voltaire) 'he could not', those heaving energies of the sublime that Pope needed both to exploit and to feel superior to.[40]

Pope's version of Milton's line is a tidy containment that may have come to be seen as diminished by the strenuous presence of the original at the foot of the page — and diminished all the more unsettlingly (perhaps) because it seemed designed as a textbook illustration of the superior excellencies of that couplet metric through which Pope liked to 'versify' earlier poets, Chaucer and Donne no less than Milton. 'Correct couplets' are not of course abandoned in 4B, but unlike those of 4A, they create an atmosphere of tension with unruly forces rather than containment of them. It seems not unlikely to me that in the final

---

[39] *Paradise Lost*, I. 56–57.
[40] Voltaire, *Lettres Philosophiques*, ed. F. A. Taylor (Oxford (Blackwell), 1946), p. 174 (n. 3 to Letter XVIII).

Dunciad 'correctness' may have come to seem as in itself reductive, and acts of containment an inappropriate response to what was becoming, for Pope, an unusually intensified perception of disorderly forces. In that strictly limited sense, he had perhaps come closer to Swift, to whom the poem had been dedicated almost from the start, and whose whole writing career, from a *Tale of a Tub* to the late poems of the 1730s, had been devoted to a flatter, non-heroic rather than mock-heroic, anatomy of the chaos dark and deep.

This last distinction, on which I won't dwell long, is one which is most effectively sensed by comparing the polluted processional majesty of Pope's London waters

> . . . where Fleet-ditch with disemboguing streams
> Rolls the large tribute of dead dogs to Thames,
>
> (II. 271–72)

with the frenetic animation of the effluences of Swift's City Shower:

> Sweepings from Butchers Stalls, Dung, Guts, and Blood,
> Drown'd Puppies, stinking Sprats, all drench'd in Mud,
> Dead Cats and Turnip-Tops come tumbling down the Flood.
>
> (ll. 61–63)[41]

Particularity is a feature of this animation, and one often regarded, by Pope and others, as inimical to grandeur. It here spectacularly differentiates two passages of not dissimilar content.

But it is a feature of 4B, and the whole paragraph to which it belongs (twice as long, I pointed out, as its 1728 or 1729 prototype), that on its own phantasmagoric plane, quite different from the headlong demented realism of the Swiftian notation, it opens up into a mode of itemisation barely present in the earlier versions, introducing not only the embryos and abortions, future odes and abdicated plays, but going on to an extended fantasy of overheated and deranged creativity, where vitality exists in a complex, half-adversarial orchestration with the lapidary doom-laden torpor, the enveloping massiveness, that is for many readers the *Dunciad*'s dominant distinctive voice:

> Nonsense precipitate, like running Lead,
> That slip'd thro' Cracks and Zig-zags of the Head;
> All that on Folly Frenzy could beget,
> Fruits of dull Heat, and Sooterkins of Wit.
>
> (I. 123ff.)[42]

[41]Swift, *Poems*, ed. Harold Williams, 2nd edn. (Oxford, 1958), I. 139.
[42]These lines do not occur in the A version.

And when, more mundanely, the hero contemplates his library and 'o'er his Books his eyes began to roll' (I. 127ff.), the list of modern authors is much longer in B than in A, and the commentary about them more ample. The process is the reverse of what we witnessed in the progression from 1A to 1B in the *Rape of the Lock*. In the later poem, Pope was neither abandoning grandeur nor even enormity: perhaps by the time of the final *Dunciad* he felt sufficiently in command to put the brakes on, and to take on competing effects without inhibition.

Enormity and grandeur are essential to the apocalyptic theme, which is if anything heightened in the B-version and culminates in its famous finale. The idea of Genesis going into reverse, the initiating Logos of St. John's gospel metamorphosed into the 'uncreating word' of the poem's close in both versions, depends for a full sense of its dire urgency on a preservation of biblical and Miltonic resonances in something like an equal and opposite order of magnitude. The idea seems to have developed from small-scale punning origins in a short poem of *c.* 1727, 'Verses to be Placed under the Picture of England's Arch-Poet', in which Pope said Blackmore 'Un-did *Creation* at a Jerk', alluding to his epic poem, *Creation*. By the time the joke had worked its way through the *Dunciad*, it had mushroomed grotesquely into the vast negative nightmare we all know.[43]

The accompanying stylistic inversion, as all readers are aware, crosses the parody barrier in a manner that seems to go beyond Dryden's observations about heroic majesties rubbing off on the satire, though it also seems a self-conscious fulfilment of the project or aspiration implicit in Dryden's *Discourse* of making satire a species of heroic poetry in its own right. In Pope's hands, this sometimes receives surprising literal applications. His couplet about Fleet Ditch taps into a large tradition of satiric writing about polluted London waters, to which Dryden, Garth, Gay and Swift all contributed, and Wakefield noted as far back as 1796 a couplet from the *Dispensary* about Fleet Ditch descending 'in sable Streams/To wash his sooty *Naiads* in the *Thames*'.[44] This is undoubtedly a germ of Pope's lines, which accented a processional movement already present in Garth, but the source of the Dunciadic couplet in its most distinctive effect comes from a much more recent line about 'the deep roar of disemboguing *Nile*' from Pope's own translation of the *Odyssey* (IV. 480). Such stylistic reversals,

[43] *Dunciad*, A III. 340, B IV. 654; 'Verses', in *Minor Poems*, ed. Norman Ault, T. E., VI. 290.
[44] *Dunciad*, ed. Sutherland, p. 133 n., citing Garth, *Dispensary*, 1699, III. 111–2 (*POAS*, VI. 86).

mirroring or even embodying the *Dunciad's* anatomy of a culture turned upside down, belong to a mode of unparodying, of upward reformulation, which I have discussed elsewhere, and of which a non-Popeian example might be Yeats's transformation of Dryden's satirical portrait of Zimri, 'A man so various, that he seem'd to be / Not one, but all Mankinds Epitome' into the Robert Gregory who was 'As 'twere all life's epitome', a positive modern incarnation of the Renaissance ideal of the complete man of which Dryden's Zimri had been seen as a travesty in the first place.[45]

That such resublimation should take place within a satire is perhaps more arresting, though the phenomenon is up to a point implicit in the mock-heroic project itself. A pompous speech by Sloth in the *Dispensary* (1699: I. 107–8), 'Thro' my Indulgence, Mortals hourly share / A grateful Negligence, and Ease from Care', may be a disfigured parody of a customary idiom for celebrating an English Augustan ideal of easy grace, sometimes conceived as a 'Horatian' urbanity in Dryden and others, in which ideas of both negligence and ease have strong positive associations. The expected phrase, amusingly modified in Garth's evocation of slothful self-indulgence, is 'graceful Ease'. It is found in Oldham's *Letter from the Country* (l. 49), and in Dryden's imitation of the *Knight's Tale, Palamon and Arcite* (III. 73), which was published the year after Garth's poem and which may, as I suggested, be an active presence in Pope's mock-heroic creations: the phrase is conspicuously added by Dryden to the Chaucerian original (ll. 2165–6), where there is no trace of it, but which Dryden otherwise follows closely at this point. Both Oldham's and Dryden's lines are cited in the Twickenham commentary as analogues to the *Essay on Criticism*'s assertion that '*Horace* still charms with graceful *Negligence*' (l. 653). I suggest that Garth's reformulation of what had become a cant phrase of the 'discourse' of politeness may also have a subtextual half-life in the imaginative hinterland of the line from the *Essay on Criticism*, and even in that of the *Rape of the Lock*'s praise of Belinda's 'graceful Ease, and Sweetness void of Pride' (II. 15), where mock-heroic answers mock-heroic in a celebrative, or at least a more subtly satirical, register, delicately poised between derision and an affirmative loyalty.[46] Such traffic, in both directions, is inevitable and commonplace in a literary

---

[45]For a fuller account, see *Satire and Sentiment 1660–1830*, p. 116; Dryden, *Absalom and Achitophel*, I. 545–6; Yeats, 'In Memory of Major Robert Gregory', ll. 86–7.

[46]*POAS*, VI. 68; Oldham, *Poems*, p. 150; Dryden, *Poems*, ed. Kinsley, IV. 1502; for the two lines by Pope, see T. E., I. 313 and n., II. 160.

culture with an almost instinctive predisposition to parody, and steeped
in allusive habits and modes of ironic inflection. It is part of a complicated relationship between eighteenth-century writers and their own
parodic forms not all of whose manifestations have received the attention they deserve, but which in the *Dunciad* also include some
subheroic itemisations which have been vividly expounded by Howard
Erskine-Hill, Emrys Jones and others. Jones for example has drawn
attention to the callow excited verbal contests in Book II, 'chatt'ring,
grinning, mouthing, jabb'ring', with 'Snip-snap short, and Interruption
smart' (II. 237, 240) and to the oddly sympathetic counterpoint this
provides to the dominant themes and tonalities of the poem.[47]

In a note to the *Iliad*, Pope observed that 'There are not only
Replies, but Rejoinders in *Homer*,... many continued
Conversations... a little resembling common Chit-chat. This renders
a Poem more natural and animated, but less grave and majestick'.[48]
The censoriousness is clear, part of Pope's patient and protracted
mission to sanitise his Homer. That such dialogue is 'natural and
animated' is conceded, but what Pope describes as animated chit-
chat, a conversation between Idomeneus and Merion (or Meriones),
is actually rendered by him in the following manner:

> To this, *Idomeneus*. The Fields of Fight
> Have prov'd thy Valour and unconquer'd Might;
> And were some Ambush for the Foes design'd,
> Ev'n there, thy Courage would not lag behind.
>
> (XIII. 353–56)

As chit-chat goes, this might be thought to be somewhat heroically
styled, and indeed rather short on animation. What Pope put down as
chit-chat in the *Iliad* note may mean no more than dialogue anyway:
the note opens with the finger-wagging remark that 'there is a great
deal more Dialogue in *Homer* than in *Virgil*'. The issue is one of
conversation vs. speeches, speeches being so important in the heroic
tradition that one of the objections against gunpowder was, in Renaissance Europe as in Japan, that it made the combatants cut down on
speeches and just shoot. As Pope put it in the 'Essay on Homer's
Battels', 'before the Use of *Fire-Arms* there was... more *Leisure* ...
for those Harangues [Homer's] Heroes make to each other in the time

---

[47]Emrys Jones, 'Pope and Dulness', *Proceedings of the British Academy*, LIV (1968), 231–63,
esp. 253ff.
[48]Pope's note to *Iliad*, XIII. 353, T. E., VIII. 122.

of Combate'.[49] I'm not sure that 'Harangues' bears a full weight of modern distaste (Johnson defines it simply as 'A speech; a popular oration'), though Pope doubtless felt for those boastful and aggressive ritual declarations the kind of ambivalence with which he viewed the whole issue of Homeric warfare.[50] But he rendered them with full honours, and they were not to be mistaken for chit-chat, as Idomeneus's reply to Merion, the furthest Pope would go in that direction, remains pretty remote from the *Dunciad*'s 'Snip-snap short, and Interruption smart', themselves animated and accorded unofficial affection, but hardly the staple idiom of that poem either.

If one wanted a *Dunciad* in chit-chat, one would have to turn to Shelley's satire on Wordsworth and his circle, *Peter Bell the Third*, a studiously flat, often brilliantly astringent downscaling. Its London is also infernal, or rather vice versa: 'Hell is a city much like London — / A populous and a smoky city' (III. i), deriving both from the *Dunciad* and from the infernal 'populous City' of *Paradise Lost*, IX. 445. The poem is a low-key patrician putdown of plebeian dunces whose Cibber is Wordsworth, another Laureate, though he wasn't yet:

> Peter was dull—he was at first
>   Dull—O, so dull—so very dull!
> Whether he talked, wrote, or rehearsed—
> Still with this dulness was he cursed—
>   Dull—beyond all conception—dull.

(VII. xi)

Not exactly, as I've argued elsewhere, the engulfing Dulness, Daughter of Chaos and eternal Night, of Pope's poem, though undoubtedly a transposition of her to the domain of mundane chit-chat.[51] Reading Colley Cibber's *Letter from Mr. Cibber to Mr. Pope*, I was recently struck by a response to Pope's attacks on him, couched in terms that seem a plaintive mimicry not of the *Dunciad* as we normally read it but as Shelley rewrote it: 'What, am I only to be Dull, and Dull still,

---

[49]'Essay on Homer's Battels', T. E., VII. 260; see also *Satire and Sentiment 1660–1830*, pp. 56–8.
[50]The word 'harangue', according to the *OED*, is 'A speech addressed to an assembly; a loud or vehement address, a tirade; formerly, sometimes, a formal or pompous speech', and derives from medieval Latin, Old French, Italian and Spanish terms for a 'place of declamation, arena'. Ironic or derogatory usages certainly seem, from the *OED*'s examples, to be in evidence in the late seventeenth and eighteenth centuries, but Pope's phrasing (which I read as mainly neutral or laudatory) and Johnson's definition show a strong survival of the non-ironic sense.
[51]*Satire and Sentiment 1660–1830*, p. 103.

and again, and for ever?'.[52] Cibber's *Letter* appeared in 1742, after the
New Dunciad (i.e. Book IV), but before the appearance of the full-
blown *Dunciad, in Four Books*, which was published the following year
with himself finally 'enthroned in the place of Theobald'.[53] It is thus a
proleptic response, but he already had much to complain of, not only
in the *New Dunciad* itself (though that had only one new offensive
line specifically about him [IV. 20], plus a long note to that line), but,
as he said in his opening remarks, 'for several Years past, in . . . [Pope's]
Poetical Works'.[54]

It's possible that he already knew, and that Pope ensured that he
knew, that a revised Cibberian *Dunciad* was in the offing, and may
even have intended the *Letter* as a warning or pre-emptive strike.[55] It
served in fact as an added precipitant, or final trigger. In a further loop
of the circle, Pope incorporated the complaint from the *Letter* in 1743
in the expanded note in *Dunciad* B (I. 109n.), as Swift had absorbed
Wotton's 'Observations' into the commentary of the expanded *Tale of
a Tub*. The proto-Shelleyan chatter was thus accommodated into the
Dunciad's ultimate version, and it would be rash to exclude the possibility that Shelley might indeed have picked it up there, since *Peter
Bell the Third* is impregnated with Dunciadic and Scriblerian elements,
transfigured and flattened to the needs and atmosphere of his own
satire. The matter of immediate interest is that Pope chose to naturalise
the Cibberian contribution to this idiom into a composition whose
dominant atmosphere might be thought inhospitable to it. I will be
suggesting that this traffic between competing moods is a feature of
the *Dunciad*, and that the notes, and the switch to Cibber, play an
important part in it.

Cibber made other interesting remarks, that Dulness wasn't actually
a crime, and that he didn't believe Pope *really* thought him dull, nearly

[52]*A Letter from Mr. Cibber, to Mr. Pope* (London, 1742), p. 53 (partially reprinted in J. V.
Guerinot, *Pamphlet Attacks*, pp. 288ff.).
[53]*Dunciad*, p. lii.
[54]Sutherland, in *Dunciad*, p. xxxiii; *Letter from Mr. Cibber*, p. 5. This recognition is already
bumptiously on display, as early as 1740, in the first edition of the *Apology*, where he
professes to admire and even enjoy Pope's attacks on him: 'Not our great Imitator of *Horace*
himself can have more Pleasure in writing his Verses, than I have in reading them, tho' I
sometimes find myself there . . . *dispraisingly* spoken of . . . I look upon my Follies as the
best part of my Fortune, . . . nor do I believe I shall ever be rhim'd out of them' (ed. Fone,
ch. 1, p. 16).
[55]*Dunciad*, pp. xxxii–xxxiii; Guerinot, *Pamphlet Attacks*, p. 290.

forty pages earlier.[56] He had proleptically become as obsessive about the term as Pope was to be relentless in applying it to him in the culminating overkill of *Dunciad* B, with its studiedly transposed slurs and its additional insults. His grievance was exacerbated by the fact that, rather remarkably, he considered the *Dunciad* 'a better Poem of its Kind, than ever was writ', reserving his main complaint for the footnotes, which he dismissed as 'Loads of Prose Rubbish'.[57] By the time of the 'am I only to be Dull, and Dull still' passage, he had cited a good deal of offending verse too. But the accents of the complaint do have a much closer match in the style of the annotation than in the atmosphere of the poem proper. One tendency of the notes is to drag down the epic pretension in various ways: through the flattening effect of the prose medium, the dimension of gossip and low journalism, the intermittent flourishes of mundane fact or bread-and-butter defamation which reintroduce an unsettling dose of the reality principle into the portrayal of the dunces, whom the poem itself had meanwhile been converting into something rich and strange.

It may have been Swift's *Battle of the Books* that taught Pope that a simultaneous activation of mock-heroic and mock-journalese was not only possible but productive of specific imaginative satisfactions. The *Battle*, itself in prose, merges the two strands in the body of the text, having announced its journalistic character, 'A Full and True Account of the Battel Fought last Friday', in the title, before the first mock-epic note is struck. The two elements are more formally separated in the *Dunciad*, whose earliest printed version of 1728 was almost if not entirely without notes. But from the *Dunciad Variorum* of the following year, for the remainder of the work's long development, and of course ever since, the poem has been read with an immense commentary, and if Cibber felt able at the start of his *Letter* to distinguish between the text and the notes, he didn't sustain the distinction for long. Indeed the satire depends so much on the interaction of the two that no accurate reading of the poem seems possible without at least some awareness of the notes, and although I suspect few readers of the poem actually read the notes *in toto*, a sense of their atmosphere will generally percolate through, if only because their massive presence on the

[56]*Letter from Mr. Cibber*, pp. 14–5; cf. *Apology*, ch. 2, p. 25, on Pope's attacks: 'I never look upon those Lines as Malice meant to me, (for he knows I never provok'd it) but Profit to himself: One of his Points must be, to have many Readers . . . a Lick at the *Laureat* will always be a sure Bait'.
[57]*Letter from Mr. Cibber*, p. 9.

page makes them unignorable: Cibber's comment that 'those vain-glorious encumbrances of Notes, and Remarks, upon almost every Line of it' have 'almost smother'd your *Dunciad*' is, forgivably, not the most enlightened way of putting it, but it's a hostile way of making the same point.[58]

Formally, the notes to the *Dunciad* suggest mock-scholarship rather than mock-journalism, though an insinuation of equivalence between the two is a recognisable Scriblerian turn, and Swift's *Battle* offered a precedent for that secondary amalgam also, so that the official mock-epic parody interacts with not one but two other generic divisions. The *Battle* helped to naturalise the principle that when a work of mock-heroic was offered as, or developed into, an edition of itself, with notes, marginalia, gaps in the MS, and the rest, its character as a mock-edition attracted attention to itself in partial competition with the epic joke, just as the mock-journalism did. The editorial routines have a way, and perhaps an actual purpose, of lowering the mock-epic tonalities, and play their part in diverting satirical energies away from the epic original. Such generic displacements, instinctive or designed, served a dual protective function in Swift, who used the various flattening agencies (prose, journalese, editorial apparatus) as much to neutralise any residual loftiness in his own text (to avoid, as he said, a figure scurvy), as to protect objects of official heroic veneration from unintended devolutions of the ironic slur.

I believe Pope didn't need to do that, his characteristic ironic style being loyalist, enhancing rather than undermining cherished cultural properties, even, and perhaps especially, in grandiloquent modes. No poet is as versatile and commanding in his ability to make irony and majesty coexist without reciprocal diminution. If Swiftian parody lowered lofty tonalities, Pope's preserved them, defiled but entire, as in the Fleet Ditch couplet, or 'Great Cibber's brazen, brainless brothers stand' (I. 32), which did not get into Book I until the B *Dunciad*, another product of Cibber's accession to full heroic honours, though the statues by Cibber's father to which it refers had stood 'over the gates of Bedlam-hospital' since about 1680.[59] When mock-heroic is thus compounded by mock-scholarly annotation, which dissipates energies of recognition and diverts parodic slurs from heroic pretension to learned self-importance, the primary majesties which Swift sought

[58]*Letter from Mr. Cibber*, p. 9.
[59]Pope's note to I. 31.

to stop in their tracks tend in Pope to receive an enabling boost, their protection from a prevailing atmosphere of derision reinforced rather than eroded by the generic displacement.

The remarkable and unSwiftian demarcation of styles between text and notes in Pope's poem additionally ensured that effects of dimin- ution could be relegated to a safe area at the foot of the page. Pope's notes can be thought of as releasing the subversive potential in a controlled environment, separate from the flow of the poem, but simul- taneously demanding to be read *pari passu*. When Cibber, having seen an advance version of 'brazen, brainless brothers', pointed out in a *Second Letter . . . to Mr. Pope* in February 1743 that the statues were of stone, not brass, Pope retorted that although Cibber had correctly 'remonstrated that his Brothers at Bedlam . . . were not *Brazen*, but *Blocks*; yet our author let it pass unaltered, as a trifle, that in no way lessened the Relationship'.[60] This put-down, transforming an atmos- phere of lapidary enormity — a term, however, which is strictly speaking more suited to stone than to bronze — into one of mundane sibling farce, is relegated not only to a note, but to a note on another passage, even more statuesquely orchestrated, the Miltonic parody which opens Book II: 'High on a gorgeous seat . . . Great Cibber sate' (II. 1–5). This belongs to a twelve-line passage, present in both main versions but not in 1728, in which Cibber's, previously Tibbald's, 'proud Parnassian sneer' modulates in the next line to 'The conscious simper, and the jealous leer' (II. 5–6), a scaling-down, not unlike that effected by the note, to more familiar presences, lower slopes of Parnassus.

The last line is somewhat more consonant with other portrayals of Cibber by Pope and others, though even it doesn't come very close, for

---

[60]*Second Letter*, pp. 3–5; Guerinot, *Pamphlet Attacks*, pp. 310–11. Pope was rightly determined, on poetic grounds, not to make any changes. The Twickenham note to II. 3 (p. 296) says William Bowyer had warned him about the inaccurate adjective, and that Pope replied on 13 November [1742?]: 'Just now I receive y^{rs} ab^t y^e *Brazen* Image. I w^d have it stand as it is, & no matter if ye Criticks dispute ab^t it'.

Cibber's *Apology* had characteristically prepared the ground for all the attention to his sculpted siblings. In ch. 1 he had remarked that 'the two Figures of the *Lunaticks*, the *Raving* and the *Melancholy*, over the Gates of *Bethlehem-Hospital*, are no ill Monuments of his [father's] Fame as an Artist' (p. 8). In ch. 3, he goes on to recount how his father, having failed to get Colley admitted to Winchester, had better success with his brother Lewis, winning the school over 'with the Present of a Statue of the Founder' (p. 36). Later, he hoped to get Colley into Cambridge, where he also executed some statues, but the plan miscarried because of unlucky timing, sparing the world some 'Sermons, and Pastoral Letters', 'instead of Plays and annual Odes' (pp. 38–9). Meanwhile, his brother Lewis became a Fellow of New College, Oxford, but died of dissolute habits in 1711 (pp. 37, 330 n.2).

example, to that 'Vanity, Impudence, and Debauchery' which Ricardus Aristarchus identified as attaching to the Cibberian hero of the 'little Epic', and from which 'springeth *Buffoonry*, the source of *Ridicule*'.[61] And Pope was more or less forced by Cibber to concede in the annotation that vivacity and pertness could be ascribed to him (it's wonderfully Cibberian to claim pertness for himself, in the very passage which contains the Shelleyan exclamations).[62] But 'proud Parnassian sneer' seems an especially awkward survival, which doesn't conform at all to the strutting hyperactive busybody of traditional accounts, or the more genial but recognisable version of this in Cibber's own *Apology*. '*Parnassian* sneer' had been recycled, between the two *Dunciads*, in the *Epistle to Dr. Arbuthnot*, not about Cibber but in an oddly coincidental proximity to a line which was fatefully offensive to him:

> Whom have I hurt? has Poet yet, or Peer,
> Lost the arch'd eye-brow, or *Parnassian* sneer?
> And has not *Colly* still his Lord, and Whore?

(ll. 95–7)

Cibber cited all three lines in the *Letter to Mr. Pope*, but only to highlight his outrage at the last line, which provoked the notorious anecdote in the *Letter* of Pope's own sexual humiliation with a whore.[63] Cibber used the preceding lines as a build-up or context, evidently without feeling that they might carry any sort of appropriate description of himself. The *Dunciad*'s 'proud Parnassian sneer' confers on the portrait, as well as attributing to the subject, a species of *hauteur*, of grandee bearing, which no one would seriously associate with this particular laureate, least of all himself. (This is hardly surprising, since the lines were applied to Cibber only as an afterthought, having originally been directed at Tibbald.)

The enormity of 'Great Cibber's brazen, brainless brothers stand' remained important to Pope. Cibber had pointed out in the *Second*

---

[61]*Dunciad*, p. 259; for Cibber on his own vanity and impudence, see *Apology*, chs. 2, 6, 11, pp. 27, 102–3, 118, 200–1 (e.g. the 'usual Effect' of attacks upon him 'is to make me vain', p. 27).

[62]*Letter from Mr. Cibber*, p. 53, cited by Pope in *Dunciad*, I. 109 n., p. 277; on accusations of pertness, see *Apology*, ch. 2, p. 29.

[63]*Letter from Mr. Cibber*, pp. 44ff. On this episode, see Mack, *Life*, pp. 779–81: 'For Pope it was dynamite: the most shattering ridicule of his wretched carcass that had ever been delivered . . . Almost overnight, engravers seized on the incident . . .' Mack describes the revelation as having a decisive impact on the four-book *Dunciad*, which 'seems to have been completed within three months of the publication of Cibber's *Letter*' (see also pp. 292–3, 871 n.)

Letter not only that the statues in question weren't bronze, but that they lay rather than stood.[64] Pope didn't pick this up, and it clearly no more suited him to go for the less dignified posture than to forego the massive alliterative resonance of 'brazen, brainless brothers', though humiliating play with the idea of prone figures would be consistent with the obvious desire to humiliate. Enormity was stubbornly preserved, though we should note that while it rubs off on Cibber, it isn't literally about him, and the sense of the line's bold massy presence was perhaps especially vulnerable to dissipation by the prose sense of things. But the passage beginning 'High on a gorgeous seat', which includes the 'proud Parnassian sneer', as well as Cibber's simpering and leering, shows the two in negotiation in the text of the poem and not only between the text and the note. A more appropriate portrayal, involving change from the A to the B text rather than an incompletely assimilated transposition, may be seen in passages 4A and 4B, where Tibbald's studious sitting, which seems almost passive under the Mighty Mother's eye, is replaced by the manic animation of Cibber's blaspheming and damning and gnawing and dashing, an energetic comic indignity coexisting con brio with the high Satanic montage. Milton offered hints for the mixture, on which Addison reported interestingly,[65] and Pope's exploitation of it in its final version is no merely predictable mock-heroic adaptation, but activates a reciprocal traffic between the familiar and the sublime of a sort Pope used to be embarrassed by when he met it in Homer.

Something of the same traffic, an ambivalence or bifurcated perspective, may be observed more crudely or strikingly in Fielding's *Jonathan Wild* (a work whose history has connections with the *Dunciad's* and which was also published, after a gestation of uncertain length, in 1743, the same year as Pope's final version). The work's official purposes similarly announce an inversely 'heroic' villain of diabolic proportions, while the poetic reality gives an inept little man, comically unsuccessful in crime and in love, and at times almost genial in his obsessive entrapment by his small-time pickpocketing compulsions. That 'poetic reality' is strikingly out of step with a prose sense in which the 'heroic' formula is largely a matter of hectoring asseveration, and which resembles the *Dunciad's* neo-Miltonic production as an iron scaffolding resembles a baroque palace. In the *Dunciad*, too,

[64]*Second Letter*, p. 4; Guerinot, *Pamphlet Attacks*, p. 311.
[65]*Spectator*, No. 303, 16 February 1712, ed. Donald F. Bond, 5 vols. (Oxford, 1965), III. 86.

you might say that the prose sense, at least as literally embodied in the prose annotation, largely carries the alternative 'little man' dimension independently of the workings of the verse, which tends towards aggrandisement. It is the dimension Shelley brought in from *hors texte*, in what looks like a modified reversion to the old burlesque, high matter in low language, discredited for the most ambitious satire in the period after Cotton and Butler, and thus unavailable for major mock-heroic expression until the time of Byron and Shelley, when epic loyalties had become less sensitive. Shelley's Cibber-analogue was, unlike Cibber himself, one of the most considerable poetic voices of his time, or of any time, even in Shelley's own grudging perception, and Shelley flattened him to a mock-lyrical-ballad-like banality, as a denizen of a flip downsized hell, much as Fielding reduced his Satanic villain to a small-time crook; whereas Pope's primary thrust was to make of Cibber a grotesque Titanic mushroom-cloud of Dulness, with universal fall-out.

As we have seen, however, the *hors texte* sometimes becomes a *sub*text in the *Dunciad*. The separations, whether in Pope's poem or in *Jonathan Wild*, are neither simple nor tidy, and the large unresolved oscillation is between the same conflicting impulses and sympathies. *Jonathan Wild* harks awkwardly back to mock-heroic, which serves it more as a verbal armature than as a live fiction, and it isn't comfortably described as a novel, though it's in that category for lack of a better that it is generally viewed. It is the work of an author steeped in Augustan and indeed Scriblerian modes, who worked elsewhere to adapt these to the novelistic genre, as Pope had no thought of doing. But there seems no doubt that in the *Dunciad*, as in *Jonathan Wild*, some scaled-down novelistic perspectives are entering, with an incompletely assimilated vitality, into the world of epic imitation.

This is a variant of a perhaps better understood process by which Sterne's *Tristram Shandy* was to incorporate the pre-emptive parody of 'L'Estrange, Dryden, *and some others*' in Swift's *Tale of a Tub*,[66] turning Scriblerian parody into an alternative novelistic mode, of self-expression and self-exploration, which Swift, had he been alive to witness it, would doubtless have reparodied with increments. The Shandean outfacing of Swift's *Tale* is indeed itself prefigured, without the Shandean folds of indirection, in Cibber's *Apology*, with its genial

---

[66]*Tale of a Tub*, Introduction, in Swift, *Prose Writings*, ed. Herbert Davis, 16 vols. (Oxford (Blackwell), 1939–1974), I. 42n.

acknowledgements of his stupidity and lack of talent, its vacuous com-placencies in the face of derision, its miscellaneous parades of self, and its fussy immediacies. When Cibber writes, for example, 'And this very Morning, where I am now writing at the *Bath, November 11*, 1738', one may wonder at the phenomenon of an author, and *a fortiori* an author conscious of his status as a Scriblerian target, so totally giving himself over to (or, you might say, unparodying) an idiom which Swift might be said to have *pre*parodied for all time in the *Tale*.[67]

The *Dunciad*, which had its own internalised ways of crossing the parody barrier, was, like Swift's *Tale*, open to *un*parodying from unlikely novelistic or Romantic sources. The Shelleyan case is instruc-tive, though it's perhaps an impure example, since the poem in which it occurs is itself a satire on a parallel theme to that of the *Dunciad*. But who would have guessed that Pope's pert pseudo-learned anno-tations, his mock-antiquarian routines, his Black Letter fabrications and his 'medieval' mimicries,

> Right well mine eyes arede the myster wight,
> On parchment scraps y-fed, and Wormius hight,
>
> (III. 187–8)[68]

would be re-enacted straight, within some twenty-five years of the final *Dunciad*, by a poet who came to be seen as a flower of Romantic genius, rebelling against restrictive Augustan canons? I mean, of course, Chatterton, who did these things without the Shandean self-awareness, or perhaps any awareness at all, but also (contrary to Romantic perception) without the hostility to Pope, whose Homer (that special object of Romantic opprobrium) he plundered for his own heroic effusions in both epic and drama.[69]

If the Romantic perceptions of a Chattertonian revolt were in some ways off target, their emergence soon after Chatterton's death is itself part of my story, a story of the eighteenth century's strange relations

[67]*Apology*, ch. 9, pp. 167–8. See *Tale*, pp. 22, 27, 132–5. For some remarks on the proleptic parody of Shandeism in Swift, see my *Gulliver and the Gentle Reader* (London, 1973), pp. 1–6.
[68]For Black Letter routines and other anti-'medieval' gesturing, see Pope's notes to I. 149, III. 187–8, IV. 18; the Caxton Appendix of 1729 and 'A Declaration' (*Dunciad*, pp. 213–6, 237–8). For bullying annotation of the kind whose tone Chatterton mimicked, see for example I. 218 n.
[69]For some discussion of Chatterton's use of Pope, see 'Schoolboy Glee', *Times Literary Supplement*, 6 May 1994, pp. 3–4. On Pope's Homer and the Romantics, see Hugh Shankman, *Pope's Iliad* (Princeton, 1963), pp. 56, 99, 144ff.; H. A. Mason, *To Homer through Pope* (London, 1972), pp. 61ff.

with its own parodic forms, and they have at least one intended and one unintended truth. The first is the obvious one that even during the medieval revival of the 1760s, to write 'medievally' was to write against the grain of an older orthodoxy (an act of rebellion of sorts, as, in its more radical way, forgery itself was). The other is that Chatterton wrote straight 'medieval' poems and learned annotations which sometimes resemble the Popeian parody of pedants more than they do any other writing, and that, since he had evidently exposed himself a good deal to Pope's works, he may partly have absorbed Popeian accents from an actual Dunciadic source. Pope would of course have reparodied the unparodying, which falls exactly within the prescription, in 'A Receit to Make an Epick Poem', to give the diction *the venerable Air of Antiquity . . . by darkening it up and down with* Old English', adding the equally literal Chattertonian touch that this is like the painter who tried to *'make his Dawbings be thought* Originals *by setting them in the* Smoak'. Even poor Chatterton's appeals, when cornered, to his poverty, would have received with increments the derision lavished in both the text and the notes of the *Dunciad* on that marriage of poetry and poverty which was to be resublimated later in Romantic mythologies of indigent genius.[70]

Whether Chatterton actually assimilated some of his effects from the *Dunciad*, as I think possible, or whether the resemblances are in some sense 'coincidental' in spite of his undoubted absorption of Pope's writings, Chatterton outfaced the parody almost as resolutely as *Tristram Shandy* outfaced the parody of *A Tale of a Tub*, though without the simpering awareness and self-elaboration, though perhaps not without a youthfully solemn version of Cibberian effrontery. Equally certainly, a potent presence of the derided element, in the *Dunciad* as in the *Tale*, lay germinating in the original.

This is not, I believe, simply to say that parody is doomed (by definition, since its mode is mimicry) to being like its targets, including future ones, though future targets complicate the issue in various ways; or that Cibber, or Sterne, or Chatterton, or Shelley were at some level adopting adversarial positions in relation to Scriblerian texts, so that their unparodying was itself conceived as a parodic enterprise, though the example of Sterne especially indicates complicated exercises of loyalty and defiance; or that Chatterton, unparodying the *Dunciad* in

---

[70]Pope, *Prose Works*, I, ed. Norman Ault (Oxford (Blackwell), 1936), p. 120; on poverty see, *inter alia*, Pope's note to *Dunciad*, II. 118.

his poems and notes, or the *Tragedy of Tragedies* in his own straight attempt at a heroic play, produced what some readers would wish to call self-parody. The undoing or resublimation of parody in non-parodic writings is as deeply ingrained in eighteenth-century authors as their well-known penchant for parodic forms. It is prefigured by a characteristic pattern of circumvention in some of the classic works of formal parody, in which the thread of bookish mockery is diverted to urgent and unbookish concerns, the nature of the human animal rather than travel books in *Gulliver's Travels*, for example, or the condition of Ireland rather than economic tracts in *A Modest Proposal*.

In the case of mock-heroic, which often in this period acted as a conduit for frustrated epic aspirations, the more likely scenario is a nostalgia for the primary form rather than a relegation of it, and the characteristic impulse is not to circumvent but to transcend the parody. The culminating effort is the *Dunciad*'s massive bid for epic status, in the teeth not only of all the expected ironic mimicries but also of its deep suppression of the epic's central subject matter of war, exceeding all Milton's anti-war motions in *Paradise Lost* in a simple breathtaking evasion or denial. It is an act of comprehensive self-division, suggesting not only split purposes but eating one's cake and having it too. And it is compounded by a host of secondary contending energies which include the generic sidetracking into mock-scholarship and mock-journalism; the vitality of powerful strands in the poem (including parts of the portrayal of Cibber, or the behaviour of the chattering dunces in Book II), which exist not as anti- or mock-heroic but outside a frame of heroic reference altogether; and the extraordinary atmosphere of unstable circularity that dominates and irradiates almost all major features of the poem.

In this is included the vast theme of uncreation, of a return to the void, of uncreating words, as it includes the issue (which never really arises in the *Dispensary* or in the *Rape of the Lock* or *Le Lutrin*) of full-scale primary epic pretension within a mock-epic form. It is insufficient to describe this in terms of contending opposites or the resolution or tension of contraries, and what I am describing is a vast wheeling indeterminacy in which all alternative possibilities are generously and perversely present much of the time. They include those primary grandeurs whose alleged disappearance is implicit in the mock-form and explicit in the poem's formal narrative. They also reveal in the perverse and the polluted, the ugly and the idiotic, qualities of surreal splendour which are not only appealing to later tastes, schooled in Modernist or Postmodern subversions or indecorums, but contain attractions to which we sometimes know Pope himself to have been responsive: the sickly feverish splendours of the 'Isles of fragrance, lilly-silver'd vales' (IV. 303), for example, part of his favourite passage in Book IV, or the couplet about barbaric invasions, 'Lo! where Maeotis sleeps, and hardly flows / The freezing Tanais thro' a waste of snows' (III. 87–8), which Johnson said Pope 'declared his own ear to be most gratified' by, in all his works, though Johnson added that *he* couldn't discover 'the reason of this preference'.[71]

These things are vivid to all good modern critics. When Maynard Mack remarks on 'the lovely movement and suggestion' of the line 'And the fresh vomit run for ever green' (II. 156), it comes home to us that there is no intelligent way of reading the line which would tell us that the 'movement and suggestion' are neutralised by the word 'vomit', as distinct from, as Mack so studiedly puts it, 'stained'.[72] The famous paragraph in Book I, which closes with the couplet about fragrant chaplets in December, and heavy harvests nodding beneath the snow (I. 77–8), is an anthology of poetic offences every bit as specifically pilloried in the *Art of Sinking in Poetry* as any Chattertonian non-language, and the notes to the passage do their relentless best to crush them under the weight of a captious derision, while readers go on responding stubbornly to what Howard Erskine-Hill has described as 'the unnatural . . . becom[ing] the beautiful' and A. D. Nuttall 'an explosion, not of absurdity, but of wild, lyric joy'.[73]

What, to ask one of the smaller, less obvious questions, do we then make of the notes, which tell us to dislike what no reader will? 'In the lower Ægypt Rain is of no use, the overflowing of the Nile being sufficient to impregnate the soil. — These six verses represent the Inconsistencies in the Descriptions of poets, who keep together all glittering and gawdy images, though incompatible in one season, or in one scene'. The note is by Scriblerus and goes on to refer to *Guardian*, No. 40, and 'our Treatise of the *Bathos*'.[74] Is Scriblerus a modern hack

---

[71]*Dunciad*, pp. 372n, 156–7 nn.; Spence, *Observations*, etc., No. 335, I. 150; Johnson, *Lives of the English Poets*, ed. G. Birkbeck Hill, 3 vols. (Oxford, 1905), III. 250.

[72]Maynard Mack, *Collected in Himself*, p. 51.

[73]Howard Erskine-Hill, *Pope: The Dunciad* (London, 1972), p. 31; A. D. Nuttall, 'Fishes in Trees', in *The Stoic in Love* (New York, 1989), p. 74.

[74]Pope's note to I. 73; see Pope's essay in *Guardian*, No. 40, 27 April 1713, ed. J. C. Stephens (Lexington, KY, 1982), p. 161; *Peri-Bathous: or, the Art of Sinking in Poetry*, in *Prose Works*, II, ed. Rosemary Cowler (Oxford (Blackwell), 1986), pp. 171ff., esp. ch. V, pp. 191ff. on the 'anti-natural'.

whose views we discount, or his author's punitive voice, or, like
Gulliver, sometimes one and sometimes the other, or is he all of the
above, impossible to disentangle, not, in a Swiftian way, in order to
induce panic from the reader's confusion, but to allow confusion
instead to open rather than close possibilities, and become an
enhancing or enabling thing, releasing the delights of things asserted
to be ugly, because for example the note might partly be read as
mocking itself and not the text it's annotating.

The winter blossoming of Pope's 'fragrant chaplets' is the kind of
thing which *Peri Bathous* describes as 'anti-natural' and may be compared with that other, almost exactly contemporary, winter blossoming,
to which Swift compares the state of Ireland in the *Short View* (1728),
falsely alleged to be flourishing: 'If we do flourish, it must be against
every Law of Nature and Reason; like the Thorn at *Glassenbury*,
that blossoms in the Midst of Winter'.[75] The passage has an eruptive,
melancholy splendour, but none of Nuttall's 'wild, lyric joy'. The pain
it expresses neutralises rather than releases a surrender to that splendour, and the idea of 'anti-nature' is one which is made difficult for
the reader to negotiate precisely because of its inappropriate festive
suggestion of fertility, sharpening the pain and constricting the mood,
rather than enlarging the scope of response. In Pope the perverse
becomes beautiful, in Swift the beautiful becomes perverse, and where
Pope's 'anti-nature' is released in play, Swift's turns in on itself. This
occurs here, unusually in Swift's writings, without the negative agency
of parodic derision, and does what Pope's negative parodic footnote
triumphantly fails to do.

---

[75] *Peri-Bathous*, V, p. 191–5; Swift, *A Short View of the State of Ireland*, in *Prose Writings*, XII.
10. See my *Henry Fielding and the Augustan Idea Under Stress* (London, 1972), pp. 50–1.

Proceedings of the British Academy, **91**, 111–134

From Text to Work:
The Presentation and Re-presentation of
Epistles to Several Persons

JULIAN FERRARO

1

IN WHAT FORM can the literary work of art be said to exist? This is a question that has often been posed before.[1] One theory of literary creation, which has perhaps received its most influential expression for modern readers in the work of the English Romantics, posits an ideal state for the literary work, in relation to which the text produced by the writer stands in a contingent relationship — as Coleridge put it in describing 'Kubla Khan' as the product of a drugged sleep in which 'all the images rose up before him as *things*, with a parallel production of the correspondent expressions'.[2] According to this paradigm, the text before the reader merely embodies the 'correspondent expressions' rather than the poem itself, which only exists in the imagination of the writer. In the terms proposed by the philosopher Charles Peirce, the text exists only as a type and any linguistic manifestation of the text is a token of that type.[3]

[1] See for example Rene Wellek, 'The Mode of Existence of a Literary Work of Art' in René Wellek and Austin Warren, *Theory of Literature*, 3rd edn. (London, 1963), F. W. Bateson, 'The New Bibliography and the New Criticism' in *Essays in Critical Dissent* (London: 1972), and Jim McLaverty, 'The Mode of Existence of Literary Works of Art: The Case of the *Dunciad Variorum*', *Studies in Bibliography*, xxxvii (1984), 82–105. For a philosophical examination of some of the problems associated with this question, see Richard Wollheim's *Art and Its Objects*, 2nd edn. (Cambridge, 1980), pp. 4–10 and 75–84.

[2] *The Poems of Coleridge*, ed. E. H. Coleridge (Oxford, 1912), p. 296.

[3] See Peirce, *Collected Papers*, ed. Charles Hawthorne and Paul Weiss, 8 vols. (Cambridge, Mass.: 1931–58), IV, paragraphs 537ff.

This conception of the mode of existence of literary works of art is comparable to the theoretical position that informs the work of textual critics in the tradition of W. W. Greg and Fredson Bowers. According to Bowers, the ultimate aim of the textual critic is to produce a text that will 'approximate as nearly as possible an inferential authorial fair copy, or other ultimately authoritative document.'[4] Thus the scholarly synthetic or eclectic text seeks to approximate to the ideal state of the work — one that is not necessarily represented in any of the historical documents, but one which accords with the author's 'final' or 'best' intentions: 'The aim of a critical edition should be to present the text, so far as the available evidence permits, in the form in which we may suppose that it would have stood in a fair copy, made by the author himself, of the work as he finally intended it'.[5] The platonic notion of text that underlies the practice of eclectic editing means that the establishment of a synthetic text in a critical edition is, paradoxically, an act of decontextualisation — variants included in the critical apparatus are seen in relation to this 'ideal' or 'preferred' text and are thus also stripped of their context. The problem with an eclectic text is that it assumes a teleological development towards whatever is chosen as the preferred text.

There is a sense in which these theoretical assumptions highlight a particular problem in considering questions about the identity and integrity of literary works. Common readers, and even professional critics, want to feel that they can talk in broad terms about the meaning or significance of a particular piece of literature, and that if there is disagreement about its meaning or significance then at least the object about which they are disagreeing is a stable one. This is, of course, a sense of security that has never been shared by textual critics. And yet, despite any acknowledgement of the complex issues raised by textual variation, literary critics are still, by and large, happy to talk of the *Epistle to Bathurst*, say, in general terms as though it were something the identity of which was somehow guaranteed — that its 'essence' (over the quality or meaning of which one might disagree) is somehow unaffected by choices that editors might have made between variant states in the 'corresponding expressions'.

This attitude often results in readers ignoring, or underestimating, the radical transformations that can take place as the work of art is

[4]Bowers, 'Textual Criticism', in James Thorpe ed. *The Aims and Methods of Scholarship in Modern Languages and Literatures*, 2nd edn. (New York, 1970), p. 33.
[5]W. W. Greg, *The Editorial Problem in Shakespeare*, 3rd edn. (Oxford, 1954), p. x.

constructed and reconstructed, presented and re-presented. Provided on the printed page with what purports to be a 'finished' text, the natural tendency of a reader in considering any variant states — if this is attempted at all — is to work backwards from the 'finished' state of the text: rather than prompting a re-interpretation of the text, the process of revision and re-presentation is itself interpreted in the light of a reading of the 'final' text, which becomes the point towards which the writer has been working all along. This approach is particularly unhelpful when it is applied to a writer for whom revision, occasionally radical revision, and reorganisation were processes ended only by death, and in whose work readings once rejected remain susceptible to reinstatement by the author in subsequent incarnations of the 'finished' text. Alexander Pope is the paradigm of such a writer.

Pope exercised an unprecedented level of control over the presentation of his work.[6] He was concerned with every element of the appearance of his poems in print, from the layout on the page and the typography to the choice of engravings and designs.[7] The result of this concern is that his texts are embodied in a physical form that might appropriately be described in terms of visual art. When dealing with the poems thus transmitted, however, it is important to recognise that there are two distinct impulses at work. Pope's concern for the book as object and his attitude to the text as field of meaning are, to a certain extent, in conflict. While the appearance of a poem on the page achieves a monumental quality, his commitment to revision leaves its text to some degree fluid.

Towards the end of his life he appears to have sanctioned an unusual procedure which of its nature places a question mark over the completeness and finality of any text chosen for publication. In the 1730s he arranged for Jonathan Richardson Jr. to collate the MSS of several poems together with the printed editions and record the variant readings.[8] A small selection of variants, all from printed texts,

[6]Pope's financial independence derived largely from his agreement with Lintot for the publication by subscription of the translation of the *Iliad*. For a full account of this venture, see Foxon, *Pope and the Early Eighteenth-Century Book Trade*, rev. and ed. James McLaverty (Oxford, 1991) pp. 51–63.

[7]Foxon provides a detailed account of Pope's relations with the book trade and his involvement with the process of production together with an extended discussion of the effects of his concern for the appearance of his text in print (*Pope and the Early Eighteenth-Century Book Trade*, esp. pp. 153–236).

[8]See *The Correspondence of Alexander Pope*, ed. George Sherburn, 5 vols. (Oxford, 1956), IV. 78 and 374, and Jonathan Richardson Jr., *Richardsoniana: Or, Occasional Reflections on the Moral Nature of Man* (London, 1776), p. 264.

was published with the notes to the 1735 *Works* (Vol. II), and in the 1736 *Works* (Vols. I and II) Pope included some variant readings rejected from his MSS. The Richardson collations most probably provided the material for the 'Variations' published by Warburton in the third and fourth volumes of the 1751 edition of the *Works*. The inclusion of 'a great number of fine verses taken from the Author's Manuscript-copies . . . communicated by him for this purpose to the Editor' seems calculated to secure this praise for Pope's judgement, as well as for the quality of his first thoughts.[9]

While it is true, as John Butt has said, that the publication of variant readings is part of a wish on Pope's part 'to present his poems as a modern classic should appear', a corollary effect of their inclusion is to extend the textual field in a way which invites a reading that goes beyond the limits of the version which is presented as the prime text.[10] Whereas the ultimate aim of the editor of a classical text is to recover the actual words used by the author, in the case of Pope's 1735 *Works* the reader is provided with alternatives, all of which derive their authority directly from the poet. The variants published in the scholarly apparatus of a work of classical literature are part of an attempt to create a stable and definitive text in the face of MS transmission at considerable remove from authorial authority. In the 1735 *Works* the author himself provides the variants and sanctions their publication. The reader must attach a different kind of significance to variant readings of this kind: paradoxically, the effect is to reverse the tendency toward stability and authority, with the result that the boundaries of the prime text become blurred.

2

The title of this paper makes reference to *Epistles to Several Persons*, a collection of poems published by Pope. However, it should be apparent that even at this level of description the designation 'Epistles to Several Persons' is a problematic one. To which poems and to what state of which poems does it refer? I want to develop three of the

[9]*The Works of Alexander Pope, Esq.*, ed. W. Warburton, 9 vols. (London, 1751), I, p. vi. Warburton's reference to a 'Manuscript-copy of the other *Ethic Epistles*' would seem more plausibly to refer to Richardson's transcriptions than to Pope's autograph drafts.
[10]Butt, 'Pope's Poetical Manuscripts', *Proceedings of the British Academy*, XL (1954), 23–40 (23).

issues that seem to me to be raised by this question. The first concerns the possible constitution of this group of poems and the ways in which variations in that constitution might affect a reading of any given poem or of the group as a whole. The second concerns textual variation within the constituent members of that fluctuating group; and the third concerns decisions about the distinction between manuscript and printed versions of the poems where manuscripts survive.

The composition of the 'Epistles to Several Persons' has a complicated history. There are essentially three different groupings made by Pope during his lifetime, according to which the collection consists of seven, eleven or four poems.[11] The first time any such collection appears is in the 1735 *Works*. In the first two editions (in folio and quarto), the *Essay on Man* — designated the first part of 'Ethic Epistles' — is followed by *To Cobham, To A Lady, To Bathurst* and *To Burlington*, together with 'To Mr. Addison', 'To Robert Earl of Oxford, and Earl Mortimer' and *To Dr. Arbuthnot* under the heading 'The Second Book'. However, in the quarto edition, the 'Directions to the Binder to place the Poems' indicate that the 'Essay on Man, or Ethic Epistles' is to be followed by 'Epistles to Several Persons', which suggests that a distinction is being drawn between the 'Ethic' epistles of the Essay and the seven 'familiar' epistles. In the volume itself, however, the 'Epistles to Several Persons' have no separate title-page, and are introduced instead with four arguments under the heading 'The Contents of the Second Book' — Epistle I 'Of the Knowledge and Characters of Men', Epistle II 'Of the Characters of Women', Epistle III 'Of the Use of Riches' and Epistle IV 'Of the Same' — which would suggest that these four poems are to be taken as a continuation of the 'Ethic Epistles' of the *Essay on Man*. Each of the poems starts on a fresh leaf and where there is space at the foot of a page on which a poem ends it is taken up by an engraving. However, on the page on which 'Epistle IV' ends the poem is followed immediately by 'Epistle V To Mr. Addison (Occasion'd by his Dialogues on Medals)', which is in turn followed, on the verso of its last page, by 'Epistle VI To Robert Earl of Oxford &c' and, on a fresh sheet, 'Epistle VII To Dr. Arbuthnot'. This arrangement sends out some strange signals in terms of the proper interrelationship of these groups of poems.

[11]For further discussion of some of the issues surrounding the constitution of the 'Epistles to Several Persons', see Donald W. Nichol, 'Pope's 1747 *Ethic Epistles* and the *Essay on Man* Frontispiece: An Abandoned "Opus Magnum"?' in Colin Nicholson ed. *Alexander Pope: Essays for the Tercentenary* (Aberdeen, 1988), pp. 222–35.

While the arrangement within the volume suggests that the second group of poems is almost a continuation of the *Essay on Man*, the directions to the binder suggest a formal separation between the two. While the 'Epistles to Several Persons' run in sequence from I to VII, the fact that the first four epistles are preceded by prose arguments — as with those of the *Essay on Man* — whereas the other three are not, suggests a distinction between these two groups, a distinction that is emphasised by the difference in titles: the first four emphasising the abstract arguments — 'Of the Knowledge and Characters of Men', 'Of the Characters of Women', and 'Of the Use of Riches' — the next three highlighting the addressee — 'To Mr. Addison', 'To Robert Earl of Oxford &c', and 'To Dr. Arbuthnot'. These anomalies suggest some hesitation about the way in which the poems are to be combined, a hesitation that seems to persist in subsequent editions.

In the 1735 octavo the title-page of the *Essay on Man* reads 'Ethic Epistles The First Book, To Henry St. John L. Bolingbroke, Written in the Year 1732'. At the end of the fourth epistle there is a note that reads 'End of the First Book'. This is followed by a title-page reading 'Ethic Epistles The Second Book', which is in turn followed by four arguments under the title 'The Contents'. Following *To Burlington* there is a further title-page reading 'Epistles, The Third Book. To Several Persons'. This third book consists of 'To Oxford', 'To James Craggs', 'To Mr. Addison', 'To Mr. Jervas', 'To Miss Blount', 'To the Same' and *To Arbuthnot*. This arrangement is maintained in the 1736 edition.

In the 1739 edition of the *Works* the *Essay on Man* is once again described as the first book of 'Ethic Epistles', while 'Epistles to Several Persons' now includes all eleven of the other poems taken together — a format that is retained in the 1740 and 1743 editions of the *Works* (Vol. II part I).

The title-page of the British Library copy of the suppressed 'death-bed edition' of 1744[12] contains 'An Essay on Man. Being the First Book of Ethic Epistles. To H. St. John L. Bolingbroke', followed by *To Cobham, To A Lady, To Bathurst* and *To Burlington* grouped under the heading 'Epistles To Several Persons', rather than 'The Second Book of Ethic Epistles' or some such title. However, an 'Advertisement' between the 'Argument' and the opening of *To Cobham* does outline the relationship of the *Essay on Man* to the 'Epistles

---

[12]BL C. 59. e. I. Used by Bateson as the copy-text for his Twickenham edition.

to Several Persons' within the framework of the abandoned 'Opus Magnum'.[13]

That Pope expected the grouping of his poems in these ways to affect the way in which they were read is clear from a letter to Swift of 16 February 1733: 'my works will in one respect be like the works of Nature, much more to be liked and understood when consider'd in the relation they bear with each other, than when ignorantly look'd upon one by one'.[14]

When the four Epistles addressed to Bathurst, Burlington, Cobham and 'a Lady' are grouped together with the *Essay on Man* what tends to be emphasised is the abstract philosophising in the poems, the way in which they advance the theory of the 'ruling passion' and the ways in which they develop and illustrate the ideas of the *Essay on Man*. That there was a period during which Pope planned to incorporate the four poems, reproduced as 'Epistles to Several Persons' in the Twickenham Edition, with the *Essay on Man* as part of an 'Opus Magnum' seems beyond doubt. That this was his 'first', 'final' or even 'best' intention is rather more contentious. There is a sense in which the relationship to the formal method of the *Essay* in which these four poems stand is as much parodic as complementary. The *Epistle to Bathurst* in particular seems to have been contrived to defy any easy accommodation within a moral scheme. Rather than providing a firm foundation for its maxims and aphorisms, Pope's re-workings of that poem seem directed towards giving full play to ironies and ambivalences. The four 'Epistles', above all else, embody an engagement between the poet and an imagined interlocutor to whose interests he responds and with whose particular point of view he disputes and engages.

A reading of the 'Epistles to Several Persons' that includes the epistles *To Addison* and *To Harley* highlights the fact that, while these poems show Pope dramatising his relationship with figures with whom he shares friendship and admiration, these are not offered uncritically — the combination of the 'Epistle to Addison' with the Atticus portrait in the *Epistle to Arbuthnot* being a particularly telling instance of this. When the collection is expanded to include the 'Epistle to Craggs', 'To Jervas' and the two epistles to the Misses Blount it can be seen to encapsulate a series of engagements of wildly differing

[13]For discussion of Pope's planned 'Opus Magnum', see Miriam Leranbaum, *Alexander Pope's 'Opus Magnum'* (Oxford, 1977). Leranbaum reproduces and discusses the 'Advertisement' (pp. 177–181).

[14]Pope, *Correspondence* III. 348.

resonance, from the personal counsel of the 'Epistle to Miss Blount with the works of Voiture' to the more politically resonant epistles to Harley and Craggs, the personal, artistic reminiscence of the 'Epistle to Jervas', and the politically charged self-revelation of the *Epistle to Arbuthnot*.

The line, 'And of myself too something must I say?' — which opens the MS poem out of which grew the *Epistle to Arbuthnot*[15] — finds an echo in the description that Pope gives of *To Arbuthnot* in 'The Author to the Reader' at the beginning of *Works* (Vol. II): ' . . . all I have to say of *Myself* will be found in my last Epistle'. Here Pope openly acknowledges the development that has taken place in the epistles that follow the *Essay on Man* — that he himself has taken centre stage. Much more than embodying philosophical precepts, aphorisms or maxims, the 'Epistles to Several Persons' — above all when read as a group of seven or eleven poems — embody the articulation of a particular poetic voice engaging with an audience of intimates and through that with the 'World beside'.

Pressure of space precludes a more detailed examination of the hermeneutic implications of editorial decisions about the composition of the 'Epistles to Several Persons', but it is worth briefly drawing attention to the anomalous practice of the Twickenham Edition in its re-presentation of these poems. Despite lamenting the effect of Warburton's title, 'Moral Essays' (which puts 'all the emphasis on the didactic elements in the poems', suggesting that they constituted 'another *Essay on Man*' and calling attention 'to all that is weakest and most pretentious in the four Epistles', while ignoring altogether 'the social satire that is their real *raison d'être*'), the Twickenham editors follow the precedent of the 'death-bed' edition by grouping the four poems with the *Essay on Man* (in parts i and ii of Vol. III) and separating them from the other epistles which are, with the exception of *To Arbuthnot*, consigned to the volume of 'Minor Poems'.[16] And yet, in deciding on the text of the four poems to reproduce, revisions of the structure of the *Epistle to Cobham* and *To Bathurst* that Pope made specifically for the 'death-bed' edition are rejected because Warburton's malign influence was deemed responsible. However, his

---

[15]Reproduced by Maynard Mack, *The Last and Greatest Art Some Unpublished Poetical Manuscripts of Alexander Pope* (Newark, 1984), pp. 419–54.

[16]*The Twickenham Edition of the Poems of Alexander Pope* (henceforth T. E.), ed. John Butt *et al.*, 11 vols. (London and New Haven, 1939–69); Vol. III. ii, ed. F. W. Bateson, 2nd edn. 1961, p. xxxvii.

influence can equally well be observed in Pope's decision to isolate the four poems in this way in the first place. As Bateson himself suggests, 'the fact is a striking example of the way the *Essay on Man* has cast its distracting shadow over what are essentially four Horatian Satires'.[17]

3

In order to address the second of my three issues — the status and effect of textual variation within the 'Epistles' — I want to begin by looking at the revisions that Pope made to the structure of the poem originally published under the half-title 'Of Taste, An Epistle to the Right Honourable Richard Earl of Burlington' and subsequently included in the 1735 *Works* under the title, 'Of the Use of Riches . . .'.[18] An examination of some of the variations between the MS version of the poem, the separately published versions, and those included in the various 'Epistles to Several Persons' highlights the difficulty of treating the poem as though it maintains a stable field of meaning.[19]

There is a sense in which the versions of the *Epistle* that Pope sent to Burlington in MS, the versions published in 1731 and the versions published in 1735 should be regarded as distinct poems — with a slightly different resonance, scope and meaning — rather than as versions of the same poem, each one supplanted by subsequent revisions in a process of correction.[20]

Howard Weinbrot's position is fairly representative of traditional readings of the *Epistle to Burlington*. While he concedes that Pope seems resigned to Burlington's Palladian example being 'distorted and degraded', he accepts as a fact that, for Pope, 'Burlington himself

---

[17]T. E. III. ii. xx.

[18]This change in title reflects a shift in the emphasis of the poem from 'taste' to 'use'.

[19]For a more detailed examination of the revisions that Pope made to this poem, in manuscript and print, see my article, 'From Taste to Use: Pope's *Epistle to Burlington*', the *British Journal for Eighteenth-Century Studies*, 19, 2 (1996), 141–159. I am grateful to the editor for permission to reproduce some of this material.

[20]Cf G. Thomas Tanselle: 'There are in general two kinds of situations in which . . . "final intentions" will prove unsatisfactory: (1) when the nature or extent of the revisions is such that the result seems, in effect, a new work, rather than the "final version" of an old work; and (2) when the author allows several alternative readings to stand in his manuscript or vacillates among them in successive editions. In the first case, one may say that there is more than one "final" intention; in the second, that there is no final intention at all'. *Textual Criticism and Scholarly Editing*, (Charlottesville and London, 1990), pp. 51–52.

remains unsullied'.[21] The tendency to take at face value the role of positive *exempla* has also characterised the work of critics presenting essentially hostile 'demystifications' of Pope's poetry. In her account of the poem, Laura Brown states that 'Pope's friend Burlington is presented as the ideal capitalist landowner' whose activities are 'indistinguishable from a corollary contribution to imperialist expansion'.[22]

The text of the poem that these scholars have made the focus of their attention is that printed in the Twickenham Edition, an eclectic text based on the 'death-bed' edition of 1744.[23] Any presentation of a 'final' text of *To Burlington*, even one that includes variant readings, tends to mask the radical nature of the changes to its structure that Pope made after its initial publication. As it evolves through the various editions, and as the force of the sequence of verse paragraphs is enhanced by internal revision, Pope engineers significant shifts in ironic emphasis. In the course of this process, the figure of Burlington acquires an increasingly equivocal position.

The surviving autograph of the poem is a fair copy, bearing the title 'Of Taste: An Epistle to The Earl of Burlington'.[24] The MS consists of a single folio sheet, containing sixty-four lines, together with a further twelve lines of marginal and interlinear additions. The text breaks off immediately before the description of Sabinus in his 'young Woods', which precedes the celebrated portrait of Timon's villa in the first edition.[25] The MS was obviously the product of considerable calligraphic labour — the title imitates typeface, as does the initial letter of the text, and the lines of verse are numbered — which suggests that the poem had reached a provisional state of completion, and that Pope had prepared the MS for circulation amongst friends. The Twickenham editors describe the MS as 'an early ... draft'; however, when Pope's revisions to the fair copy are taken into account, the MS can be seen

[21]Weinbrot, *Alexander Pope and the Traditions of Formal Verse Satire* (Princeton, 1982), p. 184. Other discussions of the poem marked by this tendency include Reuben Brower, *The Poetry of Allusion* (Oxford, 1959), pp. 243–249; Howard Erskine-Hill, *The Social Milieu of Alexander Pope* (New Haven, 1975), pp. 319–25.
[22]Brown, *Alexander Pope* (Oxford, 1985), p. 118.
[23]See the textual note in T. E. III. ii. 128–130.
[24]The MS is preserved in the Pierpont Morgan Library (MA 352, fol. 1). A facsimile and transcript have been published by Mack (*Last and Greatest Art*, pp. 156–164).
[25]The MS concludes with the catchword 'Thro', indicating that it was to have continued with what becomes line 89 of the first edition. There is a cue for the interpolation of this paragraph at an earlier point in the MS and Pope has added, and cancelled, a new catchword, 'At', which suggests that the description of Timon's villa was intended, at least at one time, to follow on immediately at this point.

to embody the text of the first half of the poem in a form fairly close to that of the first edition.[26] In addition to the autograph draft, a contemporary transcript of a complete version of the poem survives at Chatsworth among the Devonshire archives.[27]

In the MS versions and the separately published editions of the poem, its pivotal point is a more or less straightforward opposition between false 'Taste' — represented by Timon — and true 'Taste', represented by Burlington. In the revised structure that makes its first appearance in the 1735 *Works*, emphasis is much more firmly placed on the idea of 'Use', in the light of which the significance of Burlington's role as an example of true 'Taste' becomes more problematic.

When the order of verse paragraphs was revised for the 1735 *Works*, the section beginning 'You show us, *Rome* was glorious, not profuse' — which had formed part of the conclusion (following line 180) in the first edition of the poem — was moved to follow the 'standing sermon' of lines 21–22. After asserting that Burlington has demonstrated the possibility of uniting pomp and 'use', Pope immediately goes on to explain ways in which this precept will be misapplied. While he obviously makes a distinction between Burlington and the 'coxcomb' of line 22, the new structure allows only two lines of wholehearted commendation for Burlington before Pope highlights the fact that, in the world posited by the satirist, Burlington's example is destined to be travestied. His just and noble 'rules' will be barely distinguishable from the 'rules' of art by which the wealthy dunces will be pleased to starve.

In the text of the 1735 *Works*, the first line of this paragraph — which had read 'Just as they are, yet shall your noble Rules' in both the Chatsworth transcript and the first edition — is altered so that the opening couplet reads:

> Yet shall (my Lord) your just, your noble Rules
> Fill half the land with Imitating Fools:

Bateson cites the criticism, expressed in *A Miscellany of Taste*, that the sense of the first version is ambiguous.[28] In addition to making the meaning of 'just' clearer, the revised line throws greater weight on the qualification 'yet', by placing it at the beginning of the line.

---

[26] T. E. III. ii. xxvi, n 3.

[27] Devonshire MSS (1st series, 143.74 (2)). Mack also reproduces the text of the transcript (*Last and Greatest Art*, pp. 165–6). While Mack (p. 158) suggests that this version represents an intermediate stage between the autograph and the first edition, the autograph also seems to have undergone a further stage of revision that postdates the transcript.

[28] T. E. III. ii. 139 n.

The introduction of the parenthetical address '(my Lord)' disrupts the
flowing rhythm of the line, an effect that is reinforced by the repetition
of 'your' and by the painstaking hiatus between 'your just' and 'your
noble' which, leading as it does into the swifter rhythm of the following
line, makes the rhyme of 'rules' and 'fools' more telling.[29] The
revised line has an altogether different tone from the original version.
In the first edition, in which this passage had followed the description
of Timon, the tone suggests commiseration on the part of the poet for
the way his addressee's 'rules' will be misapplied; in the version in
Works (Vol. II), Burlington is much more clearly being warned of the
potentially disastrous outcome of his dissemination of the Palladian
ideal.

The revisions to the structure of the poem create a sequence in
which Pope first emphasises the role of a 'Guide' in leading wealthy
fools astray, then identifies Burlington himself as a contrasting
example — 'You show us' — and then goes on immediately to describe
the ways in which this example will inevitably, if inadvertently, result
in monstrosities such as 'some patch'd dog-hole ek'd with ends of wall'.
The fact that in the revised structure the paragraph beginning 'Oft
have you hinted . . .' now follows this dismal catalogue of misapplied
taste emphasises the impotence evoked by its opening phrase. The
word 'hinted' contrasts ironically with the extreme image of starving
'by rules of art' with which the repositioned passage ends.

When, in the first edition, this passage followed the description of
Timon, it provided a clearer contrast to it. In 1735, by its being moved
to follow the lines of generalised mockery and to introduce a series of
paragraphs outlining a method for attaining good taste, emphasis is
placed in a different way on the various elements of the passage. The
revised structure means that Villario, Sabinus and Timon exemplify the
fact that Burlington's precepts will be misconstrued. In the teleology of
the first edition, Timon and the other misguided 'Imitating Fools' had
already perpetrated their acts of tastelessness before specific mention
of Burlington's Palladian example had been made. The new structure
points out the folly of Timon and the others more clearly as a misinter-

---

[29]The repositioning of this passage sees Burlington's 'noble rules' juxtaposed with the earlier
couplet in which Pope makes a telling pun on the word 'Rule'. Ripley's 'Rule' — which will
be used as a rod to beat the 'wealthy fool' — appears in this context to suggest not only a
carpenter's implement but also a precept. In the course of the evolution of the poem, the
first gesture towards Burlington is altered from a direct address in the opening line of the MS,
to an aside in the eleventh line of the first edition, to an aside in the third paragraph of the
text printed in *Works* (Vol. II).

pretation of the same sort of 'rules' of taste that Burlington is propagating, whereas in the original order of verse paragraphs there was a much surer connection between Burlington's elucidation of the pomp and glory of Rome and the 'Imperial' conclusion of the poem.

The first edition follows the description of Sabinus with the passage in which 'laughing Ceres' re-assumes the land: it also immediately follows the 'Timon' episode with the couplet,

> In you, my *Lord*, Taste sanctifies Expence,
> For Splendor borrows all her Rays from Sense.

which continues with the section 'You show us, Rome was glorious, not profuse', that we have already seen repositioned towards the beginning of the poem in the 1735 *Works*. Thus, in the first edition Burlington's Palladian example is directly contrasted with the 'huge heaps of littleness' displayed at Timon's villa. The twofold repetition of 'you' asserts the importance of Burlington's role in a logical connection of 'Taste' and 'use'. In *his* person '*Taste* sanctifies Expence' and *he* shows that 'pompous Buildings once were things of *use*'.[30] The repositioning of the 'Ceres' passage creates a significant disjunction within the teleology of the poem between Timon's wasteful magnificence and its counteraction by Burlington's Palladian ideal.

In the revised order of verse paragraphs in the 1735 *Works*, Timon's grand folly — on which Pope has expended almost seventy lines of ridicule — does at least have one saving grace:

> Yet hence the *Poor* are cloath'd, the *Hungry* fed
> Health to himself, and to his Infants bread
> The Lab'rer bears: What his hard Heart denies,
> His charitable Vanity supplies.

These lines, which make up the first section of the 'Ceres' passage, represent the sole intrusion of the poor and hungry into the world created by the poet, one in which the only thing that arouses his overt indignation is the 'lavish cost, and little skill' of his tasteless host. The repositioning of these lines at the pivotal point of the poem ensures that they serve not merely as a coda to the abuses of wealth and the indulgence of false 'Taste', but also provide, ironically, an introduction to the theme of successful agrarian capitalism that leads the poem to its triumphant conclusion. As F. R. Leavis put it, 'Art and Nature,

[30]The emphases are mine.

Beauty and Use, Industry and Decorum, should be reconciled, and humane culture, even in its most refined forms, be kept appropriately aware of its derivation from and dependence on the culture of the soil'.[31] However, by advertising the Mandevillian irony of the fact that 'a bad Taste employs more hands and diffuses Expence more than a good one', Pope disturbs any straightforward reconciliation between 'Taste' and 'use' that the poem might be supposed to effect.[32]

When, in the MSS and the first three editions of the poem, this passage preceded the description of Timon's Villa, the scathing reference to 'Charitable Vanity' is pointed not at a third person but a second-person subject:

> ... What thy hard Heart denies
> Thy Charitable Vanity supplies.

What, in the order of paragraphs established in 1735, refers back to Timon must refer in the earlier versions of the poem to Burlington himself. Pope makes the point 'that all those who lavish money on building, including Burlington, must have hard hearts, for they could give to the poor and unemployed directly'.[33]

It has been pointed out that, in its new position, the 'Ceres' passage halts the confident momentum of the condemnation of Timon,[34] but it is its separation of the positive example of Burlington from the process of condemnation that is of greater importance. The passage can be seen to provide what amounts to an alternative eight-line version of the whole poem in which the first four lines present the unhappy compromise of things as they are, a perspective that embraces the poor as well as the wealthy and privileged, while the second four evoke the possibility of a future georgic Golden Age: in the face of this, while the efforts of Burlington and other would-be arbiters of 'Taste' are

---

[31]Leavis, *Revaluation* (London, 1935), p. 80.

[32]Pope's note in the octavo *Works* (Vol. II). For a different account of the effect of this passage within the structure of the poem, see Hibbard, 'The Country House Poem of the Seventeenth Century', *Journal of the Warburg and Courtauld Institutes*, 19 (1956), 159–174.

[33]Erskine-Hill, 'Avowed Friend and Patron', in Toby Barnard and Jane Clark, eds. *Lord Burlington: Architecture, Art and Life* (London, 1995), pp. 217–229 (p. 225). In the 'Master Key to Popery' Pope shows himself aware of the possibility, however misguided he might want to claim it to be, of applying the lines to Burlington himself. T. E. III. ii. (pp. 179–180).

[34]Erskine-Hill makes this point, *The Social Milieu*, pp. 300–301.

lauded, they are deprived of the centrality that they enjoyed in the earlier versions.[35]

In the first edition, Burlington's role in the conclusion of the poem is established by the lines 'In you, my *Lord*, Taste sanctifies Expence' and 'You show us, *Rome* was glorious, not profuse'. In the text presented in the 1735 *Works* both of these lines are removed, in one way or another, from the final section of the poem. The revision that Pope makes of the couplet,

> In you, my *Lord*, Taste sanctifies Expence,
> For Splendor borrows all her Rays from Sense.

so that the specific mention of Burlington and, more importantly, 'Taste' is removed — ''Tis *Use* alone that sanctifies Expence' — is one of the most important in terms of its effect both on the status of Burlington as *exemplum* within the poem, and on the relationship of 'Taste' to 'Sense' and 'Use'.

In a letter to Tonson, dated 7 June 1732, Pope emphasises the importance, above all else, of the positioning of the portrait of the Man of Ross within the *Epistle to Bathurst*:

> To send you any of the particular verses will be much to the prejudice of the whole; which if it has any beauty, derives it from the manner in which it is *placed*, and the *contrast* (as the painters call it) in which it stands, with the pompous figures of famous, or rich, or high-born men.[36]

It is hard to see how the figure of Burlington, who shows us 'pompous buildings once were things of Use' can escape a painterly contrast with the Man of Ross when the poem addressed to him follows the *Epistle to Bathurst* in the 1735 *Works*.[37]

---

[35]The *Argument*, added to the poem in 1735, contains the rather dismissive phrase 'even in works of mere Luxury and Elegance', T. E. III. ii. 131. Even if the suggestion of the Twickenham editors that the *Argument* was contributed by Jonathan Richardson Jr. is true, it must still have received Pope's sanction, because in one form or another it makes up part of the apparatus of the *Epistle* from 1735, onwards.

[36]Pope, *Correspondence*, III. 290.

[37]In her discussion of Pope's projected 'Opus Magnum', Leranbaum examines the changes that Pope made in the epistle in the context of its accommodation within this larger scheme, particularly in relation to the *Epistle to Bathurst*. Her concern to emphasise the importance to Pope of his 'ethic scheme' leads her to underestimate the radical nature of his revisions: 'the state of the poem as first published was from the beginning so apposite to the scheme that substantial recasting proved to be unnecessary' (*Alexander Pope's 'Opus Magnum'* p. 109).

4

As well as major re-casting, the constituent members of the 'Epistles to Several Persons' also undergo less dramatic, but nonetheless significant revision. The section of the *Epistle to Bathurst* in which Pope describes the effects on society of paper-credit is one which evolves significantly as he revises the poem for the various editions of the second volume of the *Works*. The revision of the couplet in which the poet addresses 'Blest Paper-credit' can be seen to reflect an increasingly gloomy attitude to the contemporary economic situation. What starts out in the first edition as an imagined eventuality becomes a description of the current state of affairs. The text of the first edition preserves one of the rejected revisions from the later of the two extant drafts:[38]

> Blest Paper-credit! that advanc'd so high,
> Shall lend Corruption higher wings to fly!

Here paper-credit will facilitate corruption in the future but the syntax makes the tense of 'that advanc'd so high' ambiguous. In the text of the 1735 *Works* this ambiguity is removed when Pope reverts to the original reading from the first extant draft in revising the second line, which becomes 'Now lends Corruption lighter wings to fly!'. In the 1744 text the qualification 'advanc'd so high' is removed. It is no longer paper-credit taken to extremes but paper-credit *per se* that contributes to corruption, a shift reflected in the removal of 'now' from the second line. Thus the revised couplet embraces the concept of paper-credit in a wholly ironic way, directed explicitly at the current state of affairs:

> Blest Paper-credit! last and best supply!
> That lends Corruption lighter wings to fly![39]

The changes to this couplet are difficult to accommodate within a

[38]The extensive autograph material relating to the *Epistle to Bathurst* is preserved in the Huntington Library (MSS HM6007 and HM6008). Facsimiles of the MSS together with transcriptions have been published by Earl Wasserman, *Pope's Epistle to Bathurst: A Critical Reading with an Edition of the Manuscripts*, (Baltimore, 1960). Two more or less full drafts survive together with two sheets of a third MS containing basically the description of the Man of Ross and the lines in which Pope directly addresses Bathurst, as well as all but the last six lines of the portrait of Sir Balaam. For a detailed discussion of the evolution of the poem, see Ferraro, "Rising into Light". The Evolution of Pope's Poems in Manuscript and Print' (unpublished PhD dissertation, Cambridge University, 1993), pp. 55–106.
[39]This image of paper-credit ironically echoes Proverbs 23.5: 'Wilt thou set thine eyes upon that which is not? for riches certainly make themselves wings; they fly away as an eagle toward heaven'.

model of textual revision that seeks to establish a text that represents a set of 'final intentions'. The changes that Pope makes are important as *changes* — the fact that the poet has felt it necessary to alter his text is itself a further indictment of the society that he criticises. The act of revision gives the poem a further dimension: it dramatises the relationship between 'word' and 'world', as the text can be seen responding to changes in the society with which it interacts.

A further aspect of the textual evolution of Pope's poems, his habit of retaining rejected MS readings for possible future revision, is also demonstrated by the section of the poem that follows the lines on paper-credit. Pope often returned to his original drafts when revising printed texts for new editions, and in the lines below he must have worked between both of the MS drafts of *To Bathurst*. The first draft originally continues with the following couplet:

> Pregnant with thousands, flits the scrap unseen
> And silent, sells a King, or buys a Queen.

In the margin these lines are marked for omission, presumably because, even though no king or queen is specified, they are politically dangerous. In the initial draft in the second MS the verse paragraph concludes with the couplet on paper-credit. Here, Pope marks these lines with a '1' and beside them he interpolates the following couplet, marked '2':

> Possest of both, how easy hardest things!
> They pocket States, they fetch or carry Kings,

The syntax of this couplet creates an ambiguity in the subject of the second line. The lines might suggest a passive role for, presumably, the 'dropping Guinea' of line 66 and paper-credit, which together enable a nameless 'They' to control politics at the highest level.[40] In the second draft the first line is revised to make the guineas and paper-credit clearly the subject rather than the object — 'When both unite, how easy hardest things!'. In the first edition these lines become

> Gold, imp'd with this, may compass hardest things,
> May pocket States, or fetch or carry Kings.

Pope has replaced the nebulous 'they' with his original villain. It is not

---

[40]Pope's note to this couplet, in the second octavo edition of *Works* (Vol. II) seems to strike a wistfully ironic note: 'In our author's time, many Princes had been sent about the world, and great changes of Kings projected in Europe. . . . France had set up a King of England, who was sent to Scotland, and back again'.

just the newfangled paper-credit and the corruption it facilitates that 'may' destroy established hierarchies, but the perennial evil, 'Gold'.

In the text of the 1735 *Works*, the second line of the couplet is revised in keeping with the second line of the preceding couplet, 'may' being replaced by 'can'; what is described is no longer a potential but a proven ability. In the 1744 'death-bed' edition, the lines are revised once more. Pope now addresses the lines directly to 'Blest Paper-credit' and reinforces the sense of immediacy by emphasising the power of the winged monster with a threefold repetition of the word 'can':

> Gold, imp'd by thee, can compass hardest things,
> Can pocket States, can fetch and carry Kings;

This revision re-establishes paper-credit as an agent rather than an object, giving it an identity that the poet addresses, as it were, face to face.

The evocation of 'paper-credit' as something directly addressed by the poet serves to create a moment of actual engagement — the satirist boldly confronting a virtual personification of the economic system whose vices he denounces, a physical realisation of paper-credit which Pope continues to develop in revisions to the imagery in the lines that follow. In the second draft the following couplet is interpolated to follow the first mention of paper-credit:

> Whose Leaves like Sybils, pregnant with our fates
> Bears Fates of Men and Empires to or fro.[41]

In the margin the couplet is re-ordered to follow that beginning 'Gold imp'd wth this', and between these two couplets Pope interpolates a third expounding the political significance of paper-credit:

> A single Leaf shall waft an Army o'er
> Or send a Senate to some distant shore.[42]

In the text printed in the 1735 *Works* the politically dangerous couplet, marked for omission in the first MS draft, is finally reintroduced to conclude the expanded description:

[41]These lines are in turn revised to read:
> A Leaf like Sybils, as the wind shall blow
> Scatters our Fates & Fortunes to and fro.

[42]The MS has an interesting cancelled alternative to 'a Senate' — 'hot Patriots' — which adds a further dimension to Pope's sense of the possibilities opened up by paper-credit.

> Pregnant with thousands flits the scrap unseen,
> And silent sells a King, or buys a Queen.[43]

It is clear that Pope was wary of making direct references to the monarchy in the poem, only feeling comfortable about reincorporating these lines, with their allusion to Sir Robert Knight's gift to Queen Caroline, when *To Bathurst* was printed with the other 'Epistles to Several Persons'.[44] Perhaps he wished to exclude more seriously controversial elements from this poem at a time when the furore over the application of the character of Timon to Lord Chandos would have led to close scrutiny of the poem from hostile critics. Such a hypothesis is at least supported by Warburton's recollection: 'Mr. Pope used to tell me, that when he had anything better than ordinary to say, and yet too bold, he always reserved it for a second or third edition, and then nobody took any notice of it'.[45]

In the last lines of the poem Pope again suppresses controversial — possibly treasonable — lines until the poem is incorporated in the 1735 *Works*. MS 1 reads

> His Wife, Son & Daughter, Satan! are thy own;
> His Wealth, yet dearer, forfeit to the Crown;
> The Devil and the King divide the prize,
> And sad Sir Balaam curses God and dies.

The middle two lines are marked in the margin of MS 1 for deletion and the words 'the King' are erased almost completely. Pope supplies the alternative, 'prize', above 'own' in the first line, so as to leave the two remaining lines as a couplet. The second MS reproduces this left-over couplet, with no hint of the previous reading, and it is with this that the first and second editions of the poem and the first (folio) edition of the 1735 *Works* end. Pope is not confident enough to return to MS 1 and reinstate the deleted lines until the second (quarto) edition of the *Works*. He has already implicated 'GEORGE and LIBERTY' in the bankruptcy of Cotta's son in the first edition of the *Works*,

[43]Once again, this change suggests that Pope returned to MS 1 when revising the poem for inclusion in this volume, since the couplet does not appear in MS 2.

[44]Pope's letter to Swift of 29 November 1729 suggests that he gave credence to the report of a gift from the cashier of the South Sea Company to the Queen (*Correspondence*, III, 80).

[45]Warburton to Hurd, 22 September 1751, *Letters from a Late Eminent Prelate* (London, 1809), p. 86. Cited by Bateson, T. E. III. ii. 42.

but this alliance between the King and the Devil is much more forceful.[46]

The policy of suppressing material until later editions accords such interpolated lines a problematic status. They are clearly part of the poem, and yet so is the fact of their omission. In such cases it is not merely the nature of the differences between versions of a poem that are important, but also the very fact that there are such differences.

The text of the portrait of Sporus in the *Epistle to Arbuthnot* also undergoes telling revision for the 1735 *Works*. In the course of this, Pope's satire of Hervey becomes, if anything, more ruthless. The most obvious example of this thoroughly meditated exercise of his 'proper Pow'r to hurt' is his decision to use the name 'Sporus' at all. In the first edition Pope designates his victim as '*Paris*', despite the fact that the MS refers to him only as 'Sporus'. This name, referring to Nero's palace catamite and eunuch, is among the most gloriously rude elements in the portrait. Pope's decision to reinstate it in the text of the 1735 *Works* is typical of his tendency to reserve some of his most provocative gestures for this collection.

The same strategy can be seen in the characterisation of Sporus in the lines that follow:

> His Wit all See-saw between *that* and *this*,
> Now high, now low, now Master up, now Miss,
> And he himself one vile Antithesis.

These provocative lines do not appear in the first edition, but are reintroduced from the MS in the text of the 1735 *Works*. Indeed, it is in this edition that much of the emphasis on sexual ambiguity that characterises the second half of the portrait makes its first appearance in print. Pope replaces the line from the first edition — 'Did ever Smock-face act so vile a part' — with a version of another line retrieved from the MS — 'Amphibious Thing! that acting either part' — to expand upon the hermaphrodite suggestion. He also interpolates a further couplet, again largely retrieved from the MS:

> Fop at the Toilet, Flatt'rer at the Board,
> Now trips a Lady, and now struts a Lord.

Once again, Pope suppresses the most potentially controversial and

---

[46]The line, 'Twas George & Liberty that crowns thy Cup' appears in the first MS draft. In the first edition Pope includes a compromised version: '"Tis the dear Prince (Sir John) that crowns thy cup', while the text of *Works* (Vol. II) sees a return to the MS version, with the addition of bold capitals.

provocative aspects of his satire when it is first published and would receive the closest scrutiny. In his 'Note on the Text' in the Twickenham Edition, John Butt attributes these changes to the fact that the character of Sporus was 'the last part of the poem to receive final correction'.[47] However, the existence of these additional lines in the MS suggests that the subsequent alterations can be attributed more to Pope's desire to choose his moment to include material already in existence, than to a process of 'final correction.'[48]

The changes that Pope made in the text of various poems in the 1735 *Works* are evidence of the way that he manipulated the potential resonance of elements of those poems over time. For Pope the revision process is not simply one of 'correction', but evolution; it is not so much a process tending towards a 'final' point, as an evolving dialogue with the poet's literary and political environment, between 'word' and 'world'.

5

I want to turn now to the third issue I raised at the beginning of this paper — the distinction between manuscript and print. In his preface to the first volume of the Twickenham Edition, John Butt distinguished manuscript readings as of interest only to 'the student of poetical origins', and explained their exclusion from the critical apparatus of all the volumes of the edition, except that dealing with the minor poems, by describing manuscripts as part of 'the partially formed, prenatal history of the poems ... provisional only, liable to rejection, and frequently in fact rejected'.[49] However, I think that a good case can be made for considering the elaborate MSS on which Pope lavished such careful calligraphic labour — often imitating type — and which circulated amongst a wide group of friendly readers as belonging to a rather more postnatal stage in the history of the poems. The fact that such MSS of the *Essay on Man, To Burlington, To Bathurst, and To Arbuthnot* were subsequently so heavily revised as to become in effect drafts once more only emphasises the artificiality of the notion of 'finished' states of their texts.

[47]T. E. IV. 93.
[48]For a detailed examination of the evolution of the *Epistle to Arbuthnot*, see Ferraro, 'Rising into Light', pp. 143–215.
[49]T. E. I. vii.

In his study of the 'Epistle To Robert Earl of Oxford, and Earl Mortimer', Geoffrey Tillotson reproduced the text of the MS version that Pope sent to Harley in October 1721[50] and examined the way in which, when he came to publish the poem in 1722, the revisions that Pope made to punctuation and capitalisation affect the meaning and tone of the poem.[51] The verbal changes in the published form can be seen to diminish the emphasis on Pope's personal interest in Harley's fate that infuses the MS version. In the concluding lines of this Pope, through *his* 'Muse', adopts the stance of the bold friend to virtue that one can recognise from the satires of the 1730s:

> My Muse attending strews thy path with Bays,
> (A Virgin Muse, not prostitute to praise),
> She still with pleasure eyes the Evening Ray,
> The calmer Sunsett of thy Various Day;
> One truly Great thro' Fortune's Cloud can see,
> And dares to tell, that Mortimer is He.

In the printed version this personal muse is replaced by an impersonal one whom Pope mentions only once, earlier in the paragraph, so that the conclusion is governed by muted personal pronouns:

> Ev'n now she shades the Evening Walk with Bays,
> (No Hireling she, no Prostitute to Praise)
> Ev'n now, observant of the parting Ray,
> Eyes the calm Sun-sett of thy Various Day,
> Thro' Fortune's Cloud One truly Great can see,
> Nor fears to tell, that MORTIMER is He.

Gone too is the warmth of 'with pleasure eyes the Evening Ray'. The defiance of 'And dares to tell' is also replaced by the more muted negative construction, 'Nor fears to tell', which contributes to the emphasis in the final line on 'MORTIMER', at the expense of the muse. It has been pointed out that the revised version 'both conceals and reveals Pope' and that the image of ' "The Muse" . . . emphasizes his role as recording-dignifying poet and thus dignifies his attendance'.[52] The two states of the 'Epistle' reveal Pope taking up two distinct

[50]This MS is preserved at Longleat (Portland Papers vol. 13, fos. 5–6). A further autograph MS of the poem has recently been discovered and reproduced by Michael Brennan, 'Alexander Pope's 'Epistle to Robert Earl of Oxford, and Earl Mortimer'. A New Autograph Manuscript', *Library* 15, 3 (1993), 187–205. This MS is most probably the copy used by Lintot when the poem was first printed in 1722.
[51]Tillotson, 'Pope's "Epistle to Harley". An Introduction and Analysis', in J. L. Clifford and L. A. Landa eds. *Pope and His Contemporaries* (Oxford, 1949), pp. 58–77.
[52]Griffin, *Alexander Pope: The Poet in the Poems* (Princeton, 1978), p. 119.

positions, the bold personal engagement of the private MS version and the grander self-effacement of the printed version. The changes hardly constitute a revision of the 'final intentions' of the MS version and cannot really be said to supersede it; rather, they create a different impression for a different context.[53]

In his excellent essay, 'The Mode of Existence of Literary Works of Art: The Case of the *Dunciad Variorum*', Jim McLaverty, after suggesting that it is 'valid to regard works in the post-Gutenberg era as having inscriptions as their instances', emphasises the importance of the early eighteenth century as the period in which literature begins explicitly to engage with the consequences of its mode of existence in the age of mechanical reproduction. His suggestion that the physical form of the *Dunciad Variorum* as both a serious and a mock scholarly edition is an integral part of its significance as a work of literature is both a convincing and a resonant one.[54] Pope's attitude to revision throughout his later work reveals a comparable concern with the nature of the publishing process, which creates a dividing line between what become two distinct states of a modern text: the private manuscript and the public printed version. The writer can exercise absolute control over the text of a manuscript while it is upon his or her desk, but once it is in the public domain such control becomes problematic, a fact lamented in our own century by another formidable satirist, the Austrian writer Karl Kraus: 'I do not trust the printing press when I deliver my written words to it. How a dramatist can rely on the mouth of an actor!'[55] Pope seems to try to retain some of the flexibility of a working manuscript in the published versions of his poems, not only by including rejected variants along with his prime texts in a critical apparatus, but by returning to his MSS when revising those prime texts themselves in subsequent published versions.

In his recent book, *The Textual Condition*, Jerome McGann makes a distinction between the terms 'text', 'poem' and 'work'; defining the

---

[53]In making a case for the 'suppressed' lines with which Ruffhead claimed the MS of 'To a Young Lady, on leaving the Town after the Coronation' concluded, W. W. Robson seems to be arguing for a similar distinction between MS and printed versions of this poem. In a MS version, produced with a narrow circle of readers in mind, the 'Licentiousness' of the 'suppressed' lines can be read as a further stage in the series of contrasts that define the structure of the published poem (Robson, 'Text and Context: Pope's Coronation Epistle', in Colin Nicholson, ed. *Alexander Pope: Essays for the Tercentenary* (Aberdeen, 1988), pp. 195–205). See also T. E. VI. 232–233.

[54]McLaverty, 'The Mode of Existence of Literary Works of Art'.

[55]Kraus, *Half Truths and One-and-a-Half Truths: Selected Aphorisms*, ed. and trans. Harry Zohn (Manchester, 1986), p. 50.

'text' as 'the literary product conceived as a purely lexical event', the 'poem' as 'the locus of a specific process of production (or reproduction) and consumption' and the 'work' which 'comprehends the global set of all the texts and poems which have emerged in the literary production and reproduction processes'.[56] By circulating his poems in MS versions; by revising the published versions and including textual variants, both from MSS and previous editions, in his presentation and re-presentation of those poems; by reordering and reconstituting and retitling the larger units in which those poems are grouped, by annotating his poems (and even annotating his notes), Pope seems to have had a conception of the products of his literary endeavour as 'works' very much in this sense. As Maynard Mack has put it:

> Throughout his career, the typical Pope poem is a work-in-progress. States of provisional wholeness and balance occur along the way, some more inclusive than others but each conceivable as an end stage and the one at which the poet finally rests ... never declares itself to be definitive in any absolute sense. Subtractions and accretions remain imaginable.[57]

[56]McGann, *The Textual Condition* (Princeton, 1991), p. 31–2.
[57]Mack, *Last and Greatest Art*, pp. 16–17.

Proceedings of the British Academy, **91**, 135–145

The Ambitious Pursuit:
Pope, Gay and the Life of Writing

DAVID NOKES

> And the same road ambitiously pursue,
> Frequented by the Mantuan swain, and you.
>
> > (*Rural Sports*, 1713)

1

I SHOULD LIKE to begin with an anecdote.

> Mr. Pope brought some of *The What D'Ye Call It* in his own handwriting
> to Cibber ... When it was read to the players, Mr. Pope read it though Gay
> was by. Gay always used to read his own plays. Cibber after this, seeing a
> knife with the name of J. Gay upon it, [asked,] 'What, does Mr. Pope make
> knives, too?'[1]

In a story like this, Gay is the invisible author, a kind of human
pseudonym, not so much a ghost-writer as a ghost that is written.
Hostile witnesses, like Cibber, chose to regard him as little more than
a cipher, dismissing Gay's name on a title-page as a mere Popeian
subterfuge. Gay was frequently represented not merely as Pope's ally,
but as his alias, his alter ego, or in a favourite well-worn simile, as a
burly Ajax shielding a malevolent and diminutive Teucer. In his verse
farce *The Confederates* (1717), J. D. Breval (himself adopting the
pseudonym 'J. Gay') pictured Pope gloating secretly over his skill in
making Gay take responsibility for the 'failure' of their play *Three
Hours after Marriage*.

[1]Cibber, 1748; see Joseph Spence, *Observations, Anecdotes and Characters of Books and
Men*, ed. J. M. Osborn, 2 vols. (Oxford, 1966), I. 103. (Hereafter, Spence.)

> Safe from the cudgel, [I] stand secure of praise;
> Mine is the credit, be the danger Gay's.

With monotonous regularity Gay was, (and often still is) denied responsibility for his 'own' works. In 1730 the *Universal Spectator* assured its
readers that 'Mr. Gay was not the sole author of *The Beggar's Opera*'.
In 1733, the *Daily Courant* ascribed Gay's posthumous play *Achilles*
to an unlikely theatrical collaboration between Bolingbroke, Pulteney,
Sir William Wyndham, the Duke of Queensberry, Arbuthnot and Pope.
'Mr. Gay', it pronounced, 'could not deviate into so much dulness'. In
these, and many similar comments, the name 'John Gay', like the
names 'Isaac Bickerstaff' or 'Nestor Ironside', seems to identify not an
individual but a clubland institution.

    This tradition of condescending to Gay's own literary achievements
is obvious in Johnson's 'Life of Gay'.

> Gay was the general favourite of the whole association of wits; but they
> regarded him as a playfellow rather than a partner, and treated him with
> more fondness than respect.[2]

Undoubtedly Gay himself was largely responsible for perpetuating this
image of himself as a genial literary nonentity. Authorship implies
authority; yet Gay's most characteristic literary persona is self-effacing
and self-mocking. A man who gives his works titles like *Trivia* and *The
What D'Ye Call It*, seems determined to subvert his own claims to
serious literary recognition. Moreover, Gay was a natural collaborator,
and several of his most well-known works were both inspired in their
inception and polished before publication by his fellow-Scriblerians,
Pope, Arbuthnot and Swift. Where other authors seek to stamp the
mark of their individual identity indelibly on every page, Gay chose
the anonymity of a composite literary persona. Throughout his life he
played the role of unassuming friend, a man so instinctively deferential
in his tastes and opinions that he seemed almost to surrender his own
identity. 'What will become of me I know not', he once confessed to a
friend, 'for I have not and fear never shall have a will of my own.'[3]
More often than not it was Pope who supplied the literary will-power
that Gay lacked. 'Gay they would call one of my *élèves*', he liked to
boast, despite the fact that he was actually three years younger than
his 'pupil'.[4] Early on in their relationship Pope assumed the habit of

[2]Johnson, 'Gay' in *Lives of the English Poets*, 1779–81.
[3]*The Letters of John Gay*, ed. C. F. Burgess (Oxford, 1966), p. 47 (hereafter *Letters*).
[4]Spence, item 150, vol. I. p. 62.

deploying Gay as a willing literary lieutenant, happy to fight his battles (physical perhaps, as well as verbal) by proxy. In the dedication to *The Mohocks* Gay delivered a gratuitous snub to John Dennis for no other reason than that Pope was feuding with Dennis at the time. Three years later it was Ambrose Philips that Pope was feuding with, and Gay cheerfully chipped in with his mock-pastoral burlesque, *The Shepherd's Week*. 'It is to this management of Philips that the world owes Mr. Gay's pastorals', Pope declared, as if showing off his clever pupil's work.[5]

Gay's response to such charges was itself typically self-effacing. In the advertisement to *Trivia* (1716) he affected to regard them as a form of back-handed compliment. The critics, he suggested, had 'allowed me an honour hitherto only shown to better writers: that of denying me to be the author of my own works'. If anything, he seemed almost to invite, rather than discourage, such misattributions. In the Advertisement to *Three Hours after Marriage*, he boasted of 'the assistance I have received in this piece from two of my friends' (i.e. Pope and Arbuthnot); but when, in the event, the honour of having their names joined with Gay's turned to disgrace, he promptly volunteered for the scapegoat role. 'I will (if any shame there be)', he told Pope, 'take it all to myself.'[6] One wonders whether J. D. Breval ever caught sight of this letter.

Throughout their correspondence, there is ample evidence of Pope's fondness for acting as Gay's unofficial literary agent, arranging introductions, advising on contracts and generally supervising his more indolent friend's career. And, in death, as in life, it was Pope who took responsibility for safeguarding Gay's public reputation through a determined policy of careful censorship. 'Our poor friend's papers are partly in my hands', he told Swift, 'and for as much as is so, I will take care to suppress things unworthy of him.'[7] Swift happily concurred in this policy of suppression. 'I would be glad to see his valuable works printed by themselves', he wrote; 'those which ought not to be seen burned immediately.'[8] Actually this was merely an extension of a form of Popeian censorship which had operated for much of Gay's life. For

[5]*The Correspondence of Alexander Pope*, ed. George Sherburn, 5 vols. (Oxford, 1956), I. 229. (Hereafter, Pope, *Correspondence*.)
[6]*Letters*, p. 32.
[7]Pope, *Correspondence*, III. 365.
[8]*The Correspondence of Jonathan Swift*, ed. Harold Williams, 5 vols. (Oxford, 1963–6), IV. 133, 153. (Hereafter, Swift *Correspondence*.)

example, when *Three Hours after Marriage* fell victim to a concerted campaign of critical vilification. Gay was not so entirely contrite as his penitent letter to Pope suggests. His main emotion was fury, and he was determined to take his revenge. He quickly wrote a retaliatory lampoon which ridiculed celebrated passages from plays by Addison and Steele. What happened to this lampoon? Pope suppressed it.

> Had it been published — he told Spence in 1738 — it would have made Mr. Addison appear ridiculous, which he could bear as little as any man. I therefore prevailed on Gay not to print it, and have the manuscript now by me.[9]

Not only Gay's writings, but also the details of his early career were subject to the same rigorous policy of selective disclosure. In 1736 Pope did all he could to dissuade Savage from publishing information about Gay's early career. 'As to that of his being apprenticed to one Willet, etc', he protested, 'what are such things to the public? Authors are to be remembered by the works and merits, not accidents of their lives'.[10] Instead of inconvenient facts Pope preferred the sublimity of symbols; witness his epitaph for Gay's monument in Westminster Abbey.

> Of Manners gentle, of Affections mild;
> In Wit, a Man; Simplicity a Child: ...
> A safe Companion, and an easy Friend,
> Unblam'd through Life, lamented in thy End.

This depiction of Gay as a personification of childlike innocence has had a lasting influence on his posthumous reputation; less than fifty years ago James Sutherland could still describe him as an 'Augustan Peter Pan'.[11] And, in his *Epistle to Dr. Arbuthnot* (1735) Pope established another honorific myth, casting Gay in the role of neglected genius.

> Blest be the *Great*! for those they take away,
> And those they left me—for they left me GAY,
> Left me to see neglected Genius bloom,
> Neglected die! and tell it on his Tomb;
> Of all thy blameless Life the sole Return
> My Verse, and *QUEENSB'RY* weeping o'er thy Urn.

(ll. 255–260)

---

[9]Spence, item 238, vol. I, p. 104.
[10]Pope, *Correspondence*, IV. 38.
[11]James Sutherland, 'John Gay', in *Pope and His Contemporaries: Essays Presented to George Sherburn* (Oxford, 1949), pp. 201–14.

As Brean Hammond has written, Pope's verses 'create an impression of the great man perishing in Mozartian poverty.'[12] But the facts tell a rather different story. At his death Gay left an estate worth more than £6,000 (somewhere near £200,000 at current values); and, far from being buried in a pauper's grave, Gay's funeral at Westminster Abbey was something of a grand occasion. He died, as Arbuthnot noted 'as if he had been a peer of the realm'.[13]

Our view of John Gay's life and works has thus been enormously influenced by Pope's conscious endeavours to fashion them into a form of moral myth. Gay's own words were subtly reshaped to accord with Pope's perspective on the world; Gay's own epitaph for himself ('Life is a jest and all things shew it. I thought so once, but now I know it') displaced in favour of Pope's solemn sentimentality. But was Gay really as childlike as Pope liked to present him? Was their friendship as close as it appears? And how closely did Gay follow the example of his young literary mentor?

Unquestionably Gay was grateful for Pope's early literary assistance and advice. But there is ample evidence of Gay's frustration at being regarded as one of Pope's literary under-strappers, another Broome or Fenton; or an Ajax to Pope's Teucer. And, in his later years, it is clear there was something of a rift between them. This is what I want to explore.

2

As we know, *The Beggar's Opera* was a runaway, record-breaking success, performed for sixty-two nights in its first season, 1728. Swift's attitude to Gay's triumph was unambiguous. In letter after letter he enthused over the opera's success. 'Get me ... Polly's mezzo-tinto', he demanded. 'Lord, how the schoolboys at Westminster, and university lads adore you at this juncture. Have you made as many men laugh as ministers can make weep?'[14] By contrast, Pope's reactions were more guarded. There is a tinge of jealousy in the arch way he ironically compares the new self-importance of the 'courtier' Gay with the upstart dignity of a royal boatman.

---

[12]Brean Hammond: 'A Poet and a Painter, and Ten Pound: John Gay and Patronage' in (Peter Lewis and Nigel Wood eds.) *John Gay and the Scriblerians* (London 1988), p. 25.
[13]Swift, *Correspondence*, IV. 101.
[14]Ibid., III. 277.

> The only courtiers I know, or have the honour to call my friends, are John Gay and Mr. Bowry; the former is at present so employed in the elevated airs of his own opera, and the latter in the exaltation of his high dignity (that of her majesty's waterman) that I can scarce obtain a categorical answer from either to anything I say to 'em.[15]

Even in Dublin Swift could detect the signs of a growing estrangement between the two men. 'Mr. Pope talks of you as a perfect stranger,' he told Gay in early 1730.[16] Similar remarks can be found in many other letters. My own suspicion is that the Earl of Burlington was partly responsible for this estrangement. Throughout the early 1720s Burlington had been Gay's most generous patron, providing board and lodging for him, as well as William Kent and Handel at his mansion in Piccadilly. In a previously unpublished letter, sent to Burlington in October 1722, Gay gives expression to his intense gratitude for the Earl's favour.

> ... whatever I might say or do can never sufficiently acknowledge my obligations; I believe I need not say this for I hope your lordship knows me; if you do, you must know that I love you. ... If you knew how often I think upon your lordship you would now then think of me (*sic.*) I hope you will not forget me, for I know my heart so well that it will be always sensible of your favours, though I must own I love you more for what I see in yourself than for what you have done for me, wch is more than I can ever deserve.[17]

There is something rather doggy-like about such slavish expressions of love; particularly in their explicitness. When Gay says 'I believe I need not say this', he clearly says the opposite of what he means. He obviously *does* feel a need to convince Burlington of his affection in language which suggests not the informality of an intimate but the desperation of a hanger-on. However, by the time he came to write *The Beggar's Opera* Gay had achieved at least partial independence with his job as commissioner for lotteries and his lodgings in Whitehall. And among the many motives which drove him to write such an original and mischievous mock-opera, one at least was a desire to liberate himself from the abject feeling of dependence which he had experienced at Burlington House. Burlington was a founder director and chief shareholder in the Royal Academy of Music which sponsored and promoted Italian opera in London. And in parodying Italian

[15] Pope, *Correspondence*, II. 473.
[16] Swift, *Correspondence*, III. 380.
[17] Chatsworth MSS 173.0.

opera, Gay was ridiculing Burlington's pet project. As Pat Rogers and others have shown, many of Gay's friends were opera-fans, and most of them entered heartily into the joke of Gay's affectionate pastiches. But Burlington was not amused. As audiences dwindled and the Academy went into financial collapse, Burlington turned decisively against Gay. In January 1732 Gay began a letter to Swift thus:

> It is now past nine o clock. I deferred sitting down to write to you in expectation to have seen Mr. Pope who left me three hours ago to try to find Lord Burlington, within whose walls I have not been admitted this year & a half but for what reason I know not.[18]

This is more than a little disingenuous. The reason for Burlington's displeasure was not hard to guess. But Pope, as this letter indicates, was still *persona grata* with the Earl and keen not to jeopardise this relationship by seeming to be too closely associated with Gay. And Burlington was not the only person whose goodwill Pope was unwilling to forfeit on Gay's behalf. Despite his reputation as a high-profile satirist, Pope was currently, as he told Swift, being 'civilly treated by Sir R. Walpole'.[19] All such diplomatic relations were put at risk by Gay's sudden political notoriety. The banning of *Polly* in December 1728 and all the subsequent political fall-out, including the banishment from court of Gay's new patrons, the Duke and Duchess of Queensberry, for soliciting subscriptions for a printed version of the play, only increased Gay's dangerous reputation. Throughout February and March 1729 *Polly* enjoyed the status of a *cause célèbre* and quickly became a symbolic rallying point for Walpole's political opponents. The Duchess of Marlborough pledged a subscription of £100; Bathurst, Bolingbroke, Pulteney, Sir William Wyndham and Lord Oxford all 'contributed very handsomely'.

Actually, although much is said about the 'subscribers' to *Polly*, it was not, in a formal sense, a subscription edition at all. *Polly* was printed privately at Gay's own expense, so his is the only name you find at the front; there is no proud display of well-wishers and supporters set out in a public subscription-list. Some of the confident pronouncements that have sometimes been made, claiming to identify individual subscribers, must consequently be treated with caution. It would though be very interesting to know whether Pope offered his support, since he clearly regarded this latest provocative venture by Gay with extreme

[18]*Letters*, 119.
[19]Pope, *Correspondence*, III. 81.

concern. Currently, Pope was putting the final touches to his *Dunciad Variorum*, and he was obviously mindful of the damaging repercussions of *Three Hours after Marriage*, a decade earlier. What he most feared was that some rash or heedless action by Gay might be seized on by the dunces as an opportunity for revenge against Pope himself. And so he took some tactical steps to dissociate himself from Gay's work. In a cautious, diplomatic letter to Burlington, he requested the Earl's help in obtaining legal advice on the *Dunciad* from the distinguished lawyer Nicholas Fazakerley.

> I could be glad of the decisive opinion of Mr. Fazakerly, it will otherwise be impracticable to publish the thing before Mr. G's, and I am grown more prudent than ever, the less I think others so.[20]

'Mr. G' is certainly Gay, and the implied criticism of his 'imprudence' over *Polly* could hardly be clearer.

In fact *Polly* was published on 25 March, less than a fortnight after the appearance of Pope's revised and annotated *Dunciad Variorum*; but the two satires enjoyed very different receptions. Pope's poem was presented by Walpole himself to the king and queen who had already expressed approval of the earlier draft. By contrast, Gay's banned play provoked a minor court revolution, best described in Arbuthnot's facetious account.

> The inoffensive John Gay is now become one the obstructions to the peace of Europe, the terror of ministers, the chief author of the *Craftsman* and all the seditious pamphlets which have been published against the government... He is the darling of the city; if he should travel about the country he would have hecatombs of roasted oxen sacrificed to him ... And I can assure you this is the very identical John Gay whom you formerly knew and lodged with in Whitehall two years ago.[21]

Arbuthnot drew deliberate attention to the very different reputations currently enjoyed by Gay and Pope. Far from appearing as 'the terror of ministers' Pope, whose satire had been carefully vetted by Fazakerley, was now something of a court favourite.

> Mr. Pope is as high in favour as I am afraid the rest are out of it. The king, upon perusal of the last edition of his *Dunciad* declared he was a very honest man.[22]

In much of his later poetry, Pope liked to cast himself and Gay in

[20]Ibid., III. 4–5.
[21]Swift, *Correspondence*, III. 326.
[22]Ibid., III. 326.

two distinct mythological roles. He is the fearless crusader, the lone champion of truth.

> Yes, the last pen for freedom let me draw,
> When Truth stands trembling on the edge of Law.
>
> (*Epilogue to the Satires*, II, 248–9)

Gay, on the other hand, is presented *either* as a childlike innocent:

> Of Manners gentle, of Affections mild;
> In Wit, a Man; Simplicity, Child . . .

or as a helpless victim:

> Left me to see neglected Genius bloom,
> Neglected die! and tell it on his Tomb . . .

The reality, I suggest, was rather different. Gay, despite Pope's wishes, was clearly capable of maintaining a defiant adult pose; while Pope's public boast of independence ('Tories call me Whig, and Whigs a Tory') was only made possible by a degree of diplomatic compromise or, to use his own term, 'prudence' in his private dealings with Walpole and the court. One thing is clear. Pope's instinct was always to tone down or suppress the more provocative or eccentric expressions of Gay's imagination. He warned Gay against including the crocodile in *Three Hours after Marriage*; he suppressed his intended lampoon on Addison; he censored 'unworthy' items in Gay's posthumous papers. For whatever reason, Pope saw it as his role to discourage or deter Gay from assuming the kind of adversarial literary role that he happily adopted for himself. Gay's words should be used to entertain the world with songs, not vex it with dangerous satires. There is no need to suspect ungenerous motives in this attitude of Pope's, which was no doubt well-intentioned and most probably proceeded from a concern for Gay's always precarious health. But its effect was to reinforce the impression of Gay's literary immaturity. After the *Polly* episode Gay spent increasing amounts of time with the Queensberrys at their Amesbury estate in Wiltshire. Pope seems to have distrusted the intimacy of this new friendship. 'I can give you no account of Gay', he told Fortescue in September, 'since he was raffled for and won back by his duchess, but that he has been in her vortex ever since.'[23] This reductive description of the subscriptions to *Polly* as a 'raffle' seems to suggest a certain irritation. As far as Pope was concerned, Gay's act of political

---

[23] Pope, *Correspondence*, III. 52.

defiance had merely reduced him to the status of a rich woman's toy, like a prize in one of his own lotteries. And, conscious of Gay's acknowledged lack of 'a will of my own', Pope suspected he would be tempted into acting as the headstrong duchess's agent in her current whim for anti-ministerial gestures. Three months before Gay died, Pope was still trying to wean him away from the duchess's subversive influence, and urging him to 'try his muse' at some nice safe ingratiating panegyric on the subject of the Royal Hermitage. 'Every man, and every boy,' he told him, was doing it, and 'the Queen is at a loss which to prefer. . . . Several of your friends assure me it is expected from you'; he went on, and concluded: 'one should not bear in mind all one's life, any little indignity one receives from a Court; and therefore I'm in hopes neither her Grace will hinder you, nor you decline it.'[24] It is to his credit that Gay, who had wasted too much of his life with such time-serving pieces of flummery, did decline it. His last letter to Pope includes this passage.

> As to your advice about writing panegyric, 'tis what I have not frequently done. I have indeed done it sometimes against my judgement and inclination, and I heartily repent of it. And at present as I have no desire of reward, and see no just reason of praise, I think I had better let it alone. There are flatterers good enough to be found, and I would not interfere in any gentleman's profession.[25]

Such a dignified response to what Gay clearly felt as a humiliating invitation (virtually a 'command performance') to busy himself with what 'every man and every *boy*' [my italics] was supposedly doing, is a measure of his maturity. This is not the voice of a Peter Pan, but of a man who had found himself forced into a final self-denying accommodation between the truth of his own words and the ways of the world. During his final years at Amesbury, Gay wrote several angry and outspoken works; *The Rehearsal at Goatham, The Distressed Wife, Achilles* and the final volume of the *Fables*. But he made no serious attempt to publish any of them during his lifetime. As Peter says at the end of *The Rehearsal at Goatham*: 'There is nothing to be done here; they have the power, and we must submit.' In the end Gay chose silence, rather than compromise. What he would *not* submit to was the kind of poetic acquiescence that Pope recommended. After his death, of course, his papers passed into Pope's safe keeping, and we can only

---

[24]Ibid., III. 318.
[25]*Letters*, 130.

guess at the effects of Pope's declared policy of suppressing 'things unworthy of him'. Some works undoubtedly have been lost. But many remain, and they are more unusual, more *individual* than we have often been led to believe. We will only gain a true understanding of the originality of Gay's talent if we can see past Pope's well-intentioned myth-making to distinguish Gay's own voice, and trace his own elusive strategies for dealing with the ever-fickle tastes of the town.[26]

[26]For further discussion of these points see David Nokes, *John Gay, A Profession of Friendship* (Oxford, 1995).

Proceedings of the British Academy, **91**, 147–175

Reception, and *The Rape of the Lock*, and Richardson

THOMAS KEYMER

PERHAPS THE CLEVEREST of the spate of burlesques, adaptations and critiques of *Pamela* launched by Fielding's *Shamela* in April 1741 was a late intervention in the quarrel. *Pamela: Or, The Fair Impostor. A Poem, In Five Cantos. By J—— W——, Esq.*, was published in a Dublin imprint of 1743, and a London edition appeared early in 1744.[1] The story told by J—— W—— (a skilful parodist whose identity remains unknown) was by then already familiar. Rejecting *Pamela*'s official status as a tale of *Virtue Rewarded*, he looked instead to the subversive re-reading imposed on the text by Fielding, Eliza Haywood and others. For these 'Antipamelists' (as one contemporary put it), Pamela's dealings with Mr. B. suggested not the guileless piety applauded by Richardson's supporters but instead 'the Behaviour of an hypocritical, crafty Girl, in her Courtship; who understands the Art of bringing a Man to her Lure'.[2] No longer the victim of male predacity, Pamela was redefined as the predator herself; and here is exactly the charge that J—— W—— resumes. Little is new about his tale of plebeian cunning and hypocrisy, in which a wily chambermaid draws her master 'Sir Blunder' to the snare of wedlock. In terms of plot and analysis, the poem is little more than *Shamela* versified.

What is original is the context established by the versification itself,

[1]See D. F. Foxon, *English Verse, 1701–1750: A Catalogue of Separately Printed Poems with Notes on Contemporary Collected Editions* (Cambridge, 1975), I, 551 (entries P25 and P26). The London edition was catalogued in the *Gentleman's Magazine* and *London Magazine* of January 1744; Foxon notes that the Dublin edition is likely to be later, notwithstanding the date on its title-page.
[2]Peter Shaw, *The Reflector* (1750), p. 14. The passage plagiarises Ludwig Holberg's *Moral Thoughts* (1744): see A. D. McKillop, *Samuel Richardson: Printer and Novelist* (Chapel Hill, 1936), pp. 101–2.

with its mock-heroic elaboration 'In Five Cantos'. For in J—— W——'s hands the amatory struggles of Pamela and Sir Blunder become much more than simply those of servant and master. The poem's heroic couplets bring with them the expectation of mythic analogy, and this expectation is whimsically fulfilled in verses that link the pair with Tarquin and Lucretia, Paris and Venus, Alcides and Deianira.[3] The female garb in which Mr B gains access to Pamela's bed reminds the poet of other seducers in drag: 'So once *Achilles, Thetis'* Godlike Son, / And great *Alcides*, at the Distaff spun, / And *Omphale* and *Deidamia* won' (*FI*, V, 51–3). Martial imagery further inflates the tale as one of heroic conflict. Witness, for example, the tactical circumspection with which the pair manoeuvre in an epic simile from Canto IV:

> As skilful Generals with watchful Eyes
> Concert an Ambush, or avoid Surprize,
> Feign fearful Flights, yet gain Advantage too,
> And sometimes this, and sometimes that pursue;
> Doubt their own Strength, to stand the Chance of War,
> Shun the close Fight, and skirmish from afar:
> The cautious Couple, equally afraid,
> The humble Master, and th'imperious Maid,
> Alike reserv'd, still keep the doubtful Field,
> Contend for Conquest, and disdain to yield;
> While one great End alike directs them all,
> The Hero's Ruin, or the Virgin's Fall.
>
> (*FI*, IV, 1–12)

It is in keeping with this mock-epic tone that Pamela should be seen as 'this heroic Maid' (*FI*, I, 122), while Mr B is raised to a rank that casts him as simply, and repeatedly, 'the Knight'.

Pamela's combat with Sir Blunder, moreover, plays out at super-natural as well as human levels. Avoiding the Christian machinery of Richardson's text, in which Pamela lays claim to the aid of a just and active Providence, J—— W—— turns instead to pagan forces. Blessed by Venus and cursed by Juno, his heroine finds the vigilant chastity on which her schemes depend protected by agents of the former goddess but threatened by those of the latter. And these agents clearly recall the sprites of *The Rape of the Lock*, among which, Pope writes,

> The graver Prude sinks downward to a *Gnome*,
> In search of Mischief still on Earth to roam.

[3] J—— W——, *Pamela; or, The Fair Impostor* (1744), II. 58; II. 106; IV. 58. Further references are given to this London edition (hereafter *FI*) by Canto- and line-number in brackets in the text.

> The light Coquettes in *Sylphs* aloft repair,
> And sport and flutter in the Fields of Air.[4]

These lines directly inform J—— W——'s account of Pamela's birth and the Olympian conflict that attends it:

> Thus envious *Juno*, from contracted Hate,
> Ere her first Dawn of Life, fore-doomed her Fate;
> And placed malignant Spirits at her Birth,
> Obnoxious Gnomes, and mischievous on Earth;
> Prudes in this Life, who long neglected dy'd,
> Who curse their Folly, and lament their Pride;
> Who all the Malice of their Lives retain,
> The cruel Joy of giving others Pain. [...]
> While *Venus* meditates the future Maid,
> And summons Sylphs and Sylphids to her Aid:
> "A Nymph, she cry'd, shall soon the World adorn,
> "Belov'd by me, in distant *Britain* born.
> "Thither, ye bright aërial Sprites repair,
> "And guard from future Harms the Infant Fair;
> "Nor once neglect to watch around her Bed,
> "Or on her Pillow perch, or o'er her Head:
> "Banish th'intruding Fop, and coz'ning Beau,
> "And watch the wide Extremity below.
> "There most I fear—but, much I fear, will fail
> "A guardian Spirit if the Flesh prevail."
>
> (*FI*, I, 129–52)

It is clear at such moments that J—— W—— has more than one precursor-text in mind as he writes; and in case his borrowed machinery is not enough to signal the fact, he also contrives several yet more ostentatious echoes of Pope. In Canto II, as Sir Blunder plots his nocturnal foray into Pamela's bed, Venus's servant Ariel prepares a defence,

> And warns his little Legions of the Air,
> To guard PAMELA with redoubled Care.
> "Some heavy Cloud, which yet the Fates decree,
> "She may, with Care, avoid, (he cry'd) I see
> "Impends, this Night, o'er fair PAMELA's Head,
> "Ere th'unsuspecting Maid foresakes her Bed:
> "Or if a Lover, by Appointment, meets,
> "To gain a Kiss, or slip between the Sheets;

---

[4]*The Rape of the Lock and Other Poems*, ed. Geoffrey Tillotson, 3rd edn., The Twickenham Edition of the Poems of Alexander Pope, Vol. II (London, 1962), I. 63–6. Further references are given to this edition (hereafter *RL*) by Canto- and line-number in brackets in the text.

"Or if to steal some precious, private Thing—
"—A secret Lock to beautify a Ring—
"Her Top-knot, Snuff-box, Girdle, or her Shoes,
"Or some more trifling Toy a Maid may lose:
"Of these be diligent, be these your Care,
"I'll be myself the Guardian of the Hair
"That on her Head, and that which grows elsewhere.'

(FI, II, 73–87)

It is hard to miss the immediacy with which these lines draw on a parallel moment in Canto II of *The Rape of the Lock*. Here Pope's Ariel warns his sylphs of signs similar to J—— W——'s 'heavy Cloud, which yet the Fates decree', and likewise neglects to distinguish between trivial and serious losses:

This Day, black Omens threat the brightest Fair
That e'er deserv'd a watchful Spirit's Care;
Some dire Disaster, or by Force, or Slight,
But what, or where, the Fates have wrapt in Night.
Whether the Nymph shall break *Diana's* Law,
Or some frail *China* Jar receive a Flaw,
Or stain her Honour, or her new Brocade,
Forget her Pray'rs, or miss a Masquerade,
Or lose her Heart, or Necklace, at a Ball;
Or whether Heav'n has doom'd that *Shock* must fall.

(RL, II, 101–10)

It is not only on this passage, however, that J—— W—— draws, for he also concentrates in Ariel's speech a number of further echoes. The 'trifling Toy a Maid may lose' recalls Pope's 'moving Toyshop of their Heart' (*RL*, I, 100); Pamela's 'Top-knot, Snuff-box, Girdle' recall at once the fashionable ephemera of Belinda's toilet (*RL*, I, 138) and the foppery of Sir Plume (*RL*, IV, 123–30); the hair 'which grows elsewhere' makes blatant the innuendo in Belinda's famous 'Hairs less in sight, or any Hairs but these!' (*RL*, IV, 176). And in this attentiveness to Pamela's hair and Sir Blunder's fascinated urge to steal 'A secret Lock to beautify a Ring', J—— W—— of course brings into play the stolen prize, the 'ravish'd Hair' (*RL*, IV, 10), on which Pope's great poem of sexual warfare turns.

Pamela; or, The Fair Impostor, then, is not only a witty burlesque of Richardson's novel but also a bawdy elaboration of Pope's poem. It sharpens its revision of *Pamela* through appropriations from *The Rape of the Lock*, subjecting the novel to an effect, as it were, of mock-mock-heroic, in which its protagonists suffer not only by contrast with

the noble feats of Homeric epic but also by comparison with the
debased courtliness of Popeian satire. By combining Richardson's plot
with Pope's machinery, *Pamela*'s matter with *The Rape of the Lock*'s
manner, moreover, J—— W—— implicitly credits the two texts with
some perverse and hidden affinity (and has the confidence in his
analogy to sustain it for hundreds of lines). His work thus begs an
intriguing question. Was this simply some fortuitous or gratuitous
pairing, an arbitrary juxtaposition of texts linked only by their shared
concern with amatory conflict, or had J—— W—— stumbled across
some more substantial connection?

If ever there was consensus in Pope studies, here we surely have it:
there is nothing, it would seem, to be said. When tackling questions of
reception or influence, scholars of Pope have seized on heirs more in
sight, or any heirs but Richardson. Nor has there been much interest
from the other direction. John Carroll and more recently Jocelyn Harris
have dispatched for ever old ideas of Richardson as an unlearned
genius for whom intertextual allusion was an alien resource.[5] Yet in
this case Carroll himself, whose article of 1963 remains the fullest
exploration to date of links between Richardson and Pope, makes
essentially negative conclusions. Richardson was 'as aware as [...]
Dryden or Pope of the value gained by a reference or an allusion',
Carroll rightly claims, adding that while some of these allusions are
merely casual, others make careful play on the contexts invoked.[6] He
is reluctant, however, to put echoes of Pope in this category. Puzzled
by some apparent allusions 'because the sources seem so remote from
anything Richardson would be likely to have known', he gives as his
example a passage (to which I return below) in which Clarissa seems
to remember the speech of her namesake in *The Rape of the Lock*.
Noting the coincidence not only of name but also of argument, Carroll
speculates no further, and continues to insist that there is 'no direct
indication here that Richardson is recalling Clarissa in *The Rape of the
Lock*'.[7] He leaves unexplained his suggestion that Richardson would
not have known one of the most celebrated poems of the age (an odd

[5]See John Carroll, 'Richardson at Work: Revisions, Allusions, and Quotations in *Clarissa*',
in R. F. Brissenden, ed. *Studies in the Eighteenth Century II* (Canberra, 1973), pp. 53–71, and
'On Annotating *Clarissa*', in G. E. Bentley, Jr, ed. *Editing Eighteenth-Century Novels*
(Toronto, 1975), pp. 49–66; Jocelyn Harris, 'Richardson: Original or Learned Genius?', in
Margaret Anne Doody and Peter Sabor, eds. *Samuel Richardson: Tercentenary Essays*
(Cambridge, 1989), pp. 188–202.
[6]'Richardson at Work', p. 64.
[7]'On Annotating *Clarissa*', pp. 56–7.

assumption made odder by the fact that Richardson had himself printed a commentary on this very poem, John Dennis's *Remarks on Mr. Pope's Rape of the Lock*, in 1728).[8] Carroll's probable reason for dismissing the link is clear, however, from his earlier survey of references to Pope in Richardson's letters. From these sources he compiles a picture of relentless hostility which makes him conclude, not (as one might) that Richardson was evidently fascinated by Pope, but instead that Richardson was unwilling or unable to respond with anything better than catty detraction. Although the letters discuss poems as varied as *Windsor-Forest*, *The Dunciad*, and *An Essay on Man*, Richardson's comments are marked always by reprobation on moral grounds. 'I admire Mr. Pope's Genius, and his Versification: But forgive me, Sir, to say, I am scandaliz'd for human Nature, and such Talents, sunk so low,' he tells Aaron Hill in 1744. A year earlier he tells George Cheyne that Pope makes shameful misuse of 'Talents which adorn and distinguish him above all his Cotemporaries', to the extent that some of his poems 'ought to be called in, and burnt by the Hands of the common Hangman'. Neglecting the simultaneous admiration that gives these strictures their real force, Carroll implies that Pope's was a body of work against which Richardson's predispositions and allegiances prejudiced him too violently for serious, considered response to have been within his reach.[9]

Yet there is another side to this coin. Richardson was deferential in matters of literary judgement, and his correspondence nicely illustrates the point that epistolary argument may be determined as much by the addressee as by the writer. While the letter to Cheyne is an exception, it is significant that most of the reflections quoted by Carroll come in letters to rivals, victims or adversaries of Pope within Richardson's circle (which prominently featured such champion dunces and divers as Colley Cibber and Aaron Hill). Where his correspondence moves beyond this circle, Richardson is equally likely to refer to Pope as simply 'the first Genius of the Age'.[10] Even when writing to Pope's enemies, moreover, his objection is clearly not that Pope is a poor or tedious poet. On the contrary, it is precisely because he finds Pope a

---

[8]T. C. Duncan Eaves and Ben D. Kimpel, *Samuel Richardson: A Biography* (Oxford, 1971), pp. 44, 574.

[9]'Richardson on Pope and Swift', *University of Toronto Quarterly*, 33 (1963), 19–29, quoting Richardson to Hill, 19 January 1744, and Richardson to Cheyne, 21 January 1743. Both letters are in *Selected Letters of Samuel Richardson*, ed. John Carroll (Oxford, 1964), pp. 57, 60.

[10]Richardson to Warburton, 17 November 1742, *Selected Letters*, p. 55.

great poet, a poet who demonstrably compels his interest throughout the fifteen years of his own creative life, that his remarks are consistently coloured by such extremes of anxiety and censure. One does not, after all, trouble the hangman to burn boring books. The history of censorship tells us that books are perceived as dangerous not simply when they are objectionable in political, ethical or religious terms, but when they are perceived as conveying their objectionable matter with force and skill — when, in Milton's famous formulation, they seem 'as lively, and as vigorously productive, as those fabulous Dragons teeth; and being sown up and down, may chance to spring up armed men'.[11] Richardson may not exactly have feared that Pope's poems would spring up armed men (though it is an arresting fact that the Jacobite rebellion of 1745 did indeed spring up with the *Epilogue to the Satires* at its lips).[12] It is worth exploring the thought, however, that he found in Pope (perhaps as much by projection as discovery) a voice often persuasively inimical to many of the commitments that animated his own writing, and a voice as a result that had to be challenged. What is certain is that Richardson's talk of burning Pope reflects a response that was both urgent and engaged, and of an intensity far more likely to have made him confront and contest Pope's writing in his own than simply shun it.

Work more recent than Carroll's gives good grounds for interpreting Richardson's vehemence as a sign not of peremptory dismissal but rather of reading that was sufficiently close and engaged to charge the novels themselves. *Pamela* provides a relevant (though in this case not hostile) example. Discussing the visit made to Pamela by an irate Lady Davers, Marie E. McAllister detects a whimsical echo from the *Epistle to Arbuthnot*, in which the heroine's 'Tell her I am sick in bed: tell her I am dying' picks up the beleaguered poet's opening cry of 'say I'm sick, I'm dead'. The paraphrase is no mere coincidence, McAllister suggests, but quietly compares Pamela the upsetter of hierarchies and codes with Pope the social satirist, both of whom share a way of measuring the fashionable world and their own relationship to it against

[11]*Areopagitica*, in *Complete Prose Works*, ed. D. M. Wolfe *et al.* (New Haven, 1953–80), III, 492.
[12]See Howard Erskine-Hill, 'Alexander Pope: The Political Poet in his Time', *Eighteenth-Century Studies*, 15 (1981–2), 123–48. Erskine-Hill quotes one of the Jacobite manifestos of 1745, *An Address to the People of England*, which turns to Pope to authorise its complaint that Hanoverian rule had reduced corruption 'to a regular System': 'It could never be said justly, till of late Years, that *not to be corrupted is the Shame*' (p. 148).

the uncorrupted rigour of virtuous parents.[13] Nor is this the only point
at which Richardson lends resonance to Pamela's predicament through
recollection of Pope. Earlier, her description of her Lincolnshire captivity ('this handsome, large, old, lonely mansion, that looked to me
then, with all its brown nodding horrors of lofty elms and pines about
it, as if built for solitude and mischief') brings into play the 'darksom
pines' of Eloisa's gothic prison, where 'Melancholy [...] breathes a
browner horror on the woods'.[14]

Many other congruities might be explored with reference to the
wealth of Popeian analogues noted in Jocelyn Harris's edition of *Sir
Charles Grandison* (including, in the first volume alone, unmistakable
allusions to the *Epistle to Arbuthnot*, the *Epistle to a Lady* and the
Essay on Criticism).[15] The wide distribution and the sheer number of
such echoes of a modern in a writer whose allusions are more often
to Job or Psalms makes clear the intensity and duration of Richardson's
creative response to Pope. But it is not mere frequency of incidence that
should be stressed. More important is the character of Richardson's
allusions, which on the occasions just noted may suggest simple indebt-
edness or even like-mindedness, but which in their most sustained and
complex examples show him finding in Pope not so much an authority
as a formidable antagonist, a writer whose work was more often to be
resisted or recuperated than merely endorsed. For those passages or

---

[13]'Popeian Echoes in *Pamela*: The Lady Davers Scene', *Papers on Language and Literature*,
28 (1992), 374–8. McAllister's comparison between Pamela's parental touchstone and lines
392–9 of the *Epistle to Arbuthnot* is perhaps anticipated by J—— W——. Describing Pamela's
parents, he seems to draw on Pope's remembrance of a father 'Born to no Pride, inheriting
no Strife', a 'Stranger to Civil and Religious Rage' whose austere virtue is uncontaminated
by 'Courts' or 'Suits', 'Oath' or 'Lye':

> Strangers to Frauds and Flatteries of Courts,
> To Rumours, Lyes, and busy Fame's Reports;
> The Little, Fortune gave, enjoy'd in Health,
> Far from the Pomp and Miseries of Wealth;
> From mad Ambition, and obnoxious Cares,
> From Councils, Politics, and State Affairs;
> From honest Industry drew all their Store,
> Nor, discontented, ever sigh'd for more.
>
> (*FI*, I, 67–74)

[14]*Pamela*, ed. Peter Sabor, intr. Margaret A. Doody (Harmondsworth, 1980), p. 146; *Eloisa
to Abelard*, in *The Rape of the Lock and Other Poems*, ll. 155, 165, 170. I am grateful to
Jocelyn Harris for alerting me to this echo; see also her published remarks on Eloisa and
the comparable predicament of *Grandison*'s Clementina, *Samuel Richardson* (Cambridge,
1987), p. 158.
[15]*Sir Charles Grandison*, ed. Jocelyn Harris (London, 1972), III. 478; III. 484.

aspects of his work where Richardson most clearly has Pope in mind tend also to show him at his most strenuously ideological. They show him not simply invoking but challenging 'the first Genius of the Age', almost as though to do so was indeed to stage some Bloomian slaying of the creative father, or at least to question some seemingly retrograde trend in this father's text.

Two Pamelas

Useful at this point, beyond the notion of Bloomian misreading, is Gillian Beer's model of how writers 'respond to, internalize, and resist past writing' in their arguments with the past. Beer's model is flexible enough to register competing currents of sympathy and antagonism, congruity and reorientation, and she extends it brilliantly to *Pamela* itself, finding here an attempt 'to prolong, and to dispute with, Sidney's [*Arcadia*]' in which Richardson's anachronistic reading of Sidney in terms of hierarchy and class gives focus to his own more anxious exploration of social structures. Beer's reading also demonstrates how something as simple as coincidence of name can alert us to much deeper affinities and disputes between literary texts: in light of Sidney's pastoral romance, as she notes, problems of gender, genre, and class are brought to the fore and laid open to question by the simple, single stroke of Pamela's naming.[16]

Yet Sidney is not the sole forebear in play here. Pope too offered Richardson the precedent not only for a wise and virtuous Clarissa but also for an upwardly mobile Pamela, and (as with Sidney's pastoral princess) this precedent is important in direct relation to its awkwardness for Richardson's text. Quite clearly, here is not a case of simple analogy, but rather one in which Richardson looks to Pope (as well as in other directions) for initial formulation of his subject, and then pointedly redefines this subject by means of overt and deliberate swerves from the gist of his source.

As Anna Laetitia Barbauld noted as early as 1804,[17] Pamela's otherwise unusual name is conspicuously heralded in Pope's short verse

---

[16]*Arguing with the Past: Essays in Narrative from Woolf to Sidney* (London, 1989), pp. viii, 8, 3; see also pp. 34–61.

[17]*The Correspondence of Samuel Richardson*, ed. Anna Laetitia Barbauld (1804), I, lxxviii; see also Ian Watt, 'The Naming of Characters in Defoe, Richardson, and Fielding', *Review of English Studies*, 25 (1949), 325–30.

epistle on letters, courtship and other matter close to Richardson's heart, the *Epistle to Miss Blount, With the Works of Voiture* (first published in 1712). This poem describes the hazards of marriage, on which women surrender their premarital power over suitors: then 'The fawning Servant turns a haughty Lord', while the bonds of love, when 'rais'd on Beauty, will like That decay'. A passage heralding Clarissa's moral in *The Rape of the Lock* declares: '*Good Humour* only teaches Charms to last, / Still makes new Conquests, and maintains the past.'[18] The problem on which the poem most vividly dwells, however, is that of social misalliance. For the commoner who seeks an aristocratic match will find no happiness, Pope insists, and will only debase the station to which she aspires. 'Nor let false Shows, or empty Titles please: / Aim not at Joy, but rest content with Ease', he warns, introducing his cautionary portrait of a pitifully frustrated parvenue:

> The Gods, to curse *Pamela* with her Pray'rs,
> Gave the gilt Coach and dappled *Flanders* Mares,
> The shining Robes, rich Jewels, Beds of State,
> And to compleat her Bliss, a Fool for Mate.
> She glares in *Balls, Front-boxes*, and the *Ring*,
> A vain, unquiet, glitt'ring, wretched Thing!
> Pride, Pomp, and State but reach her outward Part;
> She sighs, and is no *Dutchess* at her Heart.[19]

From a Richardsonian point of view, this is a quite extraordinary passage. In its reproof of the adventuress's shallow hankerings for glitter and gilt, its mockery of the fool who elevates his trophy wife beyond her place, and its insistence that her nominal rank can never be truly inward, the passage implies (for all its sympathy for Pamela's predicament) a strong satirical defence of established hierarchies. Such hierarchies are natural and not to be transgressed, the hint is; and in making this hint Pope anticipates with uncanny precision the terms of the *Pamela* controversy of 1741, which in *Shamela* was to begin with yet stronger patrician disdain for the levelling implications of inter-class marriage. 'Young Gentlemen are here taught, that to marry their Mother's Chambermaids [. . .] is an Act of Religion, Virtue, and Honour', protests Fielding's Parson Oliver, and he offers *Shamela* instead as a cure to 'make young Gentlemen wary how they take the

---

[18]*Epistle to Miss Blount, With the Works of Voiture*, in *Minor Poems*, ed. Norman Ault and John Butt, *The Twickenham Edition of the Poems of Alexander Pope*, VI (London, 1964), 63 (ll. 44, 61–3).

[19]*Epistle to Miss Blount, With the Works of Voiture*, ll. 47–8, 49–56 (T. E. VI. 63).

most fatal Step both to themselves and Families, by [...] improper Matches'.[20] Yet in light of Pope's much earlier poem, it is as though it is not *Shamela* but the *Epistle to Miss Blount, With the Works of Voiture* that is truly the originating Antipamelist satire. It seems to attack, proleptically, a work it antedates by three decades.

One explanation for this coincidence between poem and novel is of course that here is no coincidence at all, and that Richardson's decision to name his upstart heroine Pamela marks some quite conscious desire to take on and refute the socially conservative import of Pope's poem. There is no external proof that he knew the *Epistle*, though Aaron Hill seems to have assumed that he did when reminding him, without further explanation, that in the case of his heroine's name 'Mr. Pope has taught half the women in England to pronounce it wrong'.[21] Internal hints that the novel may not only coincide with but actually answer the *Epistle* are certainly strong enough to justify Hill's assumption. There are many straightforward parallels, as when the novel resumes the subject of Pope's 'Whole Years neglected for some Months ador'd, / The fawning Servant turns a haughty Lord': in Pamela's own paraphrase, 'the plain *English* of the politest address of a gentleman to a lady, is, I am now, dear madam, the humblest of your servants: Be so good as to allow me to be your Lord and Master'.[22] Still more interesting are those moments where Richardson seems to contest rather than endorse the words of Pope, intensifying the levelling aspect of his work through apparent reaction to, and very pointed contrast with, the *Epistle*. Two characteristics above all differentiate his heroine from her namesake in Pope. The first is that where Pope's parvenue seeks above all the baubles of wealth, Pamela remains humbly indifferent to luxury, as though to refute in advance the kinds

---

[20]*Joseph Andrews and Shamela*, ed. Douglas Brooks (Oxford, 1970), pp. 355–6, 355; cp. Lady Mary Wortley Montagu's view of *Pamela* as 'the Joy of the Chambermaids of all Nations' (*Complete Letters of Lady Mary Wortley Montagu*, ed. Robert Halsband (Oxford, 1965–7), II, 470).

[21]6 January 1741, quoted in Barbauld's introduction to *The Correspondence of Samuel Richardson*, I, lxxviii; see also Eaves and Kimpel, *Samuel Richardson: A Biography*, p. 117. The discrepancy between Pope's accentuation of the second syllable and Richardson's of the first was conspicuous enough for Fielding to joke about 'a very strange Name, *Paméla* or *Pamēla*; some pronounced it one way, and some the other' (*Joseph Andrews and Shamela*, p. 293 (Bk. IV, ch. xii)).

[22]*Epistle to Miss Blount, With the Works of Voiture*, ll. 43–4; *A Collection of the Moral and Instructive Sentiments [...] Contained in the Histories of Pamela, Clarissa, and Sir Charles Grandison* (1755), p. 18, quoting the novel's sequel, *Pamela in her Exalted Condition*, 3rd edn. (1742), III. 195.

of suspicion that underlie the *Epistle*. Where Pope's Pamela glories in 'shining Robes' and 'Pomp', Richardson's understands the semiotics of dress too well to make the same mistake. She puts aside her mistress's finery and glories instead in the bundle of homespun which marks her preference for 'poverty with honesty' over 'plenty with wickedness': 'I am sure it will be my highest comfort at my death, when all the riches and pomp in the world will be more contemptible than the vilest rags that can be worn by beggars!'[23] Again, where Pope's Pamela is seduced by 'rich Jewels' which reach only 'her outward Part', Richardson's rejects the initial proposals of Mr B in ways that seem to pick up and throw back precisely the terms of the *Epistle*. Refusing 'your rings, sir, your solitaire, your necklace, your ear-rings, and your buckles', Pamela insists that

> To lose the best jewel, my virtue, would be poorly recompensed by the jewels you propose to give me. What should I think, when I looked upon my finger, or saw, in the glass, those diamonds on my neck, and in my ears, but that they were the price of my honesty; and that I wore those jewels outwardly, because I had none inwardly? When I come to be proud and vain of gaudy apparel, and outside finery, then (which I hope will never be) may I rest my principal good in such trifles, and despise for them the more solid ornaments of a good fame and a chastity inviolate. [. . .] I am above making an exchange of my honesty for all the riches of the Indies.
>
> (*P*, pp. 229–30)

Where Pope's parvenue 'is no *Dutchess* at her Heart', then, Pamela's nobility is genuinely 'inward', and in ways moreover that precede and outweigh her merely social elevation. The militancy of her language at this point indicates the second and most audacious aspect of Richardson's claim on her behalf, at odds as it is with Pope's apparently easy equation between birth and worth. For where the *Epistle* implies that nobility is a matter of blood alone, Richardson's heroine not only redefines nobility in strictly moral terms, so making it available to the humble too; she even claims it as *peculiarly* the province of the humble, and castigates by contrast a depraved aristocracy whose conduct severs whatever links may once have existed between social and moral pre-eminence. 'My *soul* is of equal importance with the soul of a princess, though in quality I am but upon a foot with the meanest slave' (*P*, p. 197), she famously announces. She would happily become 'the wife of some clouterly plough-boy', for she would then 'have been content

---

[23] *Pamela*, ed. Peter Sabor, intr. Margaret A. Doody (Harmondsworth, 1980), pp. 65, 111. Further references are given to this edition (hereafter *P*) in brackets in the text.

and innocent; and that's better than being a princess, and not so' (*P*, p. 269). Pamela is fully equipped to become a '*Dutchess* at her Heart', the insistence is, since she is already a princess in her soul; her nobility comes from her virtue, not from her marriage, for rank alone gives no such guarantee. Richardson's emphasis here goes beyond mere talk of spiritual equality, and to this extent at least is genuinely levelling; for Pamela's virtue is seen to make her more rather than less noble than such toffs as Lady Davers, who arrives with all the trappings of rank — 'A chariot and six. Coronets on the chariot' (*P*, p. 401) — to berate her new sister-in-law as a social climber. Pamela herself has no wish for the tinsel sported by the likes of Lady Davers or Pope's fake duchess, and she prays: 'O keep me, Heaven! from *their* high condition, if my mind shall ever be tainted with *their* vice!' (*P*, p. 294). Earlier, 'smiling at the absurdity of persons even of the first quality, who value themselves upon their *ancestors* merits, rather than *their own*' (*P*, p. 84), she quotes an unnamed poet to support her claim 'That VIRTUE *is the only nobility*' (*P*, p. 83).[24]

But it is in the representation of Mr B, a gentleman 'fallen from the merit of that title' (*P*, p. 54), that the severity of Richardson's attack on a degenerate élite comes to its highest pitch. 'He intends to go to Court next birthday, and our folks will have it, he is to be made a lord', writes Pamela, resuming her characteristic uncoupling of merit and rank: 'I wish they would make him an honest man' (*P*, p. 100). She also mentions the parliamentary attendance through which Mr B advances his ambitions (*P*, p. 132), and she protests further that he is 'a Justice of Peace, and may send me to gaol, if you please, and bring me to a trial for my life!' (*P*, p. 91). All such remarks show Richardson's readiness to direct the novel's quarrel (however fleetingly) beyond the merely private conduct of rakish squires, touching instead the much larger social, legal and political structures of Walpole's England and their dangerous vesting of power with a greedy and (as Mr B's behaviour suggests) potentially rapacious élite. Pamela is no Tory satirist, however, and for the most part her complaint is simply at the dereliction of nobility inherent in her master's conduct: 'I *will* tell you, if you were a king, and insulted me as you have done, that you have forgotten to act like a gentleman' (*P*, p. 102), she insists. For men of

[24]Peter Sabor suggests George Stepney's 'Virtue alone is true Nobility', *The Eighth Satire of Juvenal Translated* (1693), l. 37 (*P*, p. 521).

his rank to act in such ways is to 'put it in the power of their inferiors to be greater than they' (*P*, p. 56).

As such passages make abundantly clear, Pamela's eventual marriage is for Richardson no transgression of categories at all; rather, it is a proper reunification of the categories, too often severed, of merit and rank. Far from debasing the aristocracy, as Pope's Pamela is seen to do, Richardson's heroine personally saves it from depravity and disrepute. As Mr B himself predicts, 'there is not a lady in the kingdom who will better support the condition to which she will be raised' (*P*, p. 297), while the alliance of noble peasant and penitent squire sealed in their eventual union bears witness to what for many Antipamelists was the novel's most alarming social message — that distinctions of rank in the end mean little, that 'we were all on a foot originally', and that 'at the last, are levelled, *king* and *slave*, / Without distinction, in the silent grave' (*P*, pp. 294–5).

It is interesting to recall that what Pope himself seemed most to value in *Pamela* was the novel's vein of social satire (if not perhaps its levelling subtext). One of his nicest put-downs was passed on to Richardson in all its ambiguity by George Cheyne: 'Mr. Pope here charg'd me [. . .] to tell you that he has read Pamela with great Approbation and Pleasure, and wanted a Night's Rest in finishing it, and says it will do more good than a great many of the new Sermons.'[25] Such words leave unclear whether *Pamela* kept Pope awake or put him to sleep, and they neglect to count how many other sermons, old or new, the novel had failed to beat. If Pope hints here at some impatience with *Pamela*'s preaching, however, his praise seems less studiously faint when William Warburton later reports their shared responses to Richardson's sequel of 1742, *Pamela in her Exalted Condition*:

> Mr. Pope and I, talking over your work when the two last volumes came out, agreed, that one excellent subject of Pamela's letters in high life, would have been to have passed her judgment, on first stepping into it, on every thing she saw there, just as simple nature [. . .] dictated. The effect would have been this, that it would have produced, by good management, a most excellent and useful satire on all the follies and extravagancies of high life; which to one of Pamela's low station and good sense would have appeared as absurd and unaccountable as European polite vices and customs to an Indian. [. . .] And what could be more natural than this

[25]Cheyne to Richardson, 12 February 1741, quoted by McKillop, *Samuel Richardson: Printer and Novelist*, p. 50.

in Pamela, going into a new world, where every thing sensibly strikes a stranger?[26]

At first sight this letter appears to recommend a further and improved sequel — a sequel perhaps that would intensify that affinity between *Pamela* and *The Rape of the Lock* on which J—— W—— was shortly to build. Yet Pope's and Warburton's idea of using the novel to satirise 'the follies and extravagancies of high life' in fact takes its cue from a significant strain of satire at work in the text from the start. Margaret Anne Doody points to the masquerade scene of *Pamela in her Exalted Condition* as already satirical in much the way that Warburton and Pope would recommend; she also mentions the moment when Pamela begins 'a Subject, which never fails to make the worst of Weather agreeable to a fine Lady; that of praising her Beauty'.[27] While as a whole this sequel may indeed draw the sting from its precursor, tactfully silencing the stridency of Pamela in her peasant condition, its occasional digs at high-life frivolity thus retain at least something of the novel's original charge. Yet Richardson's shift from forthright denunciation to gentler satire in fact begins in the volumes of 1740, towards the end of which the heroine's gradual accommodation in high life comes to mute the trenchancy of her first complaints. Focus moves from Pamela's own status as transgressive upstart to turn on the havoc played by others with natural order: one need only recall Mr B's satirical view of those who 'think it the privilege of birth and fortune, to turn day into night, and night into day, and seldom rise till 'tis time to sit down to dinner; and so all the good old rules are reversed: for they breakfast when they should dine; dine, when they should sup; and sup, when they should retire to rest; and, by the help of dear quadrille, sometimes go to rest when they should rise' (*P*, p. 393).

Games at cards return us of course to *The Rape of the Lock*, in which the game of ombre gives Pope space not only to mock 'the follies and extravagancies of high life' but also to push his satire more covertly into affairs of state.[28] It is intriguing in this context to see Richardson follow a similar route from social to political satire (if with

[26]Warburton to Richardson, 28 December 1742, *The Correspondence of Samuel Richardson*, I, 134.
[27]*A Natural Passion: A Study of the Novels of Samuel Richardson* (Oxford, 1974), p. 91; see also Terry Castle on the masquerade scene and Pamela's attempt to mount (as one masquerader puts it) 'a general satire on the assemblée', *Masquerade and Civilization: The Carnivalesque in Eighteenth-Century English Culture and Fiction* (London, 1986), p. 174.
[28]See Erskine-Hill, 'The Satirical Game at Cards in Pope and Wordsworth', in Claude Rawson, ed. *English Satire and the Satiric Tradition* (Oxford, 1984), pp. 183–95.

a somewhat heavier hand), drawing like Pope on traditional ways of encoding political reflection in games of cards:

> I had all four honours the first time, and we were up at one deal. 'An honourable hand, Pamela,' said my master, '*should* go with an honourable heart; but you would not have been up, if a knave had not been one.' 'Whist, sir,' said Mr Perry, 'you know was a court game originally; and the knave, I suppose, signified always the prime-minister.'

(P, p. 427)

It is through his own knavery, Mr B hints here, that Pamela has reached her happy state; but his point about the production of good ends from bad means only slightly softens Mr Perry's abrupt hit at a target hard to mistake.

At such moments of oppositional innuendo, one glimpses a further, political, aspect to the bizarre affinity between *Pamela* and *The Rape of the Lock*; and here too the work of J—— W—— seems peculiarly prescient. As well as the more obvious gestures of mock-heroic discussed at the start of this essay, *Pamela; or, The Fair Impostor* takes from *The Rape of the Lock* and applies to Richardson's novel two particular satirical gambits which Pope uses to voice very marked (if elsewhere mitigated) hostility to the world he describes. The most familiar is Pope's wry misapplication of forms and conventions traditionally used to celebrate epic endeavour, thereby highlighting a disparity between heroic form and post-heroic content in which the empty frivolity to which courtly society has now decayed is clearly exposed. 'There Heroes' Wits are kept in pondrous Vases, / And Beaus' in *Snuff-boxes* and *Tweezer-Cases*' (*RL*, V, 115–6): such contrasts ridicule a debased courtliness, measuring the trivial sexual warfare of Hampton Court against the truly heroic feats of a chivalric past.[29] J—— W—— points just such disparities between epic language and foppish action to achieve his own comparable belittling of Sir Blunder's world, but he also draws on the more specifically topical scope of *The Rape of the Lock*, and on those memorable moments where Pope looks beyond the vile bodies of Belinda and her set to take in the larger structures of injustice on which the leisurely high jinks at Hampton Court must finally rest. The celebrated couplet in which Pope looks

---

[29]See Peter Hughes's account (taking in both *The Rape of the Lock* and *Pamela*) of 'the long process by which the heroic mode had been transferred from war to love and sensation, from heroic fury to tendresse and sadism': 'Wars within Doors: Erotic Heroism in Eighteenth-Century Literature', in Robert Folkenflik, ed. *The English Hero, 1660–1800* (Newark, 1982), pp. 168–94, 191.

past the snuff, fans and chat of his feckless protagonists to see that 'The hungry Judges soon the Sentence sign, / And Wretches hang that Jury-men may Dine' (*RL*, III, 21–2) is not an irrelevant digression, nor is it simply a point about sloppy procedures. Beneath that obvious complaint, Pope also targets the questionable justice of laws used throughout the period to preserve the livestock and game of a propertied élite which stood in relation to these laws as both administrators and prime beneficiaries. The implication of his couplet is not simply that wretches hang that judge and jury may end their sitting early. Wretches hang as a matter of policy and public example, that the propertied may dine on the fruits of enclosure safe in the knowledge that a sanguinary body of law (shortly to culminate in the notorious Black Act of 1723) could be called on, and conspicuously enforced, to keep their feast from the dispossessed.[30] We should not need the authors of *Albion's Fatal Tree* to remind us that hanging and the threat of hanging were a primary means by which the main beneficiaries of Hanoverian rule were able to protect the gains of enclosure. And while it may have been fanciful of E. P. Thompson to read *Windsor-Forest*'s hostile depiction of Williamite rule as indicating 'what Pope's feelings might have been' about the imminent rule of the Black Act,[31] in this couplet at least one cannot escape Pope's barbed reflection on the intimidatory legislation enacted throughout his lifetime to defend the plenty of those whose privilege it was to legislate, judge and sentence.

In J—— W——'s hands, these most socially critical aspects of *The Rape of the Lock* work intriguing effects on *Pamela*. The inherent satirical tendencies of Pope's form enable J—— W—— to rewrite the novel as a mock-heroic exposure of a world increasingly close to that of Pope's poem — a debased, frivolous and self-gratifying world of titled oafs and social climbers. The elevation of Mr B as 'Sir BLUNDER, proud of an illustrious Line' (*FI*, I, 36) intensifies Richardson's original attack on aristocratic degeneracy; and this point is reiterated as the

---

[30]Compare Fielding's ironic applause for the smug frankness with which one contemporary justice hanged a wretch that jurymen might ride: ' "For it is very hard, my lord," said a convicted felon at the bar to the late excellent Judge Burnet, "to hang a poor man for stealing a horse." "You are not to be hanged, Sir," answered my ever-honoured and beloved friend, "for stealing a horse, but you are to be hanged that horses may not be stolen" ' (*The Journal of a Voyage to Lisbon*, ed. Thomas Keymer (London, 1996), p. 16.

[31]E. P. Thompson, *Whigs and Hunters: The Origin of the Black Act* (Harmondsworth, 1977), p. 291; on the gallows and judicial coercion, see Douglas Hay *et al.*, *Albion's Fatal Tree: Crime and Society in Eighteenth-Century England* (Harmondsworth, 1977), esp. pp. 17–63.

knightly combats, trials and quests which the poem affects to celebrate
are revealed as no more than a sequence of inept and clumsy gropings.
Pamela's persecutor comes to sound, in fact, like no one so much as
Sir Plume, not so much the venerable knight as upper-class twit of the
year:

> Vain of his Wealth, he ev'ry Beauty storms;
> 'Dem me, — I love you, Me'm — but I hate Forms;
> 'What say you? tell me, can you like me, Miss?
> He pauses — and then struggles for a Kiss;
> Looks at his Watch: — 'A Pox! I must be gone;
> 'Adieu, my Angel. — Call the Chariot, JOHN.'

> > > (*FI*, I, 39–4)

J—— W——'s Pamela, for her part, comes closer to her namesake in
Pope's *Epistle to Miss Blount* than to Richardson's paragon, and the
height of her ambition is represented in the kind of gaudy parapher-
nalia derided in both the *Epistle* and *The Rape of the Lock*. Both she
and her master seem locked in some mutually devious struggle of
varying lusts, for cash on her part, for flesh on his:

> With deep Designs he acts a double Part;
> To win, and to betray, PAMELA'S Heart.
> With deeper Art yet acts the cautious Fair,
> Nor bids him hope, nor bids him yet despair;
> Throws forth those Lures so seldom known to fail,
> Yet doubtful holds the Balance of the Scale.
> Sudden she darts the Lightning of her Eyes,
> Calls forth her Charms, and bids her Colour rise;
> Then looks with meek Confusion on the Ground,
> While glowing Blushes give a deeper Wound:
> With vary'd Art she plays the subtile Game,
> And e'en her Frowns but fan the rising Flame.
> The future Prospect of a happy Life,
> Of rumbling Coaches, and an honour'd Wife;
> Of Flambeaux, Titles, Equipage, and Noise,
> And a long Series of protracted Joys;
> Of Courts, Plays, Operas, Assemblies, Beaux,
> Of Lap-dogs, Parrots, Masquerades, and Shows,
> The chief Ambition of the Female Kind,
> Like flowing Tides come rushing on her Mind.

> > > (*FI*, II, 33–52)

Here the struggles of Pamela and her master come close to those
of Pope's Belinda and the Baron, whose real-life counterparts were
embroiled in games of courtship where, for all the superficial frivolity

of the manoeuvres, much indeed was at stake.[32] And J—— W—— also takes from Pope his broader sense that the struggles he describes somehow typify, indeed symbolise, the shallow and devious acquisitiveness of a whole culture shot through with corruption. Where Pope links 'the long Labours of the *Toilette*' with the similarly calculating manoeuvres of judges and merchants (*RL*, III, 21–4), or where he builds a picture of global hypocrisy from 'The Courtier's Promises, and Sick Man's Pray'rs, / The Smiles of Harlots, and the Tears of Heirs' (*RL*, V, 119–20), J—— W—— is ready to follow. Finding in Pamela and Sir Blunder the true representatives of a thoroughly spiv society, he repeatedly links their conduct with wider targets:

> Not more the Wretch who haunts a Court in vain,
> The Country Curate, or the City Dean,
> The half-pay Hero, long disus'd to fight,
> The voting Burgess, or the cringing Knight,
> Sighs for Preferment, than Sir BLUNDER sighs
> To make the fair PAMELA's Heart his Prize.
> Not more a broken Gamester longs to play,
> Nor the high Pensioner for Quarter-Day;
> Not more a Lady longs new Modes to try,
> Or the young Heir to see his Father die,
> Than he to bribe PAMELA to his Will,
> And yet keep free from galling Wedlock still!
>
> (*FI*, III, 121–32)

The opening of Canto III is similarly indebted to the equivalent moment in Pope for its survey of the noonday nation:

> Now pleading Counsels were by Fools retain'd;
> And ruin'd Clients of their Money drain'd:
> Now the new Bridegroom long had left his Bride;
> And Judges, brib'd, had set Decrees aside:
> *Betty* had stolen from her Master's Room;
> And trembling Criminals attend their Doom.
> Now busy Footmen brush th'unpaid-for Clothes,
> And the stiff Dun to's Lordship's Levee goes.
> The greasy Duchess at her Toilet now
> Repairs the wrinkled Face, and grizly Brow.
> *Phoebus* had half the teeming Earth survey'd,
> Ere yet his Beams awak'd the lovely Maid.
>
> (*FI*, III, 1–12)

Yet in using Pope to rewrite *Pamela* as a satire on high-life degeneracy,

---

[32]See Valerie Rumbold, *Women's Place in Pope's World* (Cambridge, 1989), pp. 48–82.

and more generally on the shabby enterprise culture on which it rests,
J—— W—— was not grafting something alien on to Richardson's
novel so much as drawing from it, and making more evident, an aspect
of *Pamela* inherent in the text all along. Richardson of course shows
little interest in mock-heroic and its potential to satirise the present
(though it is intriguing to find Parson Williams reading *The Rape of
the Lock*'s precursor-text, 'Boileau's Lutrin' (*P*, p. 339)).[33] He is also
far less hostile to his heroine than is J—— W—— (though it is worth
remembering that the novel is ambivalent enough about Pamela to
contain within itself all the allegations of vanity, hypocrisy and ambition
on which the Antipamelist parodists were later to play).[34] But
Richardson is, or allows his heroine to be, very openly hostile about
the dereliction of nobility of which Mr B and his sister are so conspicuously guilty, and he fully shares the mock-heroic's interest in disparities
between worth and birth. It has already been noted how, in its conspicuous valuation of plebeian virtue over aristocratic vice, the novel
repeatedly sharpens its didactic surface with a levelling edge. Merit is
a matter of conduct and not blood, and may reside more with the
disenfranchised like Pamela than with those, like Mr B, who will abuse
the role of Justice of Peace or go to Court to be made a lord. At least
until the uneasy reconciliation of the novel's conflicts in marriage
between squire and peasant, *Pamela* thus implicitly targets not just one
degenerate noble but a whole oligarchy of courtiers who preside over
society, legislate in their own interests, and feather their own nests.
The card game, in which the knavery of Mr B is fleetingly linked with
that of Walpole, makes the political point as plainly as Richardson is
prepared to allow. He then develops a coded plea for harmonious
reconciliation in the nation, and for the rule of law in a state whose
constitution should defend its people against the corruption of kings
or knaves:

> This introduced a pretty conversation, though a brief one, in relation to the
> game at whist. Mr B. compared it to the English constitution. He considered,
> he said, the *ace* as the laws of the land; the supreme welfare of the people.

---

[33]Richardson would have been acquainted, as printer, with Dennis's hostile comparisons
between *The Rape of the Lock* and Boileau's 'noble and important satirical Poem, upon the
Luxury, the Pride, the Divisions, and Animosities of the Popish Clergy' (*Remarks on Mr.
Pope's Rape of the Lock* (1728), in *The Critical Works of John Dennis*, ed. Edward Niles
Hooker (Baltimore, 1943), II. 330). Boileau is more precisely cited by Lovelace in *Clarissa*
3rd edn (1751; repr. New York, 1990), IV, 19.

[34]See Keymer, *Richardson's Clarissa and the Eighteenth-Century Reader* (Cambridge, 1992),
pp. 30–2.

'We see,' said he, 'that the plain, honest-looking *ace*, is above and wins the king, the queen, and the wily knave. But, by my Pamela's hand, we may observe what an advantage accrues when all the court-cards get together, and are acted by one mind.'

Mr. Perry having in the conversation, observed, that it is an allowed maxim in our laws, that the king can do no wrong, 'Indeed,' said Mr B., 'we make that compliment to our kings indiscriminately; and it is well to do so, because the royal character is sacred; and because it should remind a prince of what is expected from him: but if the force of example be considered, the compliment should be paid only to a sovereign who is a good man, as well as a good prince [. . .].'

(*P*, p. 428)

This is measured language, and the regenerate Mr B is scrupulous in his mediation between the sanctity of monarchy and the supreme welfare of the people; but the oppositional gist of the passage as a whole is hard to miss. So too is the change in Mr B himself, whom Pamela seems by now to have reformed not only as a moral husband but also as an anti-Walpole patriot. At any rate, if here Mr B may indeed be deem'd 'a *Whig* for my Opinion' (as he admits in the novel's first edition), he is very emphatically an opposition or 'Old Whig' of the ambiguous kind with whom Richardson was once embroiled as printer of *The True Briton*.[35]

To return to my original question, then, it would seem that *Pamela; or, The Fair Impostor* does indeed alert us to very real affinities between *Pamela* and *The Rape of the Lock* (albeit affinities complicated by nuances of style and ideology which pull in very different directions). It is not that *Pamela* itself specifically bears the mark of *The Rape of the Lock* (though it does apparently bear that of the *Epistle to Miss Blount, With the Works of Voiture*). Rather it is that in combining the two texts, J —— W —— reveals a continuity of interest between them, focusing both in a composite attack on aristocratic degeneracy and abused privilege which retrospectively illuminates (albeit by exaggeration and simplification) an important strain that these otherwise contrasting works retain in common.

[35] *Pamela*, ed. T. C. Duncan Eaves and Ben D. Kimpel (Boston, 1971), p. 336; on Richardson's oppositional (even at times crypto-Jacobite) printing in the 1720s, see Eaves and Kimpel, *Samuel Richardson: A Biography*, pp. 19–36.

Two Clarissas

One further question is whether Richardson himself, though not alluding directly in *Pamela* to *The Rape of the Lock*, subsequently saw the
connection. We cannot know for certain that he read J——— W———'s
parody, but we do know that he monitored Grub Street closely enough
to have recorded (in an undated manuscript note) that *Pamela* 'gave
Birth to no less than 16 Pieces, as Remarks, Imitations, Retailings of
the Story, Pyracies, &c.'[36] It is not unlikely that the poem reached him,
and if so it could not have failed to put him once more in mind of *The
Rape of the Lock*, and at the very time when his second and more
devastating novel about aristocratic rapacity and sexual warfare (parts
of which began circulating in manuscript late in 1744) was being drafted
and first revised. Certainly Pope was in his mind at this time for other
reasons: the revised *Dunciads* of 1742–3 and Pope's death in 1744 made
the poet's writing and reputation share with the preparation of *Clarissa*
a central place in Richardson's correspondence with Aaron Hill
throughout the middle of the decade.[37] The published *Clarissa* bears
obvious traces of these interests: the Postscript has a lengthy quotation
from the *Epistle to Augustus*, and Richardson privately identified as a
reference to Pope a reflection of Anna Howe's on the excessive vanity
of 'a celebrated Bard'.[38]

More interesting is the shadowy presence in the novel's ideological
struggles of the *Epistle to a Lady*. Lovelace looks to Pope as an
authority to support his rake's creed, and one maxim in particular
bolsters the confidence with which he sets himself to prove Clarissa
fallible. 'And this made the poet say, That every woman is a Rake in
her heart' (*C*, III, 106), he reminds Belford, drawing conspicuously on
Pope's 'But ev'ry Woman is at heart a Rake'.[39] Earlier, as he laughs at
Clarissa's confused and hesitant flight from Harlowe Place, his exclamation '*The Sex! The Sex, all over*! — Charming contradiction!' (*C*,
III, 30) may recall and conflate the same poem's 'Woman's at best a
Contradiction still' and ''Tis to their Changes that their charms they

[36]Victoria and Albert Museum, Forster MSS, XVI, 1, fo. 56.
[37]Eaves and Kimpel, *Samuel Richardson: A Biography*, pp. 576–7.
[38]*Clarissa*, 3rd edn. (1751; repr. New York, 1990), VIII. 285–6; II, 13; *Selected Letters*, p. 227
n. Further references are given to this edition of *Clarissa* (hereafter *C*) in brackets in the
text.
[39]*Epistle to a Lady*, in *Epistles to Several Persons*, ed. F. W. Bateson, 2nd edn. (London, 1961),
l. 216.

owe'.[40] In this context, at any rate, it is hard not to think again of the *Epistle to a Lady*'s portrait of dissimulating femininity, 'Bred to disguise',[41] when on the other side of the novel's great debate about gender and virtue Clarissa quotes a verse epistle by a friend, 'Miss Biddulph's answer to a copy of verses from a gentleman, reproaching our Sex as acting in disguise' (*C*, I, 11). The verses in question allow this reproach, but they blame female disguise on conditions determined by men: '*Your own false hearts* / Compel *our Sex to act dissembling parts.*' Whether or not one finds a hit at Pope in these particular lines, Lovelace's own more overt use of the *Epistle to a Lady* proves not only Richardson's imaginative attraction to the poem but also his association of its argument with modes of thought and conduct he seeks to discredit.

Yet if *Clarissa* may be read in part as engaging in dialogue with the *Epistle to a Lady*, or as drawing the *Epistle* directly into its own dialogic narrative structure, something similar may also be said of *The Rape of the Lock*. It need not be significant that the name of Richardson's saintly martyr echoes that of Pope's 'grave *Clarissa* graceful' (*RL*, V, 7), or indeed that the names of the quarrelling lovers at the novel's start, Arabella Harlowe and Robert Lovelace, echo those of Pope's real-life protagonists, Arabella Fermor and Robert Lord Petre. But, as with the precedent of Pope's Pamela, such coincidences may at least alert us to important connections between the basic dilemmas explored in both these texts. Both are profoundly concerned with the constraints placed on individuals in a culture where marriage secures not simply emotional attachments but also transmission of property, title and wealth. By the same token, both combine evident hostility to aspects of their heroines' conduct with evident sympathy for her entanglement in the unyielding laws of courtship and marriage of interest. As Christopher Hill argued long ago, the early stages of Richardson's novel examine the competing claims of inclination and money, pitting Clarissa's case for self-determination against the Harlowe 'darling view [...] of *raising a family*' (*C*, I, 72) through alliance of interest to Solmes. More recently, Valerie Rumbold's discussion of the social and economic background to *The Rape of the Lock* makes plain the real tensions and stakes that underlie the erotic combats of Pope's beleaguered Catholic heirs, as well as the genuine gravity of a situation that

[40]*Epistle to a Lady*, ll. 270, 42.
[41]*Ibid.*, l. 203.

leaves Belinda 'a degraded Toast, / And all your Honour in a Whisper lost!' (*RL*, IV, 109–10).[42] Both works, moreover, pursue their treatment of marriage markets into the murkier psychological realms of sexual obsession, struggle and rape, and for all the differences of tone between Pope's ostentatious whimsy and Richardson's tragic turn, the under-lying seriousness in each case is beyond doubt. (It is perhaps an indication of this seriousness that the *locus classicus* of Lucretia is an important point of reference in each case, though with Pope it becomes explicit only in his supplementary verses 'To Belinda on the Rape of the Lock'.)[43] Finally, both works share a common concern with the lost vocation, in a post-heroic age, of an increasingly delinquent nobility — a nobility which in Pope sinks to the trivial pursuits of Hampton Court and in Richardson to an utterly destructive libertinism.

Like the *Epistle to Miss Blount* in relation to *Pamela*, *The Rape of the Lock* presents Richardson with a distinguished precedent for *Clarissa*'s subject, but at the same time one very different in genre, tone and implication, and one that Richardson seems to have been as anxious to contest as to follow. It is perhaps unlikely that Clarissa's bizarre exclamation, 'Were ours a Roman Catholic family, how much happier for me' (*C*, I, 84), is a hint that the very Protestant context of Richardson's novel must be seen to pose dilemmas of courtship yet more acute than those of Pope's poem. But there is unmistakable reference to *The Rape of the Lock*, and reference by extension to *The Rape of the Lock*'s own use of *Paradise Lost*, in the novel's grim depiction of post-heroic depravity. Linking Lovelace's rape of Clarissa with the Baron's rape of the lock, and looking past both to a mythic primal scene, Richardson rewrites his Popeian source in ways that

---

[42]Hill, 'Clarissa Harlowe and Her Times', *Essays in Criticism*, 5 (1955), 315–40; Rumbold, *Women's Place in Pope's World*, pp. 48–82. Here too J—— W—— finds occasion to link Richardson and Pope, describing how Pamela risks exactly Belinda's fate. 'I'm now amongst the Beaux a reigning Toast, / Must make my Fortune e'er my Beauty's lost' (*FI*, III, 51–2), she resolves, and is anxious to avoid the situation of those who

> find it fatal, to their Cost,
> When Virtue, Honour,—all that's dear is lost:
> Like Roses pluck'd, the Fav'rites of a Day,
> A while admir'd, then cheaply thrown away;
> The pointed Mark of all malicious Sneers,
> And the sad Subject of dull Sonnetteers.

(*FI*, I, 53–8)

[43]See Ian Donaldson, *The Rapes of Lucretia: A Myth and Its Transformations* (Oxford, 1982), pp. 57–82, 97, 183.

conspicuously polarise, and implicity censure, the moral ambiguities of the text he recalls.

Refusing in this second novel to draw the sting to bring his plot to the wishful reconciliation of penitence and reform, Richardson creates in Lovelace a high-born anti-hero whose violent libertinism marks an extreme depth of aristocratic degeneracy, a falling away from traditional heights of chivalric virtue that is precisely Satanic both in its direction and in its depth. It is striking that, in so doing, he follows Pope by focusing his rake's destructive will as though with symbolic force on his victim's locks, desired as something at once vulnerable, forbidden, and of course (as Pope's 'Hairs less in sight' make plain) profoundly sexual. Unlike Pope, however, Richardson scrupulously avoids identifying these locks as those of a partly culpable temptress, thereby refusing to dilute the absolute culpability of her assailant. Significant here are the lines from Canto II of *The Rape of the Lock* in which Pope imbues Belinda's hair with an ominous mythic import:

> This Nymph, to the Destruction of Mankind,
> Nourish'd two Locks, which graceful hung behind
> In equal Curls, and well conspir'd to deck
> With shining Ringlets the smooth Iv'ry Neck.
>
> (*RL*, II, 19–22)

Belinda is credited here with a ruinous allure that looks back to the Fall, her Eve-like 'Ringlets' 'conspiring' together in ways that threaten 'the Destruction of Mankind'. Similar connotations of danger and entrapment are involved in the precedent faintly recalled by Pope at this point, when Milton's Eve 'Her unadorned gold'n tresses wore / Dissheveld, but in wanton ringlets wav'd / As the Vine curles her tendrils';[44] and the 'Destruction of Mankind' on which Pope plays here is comically recapitulated in the helpless temptation of the Baron, for whom Belinda's locks act like those 'hairy Sprindges' or 'Slight Lines of Hair' which betray fowl and fish to their hunters (*RL*, II, 25–6). If Pope leaves room to see the Baron as at least in part the victim of some Eve-like temptress, however, Richardson leaves no doubt, by way of emphatic contrast, that Lovelace must be exclusively seen as tempter rather than tempted. Whatever Clarissa herself may think when she talks of quarrelling with Lovelace 'like the first pair (I, at least, driven out of my paradise)' (*C*, III, 15), Richardson is careful to

---

[44]*Paradise Lost, The Poetical Works of John Milton*, ed. Helen Darbishire (London, 1958), IV. 305–7.

reformulate the language of Fall in ways that very clearly cast the rake in Satan's, not Adam's, role.[45] It is in this role that he sees Clarissa as an Eve of some thoroughly innocent kind, tricked helplessly beyond the realm of her father's garden, and he seems to conflate Pope's 'shining Ringlets' with Milton's 'wanton ringlets' as he fantasises greedily about 'the wavy Ringlets of her shining hair [. . .] wantoning in and about a neck that is beautiful beyond description' (*C*, III, 28). Here Richardson refuses to laugh away his rake's possessive desires as partly provoked by their object, and as the novel progresses he seems almost to censure Pope's comic indulgence towards the Baron by insistently associating the trivial crime of *The Rape of the Lock* with the great one of his own novel. For Lovelace's later failure to win his victim's love, as opposed to her body, is chillingly voiced in the mad obsession that seizes him, after the rape, to possess again these talismanic locks. He demands (as though in grisly recapitulation of the rape) 'that my ever-dear and beloved Lady should be opened and embalmed', and he sends to Belford meanwhile for 'a lock of her hair instantly by the bearer' (*C*, VIII, 44, 46). 'But her dear heart and a lock of her hair I will have, let who will be the gainsayers!' (*C*, VIII, 47), he repeats, plainly betraying his catastrophic failure to distinguish between physical possession and volunteered love.

Earlier, Lovelace seems more knowing about his status as some second Baron, redrawn, with new hostility, as one whose rapacious obsessions precipitate a far more calamitous loss. In a flight of fancy clearly indebted to Pope, he exclaims: 'Why, Belford, the Lady must fall, if every hair of her head were a guardian angel, unless they were to make a visible appearance for her, or, snatching her from me at unawares, would draw her after them into the starry regions' (*C*, III, 104–5). His words again bizarrely recall Belinda's lock, while also suggesting the sylphs who guard it and the lock's inevitable ascension 'to the Lunar Sphere, / Since all things lost on Earth, are treasur'd there' (*RL*, V, 113–4). The irony of this echo is very much at Lovelace's expense, for his joking prediction is later fulfilled in Clarissa's death and his own dream of her saintly ascension 'to the region of Seraphims' (*C*, VII, 148). Clarissa must indeed be drawn to these regions, to the lunar sphere, for in Richardson's tragic resumption of Pope's subject it is not simply a lock of hair that is lost to the world but the world's

---

[45]See Gillian Beer, 'Richardson, Milton, and the Status of Evil', *Review of English Studies*, NS 19 (1968), 261–70, reprinted in *Arguing with the Past*, pp. 62–73; Keymer, *Richardson's Clarissa and the Eighteenth-Century Reader*, pp. 111–4, 190–6.

brightest ornament. The point is further reinforced when Lovelace whimsically foresees his victim's loss in ways that echo the comparable 'upward rise' of Belinda's lock ('A sudden Star, it shot thro' liquid Air, / And drew behind a radiant *Trail of Hair*': V, 123, 127–8). In his own words, Clarissa too becomes some such sudden star, who soars to the lunar sphere: 'I was *in danger of losing my Charmer for ever.* — She was soaring upward to her native Skies. She was got above earth, by means, too, of the *Earth-born*: And something extraordinary was to be done to keep her with us Sublunaries' (III, 276).[46] The association, again, is inescapable: drawing insistently on the connotations of Pope's poem yet at the same time resisting its comic tone, Richardson seems at such moments to offer his novel as some tragically literal resumption of what in Pope remains largely *jest*.

As these uneasy echoes of Pope make plain, *Clarissa*'s relationship to *The Rape of the Lock* is real yet also evasive, as though unable to settle itself finally between homage and critique. On the one hand, the richness of significance attached by the novel to its heroine's locks shows profound understanding of the subtlety with which Pope had used the lock and its rape to hint at larger, darker conflicts. Yet at the same time Richardson's allusive rewritings of certain lines shy away from Pope's playful obliqueness, as though to insist that here is no laughing matter, and that the full seriousness of the subject they share can only be reached through *Clarissa*'s distinctive mode of Christian tragedy. In one point, however, the two texts seem to meet in at least approximate accord, with the readiness of Richardson's heroine to echo (albeit in starker form) the conclusions of her namesake in Pope. Perhaps by now we may dispense with John Carroll's assumption that Richardson's heroine failed to pay serious attention to Pope in general and *The Rape of the Lock* in particular, and return in conclusion to that echo of Canto V which Carroll himself was first to note. The source is the famous moral in which 'grave *Clarissa* graceful' asks 'why are Beauties prais'd and honour'd most', going on to remind her audience that 'frail Beauty must decay' and 'Locks will turn to grey, / Since painted, or not painted, all shall fade, / And she who scorns a Man, must die a Maid'. Clarissa's purpose here is to raise the enduring virtues of 'good Sense' and 'good Humour' above the matter of mere

[46] I am indebted here to Jocelyn Harris's account of Miltonic echoes in *Clarissa*, in which she notes in passing Richardson's use of 'an image from that other poem of Fall, Pope's *Rape of the Lock*': see *Samuel Richardson*, p. 67; also 'Richardson: Original or Learned Genius?', p. 194.

evanescent beauty, and she concludes that esteem must therefore come from more than surface alone: 'Beauties in vain their pretty Eyes may roll; / Charms strike the Sight, but Merit wins the Soul' (*RL*, V, 9–34). With much of which Richardson's heroine would clearly agree. Her own version of the moral, however, is of a different tone and emphasis:

> For, as to our Sex, if a fine woman should be led by the opinion of the world, to be vain and conceited upon her form and features; and that to such a degree, as to have neglected the more material and more *durable* recommendations; the world will be ready to excuse her; since a pretty fool, in all she says, and in all she does, will please, we know not why.
>
> But who would grudge this pretty fool her short day! Since, with her summer's sun, when her butterfly flutters are over, and the winter of age and furrows arrives, she will feel the just effects of having neglected to cultivate her better faculties: For then, like another Helen, she will be unable to bear the reflexion even of her own glass; and being sunk into the insignificance of a *mere old woman*, she will be entitled to the contempts which follow that character. While the *discreet matron*, who carries *up* [. . .] into advanced life, the ever-amiable character of virtuous prudence, and useful experience, finds solid veneration take place of airy admiration, and more than supply the want of it.
>
> (*C*, I, 278)

Like her namesake in Pope, Richardson's Clarissa thus contests the value placed by her culture on mere beauty, but she does so with greater severity: for all her talk of excusing the 'pretty fool', her language of vanity, conceit and folly goes significantly beyond that of her predecessor. This is not her only departure from the Popeian moral, however, for (in keeping with Richardson's emphasis throughout the novel) her argument resists the tradition of satire against women, and the fullest weight of her censure falls instead on a decadent masculinity. Devoting as much space again to male vanity as to that of women, she further intensifies her language to speak of fops and coxcombs as 'the scorn of one Sex, and the jest of the other' (*C*, I, 279), pointedly redirecting the force of her predecessor's words. The end point of her argument, of course, is Lovelace, whose own 'despicable [. . .] self-admiration' (*C*, I, 279) will soon deny Clarissa everything, including what seems in context the happy enough outcome feared by her namesake in Pope — that 'she who scorns a Man, must die a Maid'.

Here again, then, we find Pope acting on Richardson in a role poised intriguingly between that of influence and that of antagonist, informing the direction of Clarissa's thought but also giving focus to the departures and counter-arguments which his own Clarissa's moral seems here to provoke. It is plain at this point, as in general, that Richardson's thinking about Pope was indeed marked by argument and resistance as well as influence and acceptance, but it is equally plain that we cannot take the intermittent hostility apparent in his more general reception and rewriting of the poems to mean that Richardson withheld his serious attention from the writer he called 'the first Genius of the Age'. On the contrary, we have in Richardson's novels a fine example of creative misreading and wilful rewriting of Popeian topoi, a fascinating and underexplored set of connections with much to tell us about the distinctive methods and emphases of both writers. This essay has attempted to sketch the ways in which both share common interests in conflicts of courtship and marriage, gender and class; in censure of an aristocracy that is at best (in the Baron) self-gratifying and at worst (in Lovelace) all-destroying; and in efforts to define notions of nobility and virtue, together with their problematic relationship to blood and birth. In all these matters, it is hard to escape the conclusion that Richardson's novels are significantly provoked by Pope. This, however, is hardly to exhaust the complex connections between these two vast bodies of work: there remain other stories to tell about Richardson and Pope, and perhaps also about that ingenious reader and wit, J—— W——.

Index

Addison, Joseph, 11, 16–17, 104, 138, 143
  *A Discourse on Ancient and Modern
    Languages*, 57
Aden, John M., 23
Allen, Ralph, 11
Anne, Queen, 17, 34, 35–36, 38
anti-Augustan tradition, 18
Arbuthnot, Anne, 13
Arbuthnot, John, 11, 19, 136, 137, 139, 142
Aristotle, 2
Asiento-Clause, 34, 37
Atterbury, Francis, Bishop of Rochester, 11,
  16–17
Atterbury Plot, 15
Augustus, 18, 19
Augustan Age, the, 18–19
Augustan satires, 72
authorial intention, 8, 112

Banckes, John, 83
Barbauld, Anna Laetitia, 155–56, 157
Baring, Anne, 66
Barnard, Toby, 10, 124
Bateson, F.W., 118, 119, 121
Bathurst, Allen, first Earl of, 141
Baudelaire, Charles, 91, 92
Beer, Gillian, 49, 155, 172
Behn, Aphra
  Oroonoko, or The Royal Slave, 37, 40
Belhaven, Earl of 41
Berkeley George, bishop of Cloyne 5, 11
Bethel, Hugh, 13
Betterton, Thomas, 17
Black, Jeremy, 23
Blackmore, Sir Richard, 79, 81
  Creation, 95
Blackwell, Thomas, 57
Bloch, Tuvia, 74, 78
Blount, Edward, of Blagdon, 16, 47
Blount, Martha, 4, 9, 12–13, 37, 67, 68
Blount, Teresa, 12–13, 37
Boccaccio, Giovanni, 58, 76, 77
Bodin, Jean
  Six Livres de la République, 2, 32–34, 42
Boileau-Despréaux, Nicolas, 81, 84
  Art Poétique, 81

Le Lutrin, 77, 79, 81, 108, 166
Bolingbroke, Henry St. John, Viscount, 3,
  11, 21, 36, 45, 116, 136, 141
Bowers, Fredson, 8, 112
Bowry, Mr., 140
Bowyer, William, 102
Brennan, Michael, 132
Breval, John Durant, 137
  Henry and Minerva, 63
  The Confederates, 135
Britannia, myth of, 63
Brooks-Davies, Douglas, 23
Broome, William, 66, 83, 139
Brower, R.A., 18, 120
Brown, Laura, 39, 120
'Brown and Mears', 83
Brownell, Morris, 17
Buckingham, Catherine Sheffield, Duchess
  of, 13
Burlington, Richard Boyle, third Earl of, 10,
  13, 24, 119–125, 140–41, 142
burlesque, 81, 105, 147
Butler, Samuel, 105
  Hudibras, 81
Butt, John, 114, 118, 131
Byron, George Gordon, Lord, 105

Caesar, Mary, 13
Caroline, Queen, 129
Carroll, John, 151–52, 173
Caryll, John, second Lord Caryll of
  Durford, 10, 34, 47, 48
'Caryll Papers', 31
Cashford, Jules, 66
Castle, Terry, 161
Catherine the Great, 27,
Caxton, William, 82, 83, 106
Chandos, James Brydges, Lord, 129
Chapman, George, 28, 66
Charles I, King, 30–31, 35, 40
  Eikon Basilike, 31
Charles II, King, 17
Chatterton, Thomas, 106–8, 109
Chaucer, Geoffrey, 58, 75–77, 82, 93
  Knight's Tale, 74, 77, 96

Chesterfield, Philip Dormer Stanhope, Lord, 84
Cheyne, George, 152, 160
Cibber, Coley, 77, 82, 89–91, 98–108, 135, 152
   Letters to Mr. Pope, 83, 98–99, 100–101, 102, 103–4
   Apology, 90, 99, 100, 102, 103, 105–6
   'Broglio MSS', 90
Cibber, Lewis, 102
Clarke, Howard, 57
Clark, J.C.D., 22, 23
Clark, Jane, 10, 124
Clifford, J.L., 132
Coleridge, Samuel Taylor
   Kubla Kahn 111
Colley, Linda, 22
Cotton, Charles, 2, 14, 105
Columbus, Christopher, 33, 38
Comedy, 20
conquest, 2, 36, 44
Corp, Edward, 31
Cowley, Abraham
   Davideis, 92
Cowper, William
   Odyssey, 59
Cross, A.G., 27
Cromwell, Oliver, 40, 41
Creech, Thomas, 20, 51
Cruickshanks, Eveline, 22–23, 31

Damrosch, Leopold, 18, 24
Daniel, Samuel, 46
Davenant, Sir William
   Gondibert, 82
Davis, David Brion, 33, 34, 39
Davis, Herbert, 69
deism, 3
de las Casas', Bartholomé, 33
de Forest, George, Lord, 66–67
de Lyra, Nicholas, 82, 83, 85
Dennis, John, 137, 152
   Remarks on Mr. Pope's Rape of the Lock, 152, 166
Dickinson, H.T., 12, 37
Dilke, C.W., 10
Dixon, Peter, 6
Donaldson, Ian, 170
Donne, John, 3, 93
   Satyre IV, 44
Doody, Margaret Anne, 161
Dryden, John, 4, 28–32, 45, 57–58, 62, 72, 75–77, 79, 81, 88, 92, 95, 105, 151
   Discourse, 95
   Fables, 28, 58, 74
   Absalom and Achitophel, 31, 35

   Iliad, 28–30
   Mac Flecknoe, 82, 84, 92
   Palamon and Arcite, 74, 96
   The Hind and the Panther, 35
   and Anne Killigrew, 4

Erasmus, Desiderius, 3, 20
Ehrenpreis, Irvin, 11
eighteenth-century historiography, 22
Eliot, T.S.
   The Waste Land, 82, 91, 92
English Romantics, 111
epic, 72, 73, 77, 79, 81, 82, 88, 100, 101, 108, 151, 162
Erskine-Hill, Howard, 12, 18, 21, 23, 27–53, 69, 97, 109, 120, 124, 153, 161
Exclusion Crisis, 32

Fairer, David, 18, 24
feminist criticism, 4
Fénelon, François de Salignac de La Mothe, Archbishop, 56
   The Adventures of Telemachus, 55, 62
Fenton, Elijah, 59, 66, 139
Ferraro, Julian, 7, 111–34
Fielding, Henry, 20, 79, 81, 105, 110, 157
   Jonathan Wild, 88, 104, 105
   Shamela, 147, 156, 157
   The Tragedy of Tragedies, Or ... Tom Thumb the Great, 88
Filmer, Sir Robert
   Patriarcha, 40
Flaubert, Gustave, 74
Ford, Charles, 12
form, (importance of), 1–2
Fortescue, William, 13
Foxon, David, 7, 8, 25, 37, 113, 147
France, Peter, 2
Frederick, Prince of Wales, 42
French Revolution, 22
friendship, 55–68
Fuchs, Jacob, 20, 44

Garth, Samuel
   Dispensary, 77, 79, 81, 92, 95, 96, 108
Gay, John, 8, 11, 13, 95, 135–45
   Achilles, 136, 144
   Fables, 144
   Polly, 141, 142, 143
   Rural Sports, 135
   The Beggar's Opera, 136, 139, 140
   The Distressed Wife, 144
   The Mohocks, 137

The Rehearsal at Goatham, 144
The Shepherd's Week, 137
The What D'Ye Call It, 136
Three Hours after Marriage, 135, 137, 142
Trivia, 136, 137
gender, 13
George I, King, 45
George II, King, 18, 45
Gerrard, Christine, 21
Gladstone, W.E., 64
Studies on Homer, 64, 66
Godwyn, Morgan, *The Negro's and Indians Advocate*, 36
Gregg, W.W., 8, 112
Griffith, Philip Malone, 31
Griffin, John, 132
Grub Street, 91
Guerinot, J.V., 83, 99

Hadrian, 47–49
Holland, Philemon, 83
Halsband, Robert, 13, 157
Hammond, Brean, 21, 139
Hammond, Paul, 10
Handel, 140
Hanoverian opposition, 17, 21, 153, 163
Hara, Eiichi, 23
Harley, Robert, 36, 38, 132
Harpsfeld, Nicholas, 82
Harris, Jocelyn, 151, 154, 173
Haywood, Eliza, 147
Hervey, John, Lord Hervey of Ickworth, 11, 130
Herzen, Alexander, 41, 42
Higgons, Bevil, 38
Hill, Aaron, 152, 157, 168
Hill, Christopher, 169
Holberg, Ludwig, 147
Homer, 17, 19, 27, 40, 46, 52, 57, 58, 77, 79, 82, 83, 88, 97, 104, 151
Odyssey, 28, 45, 64, 67
Iliad, 58
Horace, 2, 3, 9, 18, 42, 43, 44, 51, 52, 96
Epistle to Florus, 49
Odes, 84
Houston, Jean, 58, 63
Howe, Anna, 168
Hughes, John
Calypso and Telemachus, 62
'Inventory of a Beau' Tatler, 73
Hughes, Peter, 162
Hutton, Sir Richard, 30

Irish Catholics, 40–41

Jacobitism, 22–24, 30, 32, 45, 50, 153, 167
James, Henry, 13
James II, King, 31, 40, 41, 44
James III, the Old Pretender, 17
Johnson, Samuel, 31, 34, 57, 62–63, 83, 109, 136
Dictionary, 31, 34, 36
Jones, Emrys, 97
Jones, Hester, 4, 55–68
Joyce, James
Ulysses, 82
Juvenal, 44, 75

Kent, William, 140
Keymer, Thomas, 25, 147–75
King, William, Archbishop of Dublin, 11
Kinsley, James, 74, 75
Knight, Sir Robert, 129
Kraus, Karl, 133
Kutuzov, A.M., 27

Landa, L.A., 132
Lang, David Marshall, 27, 45
Langhorne, William, 56
Leavis, F.R., 123–4
Lees-Milne, James, 12
Leranbaum, Miriam, 21, 117, 125
L'Estrange, Sir Roger, 105
Lintot, Bernard, 113, 132
Locke, John, 38, 39, 40
Two Treatises of Government, 31–32, 33, 39, 41
Louis XIV, 40
Longinus, 2, 46

M., B., *The Planter's Charity*, 37–38
Machiavelli, Niccolo, 3
Mack, Maynard, 2, 3, 6, 7, 9, 11, 14–17, 18, 24, 28, 30, 61, 69, 74, 84, 85, 86, 103, 109, 118, 134
Mainwaring, Arthur, 29–30
'Man of Ross', 125, 126
Mandeville, Bernard, 124
Manilius, 20, 51
Marchmont, Earl of, 27
Marlborough, Sarah Churchill, Duchess of, 13, 141
Martin, Peter, 17
Marvell, Andrew, 3, 4, 47
Maynard, J., author of *Assiento, sive commercium Hispanicum*, 38
Mason, H.A., 19
McAllister, Marie, E., 153, 154

McCabe, Richard, A., 21
McDonald, Peter, 49
McGann, Jerome, 133–4
McLaverty, James, 7, 8, 25, 113, 133
Milton, John, 5, 49, 74, 80, 92–93, 102, 104, 108, 153, 173
   Paradise Lost, 45, 46–47, 72, 77, 91, 93, 98, 108, 170–73
   Sonnet VII, 52
mock-epic, 20, 74, 87, 88, 89, 92, 100, 101, 108, 148
mock-heroics, 20, 72, 73, 77, 78, 79, 80, 81, 82, 84, 87, 88, 91, 94, 96, 100, 101, 105, 108, 148, 150–51, 162, 163, 166
Modernism, 109
Money, D.K., 37
Monod, Paul Kléber, 23
Montague, Lady Mary Wortley, 4, 11, 13, 84, 157
Montaigne, Michel Eyquem de, 2, 3, 14, 20
Morris, D.B., 18
multiple biography, 12, 16
Murray, William, Earl of Mansfield, 43
   Lewis's Case; Sommersett's Case, 43

nationhood, 22
Nichol, Donald, W., 24–25, 115
Nicholson, Colin, 21, 24
Nokes, David, 13, 135–45
novelistic genre, 105
Nuttall, A.D., 109, 110

Ogilby, John, 83
   Homer his Odysses translated, 59
Oldham, 84, 87–88
   Letter from the Country, 96
opposition culture, 3
Osborn, J.M., 19, 47, 83, 135
Otto, Walter, 64
Ovid
   Metamorphoses, 77
Oxford, Robert Harley, Lord of, 141
Ozawa, Hiroshi, 23

Parnell, Thomas, 38, 61
   Essay on Homer, 56, 57
   To Mr. Pope, 55
   Battle of the Frogs and Mice, 84
parody, 72, 105–06
Partridge, Monica, 27, 42
Peirce, Charles, 111
Persius, 52
Philips, Ambrose, 137

Pittock, Murray, G.H., 23
Plowden, J.F.C., 20, 51
Pomey, François Antoine
   The Pantheon, 63, 64
poets as moralists, 5
Pope, Alexander
   and Freemasonry, 28
   and politics, 21
   and the 'Adrian verses', 47–49
   and the literature of Greece and Rome, 18, 72, 82
   and the South Sea Company, 37, 129
   and the visual arts, 17
   as autobiographical poet, 3
   as moralist, 1
   as satirist, 52–53, 95, 118, 121, 128, 151, 153
   biographical study of, 11–17
   Caryll transcripts of letters, 10
   collaboration on *Three Hours after Marriage*, 135, 137–38, 142, 143
   control over printed form of his works, 8, 113–131, 133
   arrangement of poems, 115–19
   correspondence, 4, 9–11, 15–16, 47, 62
   critical works on, 17–25
   decorations accompanying texts, 8, 113
   editors, modern, 6, 10
   estrangement from John Gay, 139–45
   first editions, 9, 122
   Homer project, 17, 28, 55–68, 106
   manuscripts, 6–9, 29, 46, 85, 93, 113–14, 118, 119–22, 124, 126–34
   maternal forbears, 16
   poetry of friendship, 4, 55–68
   Pope symposium (Binfield), 24
   presentation of women, 3–5
   Renaissance, influence upon Pope, 14
   recent discussions of, 1, 5, 6–25
   treatment of epic material, 71–72
   typography, 8–9, 113
   use of footnotes, 100–101
   use of rhyme, 25, 26, 46–53, 93, 122
   vision of past, 35
   vision of peace, 2
   vision of world, 1
Pope, Alexander (works)
   An Essay on Criticism, 2, 6, 96, 154
   An Essay on Man, 2, 6, 7, 14, 21, 39, 41, 42, 115, 116, 117, 118, 119, 131, 152
   Correspondence, 10, 27, 37, 48, 117, 125, 129, 137, 138, 140, 141, 143
   Eloisa to Abelard, 42, 154
   'Epilogue to the Satires', 44, 143
   Epistles to Several Persons, 114, 116–17, 118, 119, 126, 129

Iliad translation, 19, 27–31, 37, 58, 65, 77, 80, 84, 88, 97
Imitations of Horace, 9, 18, 42, 49, 51
Miscellany (1717), 60
Odyssey translation, 4, 45–46, 55, 58, 67, 78, 96
'Of the Characters of Women', 115
'Of the Knowledge and Characters of Men', 115, 116
'Of the Uses of Riches', 115, 116, 119
On receiving from the Right Hon. Lady Francis Shirley a standish and two pens, 62
On the Benefactions in the late Frost, 1740, 45
'Postscript' to the *Odyssey*, 65
Sappho to Phaon, 7
The Art of Sinking in Poetry, 109
The Dunciad, 3, 4, 6, 7, 14, 69–72, 74, 77, 78, 80–87, 89–101, 103–109, 142, 152, 168
'The Dying Christian to his Soul', 48
The First Satire of the Second Book of Horace, Imitated, 7, 14
The Pastorals, 7
The Rape of the Lock, 4–5, 22, 25, 69, 73–75, 76, 77, 79–82, 86–90, 92, 95, 96, 108, 148–52, 154, 156, 161–75
The Second Satire of the Second Book of Horace, Imitated, 37
The Temple of fame, 49–50, 51
To a Lady, 4, 67, 115, 116, 117, 154, 168–9
'To a Young Lady, on leaving the Town after the Coronation', 133
To Augustus, 9, 18, 168
To Bathurst, 6, 112, 115, 116, 117, 118, 125–30, 131
'To Belinda on the Rape of the Lock', 170
To Bolingbroke, 47, 53
To Burlington, 7, 115, 116, 117, 119–25, 131
To Cobham, 115, 116, 117, 118
To Craggs, 117, 118
To Dr. Arbuthnot, 7, 8, 50, 103, 115, 116, 117, 118, 130, 131, 138, 153, 154
To Harley, 117, 118
To Jervas, 7, 116, 117, 118
To Miss Blount, 116, 117–18, 156–58, 164, 167, 170
To Mr. Addison, 49, 115, 116, 117
To Mr. Bethel, 37
To Robert Earl of Oxford, and Earl Mortimer, 115, 116, 132–33
Windsor-Forest, 2, 6, 22, 34, 35, 37–39, 44, 152, 163
Works (1735), 8, 113, 114, 115, 116, 119, 121, 123, 125, 126, 128, 129–31

Works (1736), 114, 116
Works (1739), 116
Works (1744), 126, 128
Works (1751), 4, 114
Postmodernism, 109
Prior, Matthew, 36
progress, idea of, 21
progressivist accounts of eighteenth century, 22
Pulteney, William, 136, 141

Quarles, Francis, 83
Queensberry, Charles Douglas and Catherine Hyde, Duke and Duchess of, 136, 141, 143

Rabelais, François, 20
Radishchev, Alexander, 27, 32, 45
    Journey from St. Petersburg to Moscow, 45
    Ode to Liberty, 45
Ramsay, Andrew Michael, 56
Rawson, Claude, 19, 20, 24, 69–110, 161
Reformation, 35–36
Renaissance mysticism, 23
Restoration heroic tragedy, 88
Revolution of 1688, 22, 32
Richardson, Jonathan (the younger and elder), 6, 7, 13, 83, 85–86, 93, 113, 114, 125
Richardson, Samuel, 25, 147–75
    Clarissa, 168–75
    Pamela, 153–70
    Pamela in her Exalted Condition, 160–61
    Sir Charles Grandison, 154
Rideout, Tania, 8
Robson, W.W., 133
Robinson, Peter, 23
Rochester, John William, Earl of, 84, 92
Rogers, Pat, 10, 12, 20, 21, 24, 36–3, 41, 69, 141
Roman Catholicism, 16, 22, 35, 51
Roman Republic, 19
Ross, Anthony, 63
    Muses' Interpreter, 64
Rousseau, George S., 6, 7, 9, 11, 12, 24, 41
Rumbold, Valerie, 12, 13, 19, 165, 169
Ruskin, John
    Queen of the Air, 64, 68

Savage, Richard, 138
Scarron, Paul and Cotton, Charles
    Virgil Travestied, 81
Seneca, 51

Settle, Elkanah, 83
Shaftesbury, Anthony Ashley Cooper, third
    Earl of, 5, 32
Shakespeare, William, 14, 33–34, 52, 85
    Merchant of Venice, 33, 44
    Othello, 33
    The Tempest, 34
Shankman, Hugh, 106
Shankman, Steven, 19
Sharp, Granville, 43
Shaw, Peter
    The Reflector, 147
Sherburn, George, 9, 19, 34, 113, 138
Shelley, Percy Bysshe, 105, 107
    Peter Bell the Third, 98–99
Sherbo, Arthur, 34
Sidney, Sir Philip, 155
    Arcadia, 155
slavery, 2, 22, 25–53
Sophocles, 85
Spadafora, David, 21
Spence, Joseph, 19, 47, 56, 83, 135, 135, 138
    An Essay on Pope's Odyssey, 61
Spenser, Edmund, 5, 52, 58
Stack, Frank, 19
Stanford, W.J.B., 64
Statius, 76
Steele, Sir Richard, 138
    The Spectator, 48
Sterne, Laurence, 107
    Tristram Shandy, 105, 107
Stewart, Douglas, J., 58
Storey, Graham, 31
Suffolk, Henrietta Howard, Countess of, 13
Sutherland, James, 69, 74, 85, 90, 99, 138
Swift, Jonathan, 11, 12, 15–16, 20, 33, 36, 62,
    79, 84, 88–89, 92, 94, 95, 117, 129, 136,
    139, 140, 141
    A Short View, 110
    Battle of the Books, 74, 79, 80, 83, 88, 89,
        100, 101
    Correspondence, 137, 139, 140, 142
    Gulliver's Travels, 87, 108, 110
    Modest Proposal, 34, 108
    Tale of a Tub, 83, 94, 99, 105, 106, 107
Szechi, Daniel, 23

Tacitean view, 18–19
Tacitus, 3
Tanselle, Thomas, 119
Tassoni, 84
Temple, Sir William, 47
Theobald, Lewis, 77, 83, 85, 89, 99, 102, 103
Thompson, E.P., 20, 163

Thompson, Francis, 62
Thomson, James, 42
Tickell, Thomas, 30, 38, 41
Tillotson, Geoffrey, 25, 49, 69, 74, 77, 81, 88,
    132, 149
Tonson, Jacob, 125
Tory views, 22, 34, 143, 159
Treaty of Utrecht, 2, 34–35, 36, 37, 38
Trumbull, Sir William, 9, 11
Turner, Edith (Pope's Mother), 12

Vander Meulen, David L., 7, 83, 85, 91
Virgil, 3, 19, 88, 97
    Aeneid, 88
    Eclogues, 36
Voltaire, François Marie Arouet, 93

W., J. author of *Pamela: Or, The Fair
    Imposter*, 147–50, 154, 161–70, 175
Wakefield, Gilbert, 92, 95
Walwyn, William, 30
Walpole, Sir Robert, 3, 13, 17, 21, 43, 44,
    141, 142, 143, 159, 166, 167
Warburton, William, 11, 22, 118, 129, 152,
    160–61
warfare, 2, 35, 44, 78, 80, 82, 98, 108
Warton Lecture (British Academy), 24
Warton, Thomas, 28
Wasserman, Earl, 6, 126
Watts, Isaac, 83
Weinbrot, Howard D., 18, 21, 22, 44, 119–20
Wesley, Samuel, 83
Whig views, 14, 16–17, 22, 30, 34, 38, 143,
    167
William I, King, 35
William II, King, 35
William III, King, 34, 35, 51, 51
William and Mary, 38
Williamite rule, 163
Williams, Aubrey, 18
Williams, Carolyn, D., 19
Winn, James, A., 24
Wood, Robert, 57
Woodman, Thomas, 20
Woolf, Virginia, 13
Wordsworth, William, 5, 98, 161
Wycherley, William, 11
Wyndham, Sir William, 136, 141

Yates, Frances, 23
Yeats, William Butler, 96
Young, Edward, 38